SANCHI AND ITS REMAINS

SANCHI AND ITS REMAINS

A FULL DESCRIPTION OF THE ANCIENT BUILDINGS, SCULPTURES, AND INSCRIPTIONS
AT
SANCHI, NEAR BHILSA, IN CENTRAL INDIA

WITH REMARKS ON THE EVIDENCE THEY SUPPLY AS TO THE COMPARATIVELY MODERN DATE OF THE

BUDDHISM OF GOTAMA, OR SAKYA MUNI

WITH FORTY PLATES

BY

GENERAL F. C. MAISEY
H. M. INDIAN ARMY

AND AN INTRODUCTORY NOTE BY MAJOR-GENERAL SIR ALEX. CUNNINGHAM, K.C.I.E., C.S.I., R.E.

GYAN

Published by

GYAN

Gyan Publishing House
5, Ansari Road
Daryaganj, New Delhi-110002
Phone: 011-47034999, 9811692060
E-mail: books@gyanbooks.com

Distribution Network
gyanbooks.com
India, USA, Canada, UK, Australia, France

ISBN : 978-81-212-2612-7 (HB)
First Published, 1892

2nd Impression 2021

Printed at: Gyan Press, Delhi.

Sanchi and its Remains
Author: General F. C. Maisey

SÁNCHI AND ITS REMAINS

A FULL DESCRIPTION OF THE ANCIENT BUILDINGS, SCULPTURES, AND INSCRIPTIONS

AT

SÁNCHI, NEAR BHILSA, IN CENTRAL INDIA

WITH REMARKS ON THE EVIDENCE THEY SUPPLY AS TO THE COMPARATIVELY MODERN DATE OF THE

Buddhism of Gotama, or Sákya Muni

WITH FORTY PLATES

BY

GENERAL F. C. MAISEY

H.M. INDIAN ARMY

AND AN INTRODUCTORY NOTE BY MAJOR-GENERAL SIR ALEX. CUNNINGHAM, K.C.I.E., C.S.I., R.E.

LONDON

KEGAN PAUL, TRENCH, TRÜBNER & CO., LTD., CHARING CROSS ROAD

1892

PREFACE.

THE most important of the many Buddhist memorials in India are those at Sánchi in Bhupál, Bharhut in Bhagelkhand, and Buddha Gayá in Behar; which, whatever their relative age, are all over 2,000 years old; and those at Amarávati in Southern India, which are several centuries more recent.

Considerable difference of opinion exists, among the learned authorities who have treated of these antiquities,(1) both as to the relative age and importance of the earlier remains, and as to the nature and date of the form of religion which they indicate: and I venture to hope that this book, whatever its shortcomings, may be of some use in clearing up disputed points. Its objects are as follows:—

1st. To place on record a full and connected description of the Sánchi memorials; and to show their connection with religious systems antecedent to what is now called Buddhism.

2nd. To give accurate illustrations, from my own hand-drawn originals, of the Sánchi buildings, and sculptures.(2)

3rd. To invite attention to the evidence, which the Sánchi remains supply, that the Buddhism of Sákya—which is usually attributed to the sixth century B.C.—was introduced, as a reform of the pre-existing semi-Mithraic faith, about the commencement of the Christian era; that is, shortly before the time when the gateway sculptures of Sánchi were executed.

Since my book has been in print, Sir A. Cunningham has brought out a new work, entitled, "Mahábodhi; or the Great Buddhist Temple under the Bodhi-tree,

(1) Cunningham's "The Bhilsa Topes" (1854); Fergusson's "Tree and Serpent Worship" (1868, 1873); Rájendra Lál Mitra's "Temple of Buddha Gayá" (1878); and Cunningham's "Stúpa of Bharhut" (1880): many notices of Buddha Gayá are also contained in Cunningham's Reports of the Archæological Survey of India (Vols. I., III., and XI.).

(2) In "Tree and Serpent Worship," most of the plates relating to Sánchi were copied from my original sketches: but not a few of them were, more or less, incorrectly reproduced; with the result that they led to erroneous conclusions.

at Buddha Gayá." I can but regret that when drafting my own chapters, I had not the advantage, which, by the courtesy of the learned author, I now have, of studying this valuable addition to the literature of Indian Buddhism.

It raises anew the question as to the comparative antiquity and importance of the remains at Buddha Gayá, Bharhut, and Sánchi; which is too long for discussion in a preface: but I must take the opportunity of saying, that, so far as I have seen, I have no reason to modify the views, as to the nature and date of Sákyan Buddhism, expressed in the following pages.

While drafting this preface, I have seen, for the first time, Colonel Cole's Report, on the work done by him, at Sánchi, as Curator of Ancient Monuments in India. (See my p. 4.) This publication gives numerous fine photographs of the Sthúpas, and the sculptured gateways; and should have been included in the detail of books treating of Sánchi, given in my page 2.

FRED. MAISEY,

GENERAL.

London, 18*th July*, 1892.

CONTENTS.

PAGE

INTRODUCTORY NOTE xi

CHAPTER I.

INTRODUCTORY 1

CHAPTER II.

GENERAL DESCRIPTION OF THE ANTIQUITIES AT SANCHI 5

CHAPTER III.

THE PRINCIPAL, OR NO. 1 STHUPA 9

CHAPTER IV.

THE NORTHERN GATEWAY OF NO. 1 STHUPA; AND ITS SCULPTURES 18

CHAPTER V.

THE EASTERN GATEWAY OF NO. 1 STHUPA; AND ITS SCULPTURES 42

CHAPTER VI.

THE SOUTHERN GATEWAY OF NO. 1 STHUPA; AND ITS SCULPTURES. 53

CHAPTER VII.

THE WESTERN GATEWAY OF NO. 1 STHUPA; AND ITS SCULPTURES 58

CHAPTER VIII.

STHUPAS NOS. 2 AND 3; AND THEIR DETAILS; AND THE REMAINS OF STHUPAS 4 TO 8 . 67

CHAPTER IX.

ISOLATED PILLARS: CHAITYA, AND OTHER TEMPLES: VIHARAS, OR MONASTERIAL BUILDINGS: AND OTHER MISCELLANEOUS REMAINS, NOT ELSEWHERE DESCRIBED . . . 72

PAGE

CHAPTER X.

The Disc-and-Crescent Symbol 78

CHAPTER XI.

Inscriptions, unconnected with Relic Deposits 94

CHAPTER XII.

Funereal Relics; and their Inscriptions 108

CHAPTER XIII.

The Age, and Purport of the Sanchi Sthupas; their Enclosures; and Gateways 116

CHAPTER XIV.

The Mithraic Nature of Primitive Buddhism: and the Comparatively Modern Date of the Buddhism of Gautama or Sakya 123

Index 135

INTRODUCTORY NOTE.

Towards the end of October, 1850, Lieutenant Maisey, on his way to Sánchi, stopped a few days with me at Gwalior. I was then the Executive Engineer of the Gwalior State, and as I had to visit the out-stations of Augar near Ujain, and Lalitpur near Chanderi, I arranged to pay a visit to Sánchi on my way from Augar to Lalitpur. As I was naturally anxious to examine the numerous Buddhist Stúpas at Sánchi and its neighbourhood, Lieutenant Maisey kindly agreed to defer all explorations until my arrival. Accordingly he occupied himself in the measurements of the Stúpas and in making drawings of the sculptured bas-reliefs on the Toran gateways of the Great Stúpa.

I arrived at Sánchi on the 23rd of January, 1851, and the same morning, after only a few hours' work, we found the relics of Sáriputa and Mogalána, the two chief disciples of Buddha, in the ruins of No. 3 Stúpa. As this discovery and all our subsequent explorations are fully described in my "Bhilsa Topes," I only refer to them here to explain how it happened that I became associated with Lieutenant Maisey in the exploration of "Sánchi and its Remains."

During our intercourse I found that my companion had read carefully all the books that promised to yield any information which would be of use in his explorations. He had already noted that the Sanchi hill on which the Great Stúpa stood was very probably the *Chetiya giri*, or "Chaitya hill," of the Mahavanso,(¹) where Asoka had halted for a short time on his way between Pátaliputra and Ujain. As this resting-place is named *Wessanagara* by Buddha Ghosha,(²) the identification seems to me to be quite certain; for the ruins of *Besnagar* still exist, only two miles to the north of Bhilsa. I have made this identification myself in "Bhilsa Topes," p. 270, where I have drawn attention to its great importance towards fixing the age of the Stúpa. For as the hill must have received its name of *Chetiyagiri* from the Chetiya (or Stúpa) which was standing on it, we learn that the Stúpa was already in existence before Asoka came to the throne. His accession has now been fixed by M. Senart [3] in B.C. 273; the Stúpa must have been in existence in B.C. 280, and most probably many years earlier.

During our intercourse, which was daily from 23rd January to 12th March, 1851, Lieutenant Maisey and myself were in perfect accord as to the probable age of the Sánchi Stúpas. We agreed that:

> The Toran gateways were set up in the first century A.D., say 80 A.D.
>
> The stone railings round the Stúpa, by Asoka, about 250 B.C.
>
> The Great Stúpa, some time before Asoka, perhaps as early as 500 B.C.

Between 1851 and 1871 I met Maisey only once, for a few hours in 1856, when he was an Assistant Commissioner at Ambala. During the forty years that have passed, his reading has

(¹) Turner's "Mahavanso," p. 76. (²) Turner's "Pali Annals," J.P. vii. 930. (³) "Ind. Ant." xx. 241.

apparently led him to look to foreign sources for the origin of symbols which I accept as undoubtedly Buddhist. His early opinions were evidently shaken by the scepticism of Wilson, who considered it doubtful whether the edicts of Priyadarsi have any connection with Buddhism, (Royal Asiat. Soc. Jour. xii. 236), and that they contained "nothing exclusively characteristic of Buddhism," and also that the identification of Asoka with Priyadarsi rests upon a passage of the Dipawanso, which he calls "a work of rather doubtful character."

Maisey's views must have been changed very early, as he states that one of the main objects of the present work is to illustrate and maintain the following views:—

I. The Buddhism of Sákya Muni does not date from the sixth century B.C., but from about or shortly before the Christian era.

II. There is no sufficient proof that the *Devánampiya* of the Edicts is the *Asoka* of history, or that the religion inculcated is the Buddhism of Sákya.

When General Maisey adopted these views, he does not seem to have been aware of my discovery of three inscriptions of Priyadarsi, dated in the year 256, which can only be referred to the era of Buddha, nor of the contemporary edict of Bairát, which mentions all the names of the Buddhist triad, Buddha, Dharma, and Sangha, proving (as stated by M. Senart) that at that time Priyadarsi "was a declared Buddhist." M. Senart further refers to the 11th rock edict, which states that in that year Priyadarsi "set out for the *sambodhi*," a term which inevitably links Piyadasi with Buddhism. The Bairát edict also mentions the four-fold division of Buddhists as *Bhikshus* and *Bhikshunis*, *Upásakas* and *Upásikás*.(1) But these edicts of Priyadarsi, which are so undeniably Buddhist, belong to the period between 260 and 258 B.C., as they mention the names of five different Greek kings his contemporaries.(2) The Buddhism inculcated in them is therefore two centuries and a half older than the period of "shortly before the Christian era."

The second doubtful point, which was first put forth by Wilson, is the want of sufficient proof that Priyadarsi was identical with Asoka. The identity is affirmed by the Dípawanso; and it is most convincingly proved by the fact that the two were contemporary sovereigns who reigned over the same country (N. India) at the same time. Both Brahmans and Buddhists make Asoka the grandson of Chandra Gupta Maurya. Deducting the sum of their reigns, 24+28=52 years, from B.C. 235 we get 273 B.C. for Asoka, whose reign includes the period of 259 B.C., when the agreements were made with the Greek kings.

Whether the Buddhism inculcated in the edicts of Priyadarsi is the same as the Buddhism of Sákya we have no means of ascertaining. But, as M. Senart observes,(3) "these monuments represent a stage of Buddhism different from that developed in later times." One difference noted is that they contain no allusion to *Nirvána*, but refer only to *Swarga*.

The great Stúpa at Sánchi is undoubtedly old. General Maisey thinks that it was pre-Buddhist, and belonged to the old fire and serpent worship. It was at first a simple hemisphere, which, after it was taken possession of by the Buddhists, was truncated. A berm or raised terrace was then made all round for the purpose of perambulation; and lastly, a stone railing or enclosure was added, with four entrances. The four Toran gateways were a much later addition. I see no objection to this description. But when he goes on to say (p. 117) that "the *inscriptions* of the railed enclosure show that the religion *then existing* was closely allied to *Sun*, *Fire*, and *Elemental* worship," I must confess that I cannot find the faintest allusion in any of them to these objects. But I believe that the notions about *Sun-worship* have arisen from a

(1) Senart, "Ind. Ant." xx. 259. (2) Senart, 247. (3) "Ind. Ant." xx. 246.

simple mistake, while those about *Fire-worship* and *Element-worship* have been founded on faulty translations.

SUN-WORSHIP.—I remember that when Maisey and I were together at Udayagiri (near Sánchi) in 1851, we both looked upon the four-armed figure holding a club and discus as a representative of *Súrya* or the "Sun." But I long ago discovered that the figure was that of the four-armed Vishnu holding the "club," as *gadá-dhar*, and the "discus," as *chakra-dhar*; and so I have described it in my "Archæological Survey," vol. x., p. 50, which was published in 1880. It is this same figure which is given in Maisey's Plate XL., fig. 8, where it is described as "Figure of *Súrya* from Udayagiri." But the *chakra*, or "wheel," was a very prominent symbol of Buddhism, as it represented *Dharma.* A reference to my "Bharhut Stupa," Plate XIII., inner face of Prasenajit's Pillar, which has, over the figure of the wheel, the legend *Bhagavato dhama-chakam* "the Dharma Chakra of Bhagavat," is decisive on this point. General Maisey refers to the Bharhut sculptures, Plate XXXIII. 3, Plate XXXI. 2, and Plate XXXIV. 4, and also to his own Plates IV., VIII., XIII., XXVI., as confirming his opinion; but all of these examples are simple *dharma-chakras* with Buddhist worshippers.

FIRE-WORSHIP.—General Maisey based his opinion as to the existence of fire-worship at Sánchi on the representations of two temples shown in Plate XIII. But his chief reliance is on an inscription dated S. 93=A.D. 411, which exists on one of the bars of the railing round the Great Stúpa. In the opening paragraph of this record the word *ávasatha* is taken to be a "fire temple," in accordance with one meaning assigned to the word in Wilson's Sanskrit Dictionary. But its common and primary meaning is simply a "house or abode," and so it is translated by Mr. Fleet (¹) as "the abode of most excellent Sramanas." As Sramana is a specially Buddhistic term, Buddha himself being called the *Mahá-Sramana* or "Great Ascetic," this inscription is fatal to Maisey's belief that "Fire-worship was still a part of Buddhist ritual in the fifth century of the Christian era." (²)

With respect to the temple in Plate VIII., from which flames *appear* to be issuing (see Fergusson's "Tree and Serpent Worship," Plate XXIX. Fig. 1), I am very doubtful, as none of the figures are in the well-known fire-worshippers' dress. But in the two scenes shown in Fergusson's Plate XXXII. there can be no doubt, as the flames issue from their proper outlets in the upper openings of the roof, while all the people are in fire-worshippers' costume. I believe that the two bas-reliefs refer to the two legends of Buddha, who, by his mere wish, *arrested* the lighting of the fire, and the splitting of the wood. The two legends are told in Spence Hardy's "Manual of Buddhism," pp. 190-191.

ELEMENT-WORSHIP.—General Maisey's opinion, that element-worship formed part of the Buddhist cult down to the fifth century A.D., is based chiefly on an erroneous translation by Abel Remusat of a passage in the Travels of the Chinese pilgrim, Fa Hian. In Chapter XX. he relates that the first representation of Fo made by Raja Prasenajit of Kosala, was the "*head of an ox*" *carved in sandal-wood.* But the "Bull's head" is the well-known name of the dark red sandal-wood, and the true translation is that the figure of Buddha was carved in *Go-sirsha-chandan*, or "Bull's-head sandal-wood." (See Beal's "Fa Hian," I., p. xliv., and Giles, p. 42.)

Putting full faith in Remusat's translation, the author concluded that Buddha continued to be worshipped in the form of a "Bull's head," down to the time of Fa Hian, or A.D. 399-410, and accordingly he states (p. 16) that there were no images of Buddha in India until the fifth

(¹) "Gupta Inscriptions," p. 32. (²) See p. 105, Note.

century. He was aware that Buddha was represented on the coins of Kanishka, towards the end of the first century A.D., and as he saw that there were no figures of Buddha amongst the sculptures of the Sánchi Stupas, he thought that the Indians had not adopted the practice of the Indo-Scythians. But the discovery of a colossal figure of Buddha at Mahábodhi, with an Indo-Scythian inscription dated in s. 64, or A.D. 142, shows that the Indians had already adopted the style of the Gaudhára sculptures as early as the reign of Huvishka. A colossal figure of Buddha, with an early Indo-Scythian inscription, was also exhumed by me in the ruined temple of Gaudhakuti in Srávasti.

In adopting the Bull's head figure as the representation of Buddha, Maisey was naturally led to the conclusion that the common taurine symbol of a circle surmounted by a crescent was the simple form of the old elemental worship of the "Sun and Moon"—which he further identified with the common three-pronged symbol of Buddhism. But in doing this he ignores the central limb, which changes the two-horned *crescent* into a *trisul* or *trident*. He notes that Prinsep named this symbol the "Buddhist monogram," while he objects to its "being treated as an exclusively Buddhist symbol." It is now, I believe, generally accepted as a symbol of the *Tri-ratna*, or "Three jewels," in allusion to the Buddhist triad of *Buddha, Dharma*, and *Sangha*. In all the examples of this symbol that I have seen, the central prong is never wanting. It is used as a common pendant for a neck-ornament; it forms the pinnacle of the standard; and is very common on coins.

With respect to the age of the *Relics* which were found in the Stúpas at Sánchi and its neighbourhood, the author is constrained by his recognition of the Buddhist symbols of the *Dharma-chakra* and the *Tri-ratna* as symbols of the *Sun* and the *Elements* to assign a very late date, even posterior to the Christian era. He admits (p. 95) that the edicts of Piyadasi are of the third century B.C., and then goes on to say that the same alphabetical characters continued in use "all over India for *several centuries after* the date of the Piyadasi edicts." This statement is certainly incorrect, as I have shown that as early as 100 B.C. the Indian letters had already received *mátras*, or headstrokes. These *mátras* are also found in the inscriptions of Rajubul and his son Sodása, of the first century preceding the Christian era, and in all the Mathura inscriptions of the Kushán kings, Kanishka, Huvishka, and Vasu Deva. The absence of *mátras* is a sure proof of antiquity, and it was on this evidence that I established the date of the Bharhut Stúpa, which was erected during the rule of the Sunga kings, who succeeded the Mauryas, in B.C. 178.

Now the Sánchi inscriptions show both of these forms of letters, the *earlier*, of Asoka's time, without *mátras*, as shown in the records on the railings and in the labels on the relic caskets, and the *later*, with *mátras*, as shown in all the records on the gateways.

General Maisey would appear to have been influenced by Wilson's hasty statement that I had inferred the date of the *Relic caskets* from the *names* inscribed upon them. As I have pointed out upwards of twenty years ago, I relied on the *fact* that the inscriptions on the caskets were in characters of Asoka's age.(1) I now repeat my assertion that the alphabetical characters used on all these caskets are of Asoka's age. From this fact I inferred that the names inscribed on the Relic caskets must be those of eminent Buddhists of the same period. And so they proved to be, as they included *Mogaliputra*, the head of the Buddhist Church in Asoka's reign, and *Kásyapa* and *Madhyama*, two of the five missionaries who were sent to the *Hemawanta*

(1) See "Archæol. Survey," I. p. xxxix.

country after the meeting of the Buddhist Synod in Asoka's reign.(¹) This identification is rendered quite certain by the description of *Kásyapa*, as *Sava Hemavatácharíyasa*, "the Teacher of the whole Hemawanta." This fact was recently quoted with approval by Prof. Max Müller in his Presidential Address to the Oriental Congress.

General Maisey (p. 114) thinks it "probable that the Buddhists who brought these relics to Sánchi, *appropriated*, as their relic-shrines, buildings already ancient, and sacred in connection with the older form of worship." He also thinks (p. 105) that "the *inscriptions* at Sánchi contain no indication of an *exclusively Buddhist* allusion." Here he must have overlooked the significant Buddhist titles of many of the donors—amongst which I find

Budha-rakshita	*Budha-mitra*	*Budha-pálita*
Dharma-rakshita		
Sangha-rakshita	*Sangha-mitra*	

besides *Upásika* and *Upasiká*, and the eminently Buddhistic *Budhopásika*, with numerous *Bhikshus* and *Bhikshunis*.

I have made this rather long examination of Maisey's views for the purpose of showing wehre and how they differ from the generally accepted belief as to the successful establishment of the Buddhist religion by Asoka in the third century B.C. I think that his views may have been biassed by the pious wish to prove that Christianity was prior to Buddhism. Although I do not agree with the author's views on this point, I consider that it is an advantage to have them stated so fully by one who was intimately acquainted with all the Stúpas and other remains at Sánchi, and who had carefully studied the subject for many years. The numerous plates add very considerably to the value of the book, as they give very faithful copies of the sculptures on a large scale.

A. CUNNINGHAM.

(¹) "Bhilsa Topes," p 285.

SANCHI AND ITS REMAINS.

CHAPTER I.

INTRODUCTORY.

In 1849, while employed under the Government of India, in archæological work in the Upper Betwa Districts of Central India,[1] I first heard of the Buddhist antiquities of Sánchi, from the then Political Agent at Bhupál, Captain J. D. Cunningham; and, at his suggestion, I was directed to suspend my other work, and proceed as soon as possible to Sánchi, and prepare for Government an illustrated report upon its buildings, sculptures and inscriptions.

I spent the cold seasons of 1849-50 and 1850-51 at Sánchi; and in October, 1851, submitted to Government the report and annexures which are the basis of this book.

In January, 1851, I was joined at Sânchi by Major Alexander Cunningham, then Executive Engineer at Gwáliyar—now General Sir A. Cunningham, K.C.S.I., C.I.E. —and we together dug carefully into the Sthúpas at and near Sánchi, and disinterred a number of interesting relics, which will be described in a subsequent chapter.

These *trouvailles*, and the inscriptions at Sánchi, were to have formed the subject of a second report; which I undertook to prepare as soon as I had completed all the fair copies of my Sánchi drawings, and had received from the Bengal Asiatic Society translations of the inscriptions.

The proposed supplementary report was never prepared. I did not receive the promised translations; and as I was away on active service in Burmah from March, 1852, to May, 1854, it was not until October, 1854, that I was able to send in the last batch of finished drawings; and soon after this, my special archæological employment was terminated, and I was transferred to other work.

The expense of reproducing my drawings caused the Home Government of the Honourable East India Company to hesitate as to the publication of my report and plates; and while the matter was still under consideration, Major Cunningham brought

(1) I was selected for this "special duty" on the recommendation of the Lieutenant-Governor of the N. W. Provinces; under [illegible] Hindú antiquities of Kálinjar, in Bun[illegible] two before, prepared an illustrated account of the [illegible] in the "Journal of the Asiatic Society of Bengal."

out his learned work on the Sânchi Sthúpas;[1] regarding which I wrote as follows, when forwarding to the Government, in October, 1854, my last batch of completed drawings:

> "In the interval that has elapsed since I first took the work in hand, Major Cunningham has written a very valuable and interesting book upon the same subject; so that my account, if published, will labour under the disadvantage of being to some extent a repetition; as, of course, we both naturally noticed the same peculiarities, and to a certain extent came to similar conclusions. My view, however, of the general subject differs so much from Major Cunningham's that I still hope to find it will possess some interest of its own; and perhaps tend to a more complete elucidation of Buddhist antiquities than could be effected by a single publication."

I quote the above, because such study of Indian Buddhism as I have had opportunities for since I first wrote about Sánchi has confirmed me in the views I then held and expressed, and which, stated briefly, are as follows:—

1st. That the Buddhism of Gautama, or Sákya Buddha, dates, not as usually supposed, from the sixth century B.C., but from about, or perhaps shortly before, the commencement of the Christian era; and

2nd. That there is no sufficient proof, either that the "Devánampiya Piyadasi" of the Indian rock and pillar edicts is the "Asoka" of Buddhist history, or that the religion inculcated in those edicts is the Buddhism of Sákya.

The importance of this view, if sustainable, not only in an antiquarian, but in a Christian sense, need scarcely be enlarged upon; and one of the main objects of this book will be to illustrate and maintain it.[2]

Since the publication, in 1854, of "The Bhilsa Topes," many notices of the Sánchi remains have appeared in books, periodicals, and newspaper articles; the principal books being, in order of date, Fergusson's "Illustrated Hand-book of Architecture" (1859); "Tree and Serpent Worship" (1868 and 1873); and "History of Indian and Eastern Architecture" (1876); Rousselet's "India and its Native Princes" (1876); Sir A. Cunningham's "Stupa of Bharhut" (1880); and Sir Lepel Griffin's "Famous Monuments of Central India" (1884).

I have not been able to study all these authorities as fully as I could have wished; but I think I am justified in saying that they have by no means exhausted the subject of the Sánchi antiquities. Some of them, moreover, contain inaccuracies which I am able to correct; and all, I believe, are based upon a general view of Buddhism which is opposed to that which I shall advocate in the following pages.

I need hardly say that it is with much diffidence, and with a full sense of the high authorities against me, that in now submitting to the public my detailed description of the remains at Sánchi, I submit also the speculations and conclusions to which they have led me. Much that I shall have to say, however, has long had the sanction of writers of established Indian reputation; and I can urge that in publishing my own views, I am following the advice of friends thoroughly versed in

[1] "The Bhilsa Topes; or Buddhist Monuments of Central India." [illegible]54.

[2] The text and plates of my 1851 Report on th[illegible] I have, with the sanction of the Right Hon. the Secretary of State for In[illegible] at my disposal for the preparation of this work.

the subject of Indian antiquities, who had read my original report and examined its numerous illustrations.

Throughout the book I shall, in alluding to Topes and Tumuli, or representations thereof, use the Sanskrit word "Sthúpa;" as the meanings attached to that term by European scholars are so various that the Sanskrit form is the most convenient.

Some of the varied renderings of "Sthúpa" (Páli Túpha) will be found in the following works: Prinsep, "Jour. As. Soc. Beng." vii. 443, 451; Rémusat, "Foe-Koue-Ki," chapter xiii., note 6; Cunningham, "The Bhilsa Topes," 9, 10, 11; and Spence Hardy, "Eastern Monachism," 217.

This introductory chapter seems an appropriate place for a few remarks on the name or names of the locality.

The inscriptions on the enclosures and gateways make no mention of "Sánchi;" and though at my first visit I thought the name "Kánakhariya" occurred in one of the inscriptions of the Eastern gateway, more careful examination has led me to doubt, if not reject, this reading.

The "Maháwanso," and other Buddhist works which mention localities in Central India, are equally silent, as to any names resembling Sánchi, or Kánakhera; and the same may be said of the itineraries of the Chinese travellers Fa Hian and Hwan Thsang, who visited India in the fifth and seventh centuries of the Christian era. Fa Hian it is true mentions a "great kingdom of Shachi;" but he locates it between the Ganges, opposite Kanoj, and the country of Kosala, or Oudh (see "Foe-Koue-Ki," chapter xix.); and speaks of it as a place which he actually passed through on his way to Kosala, and not as a distant place, only heard of. (See however, on this point, the speculations and remarks in "The Bhilsa Topes," pp. 180 to 182; and Laidlay's "Fa Hian," ch. xix., note 2; and ch. xx., notes 2, 3.)

We may therefore conclude that the names now given to the locality were not in use until after the fifth, or perhaps even the seventh century A.D. Sánchi—also called Sáchi—and Sátchi, is probably a corruption of Sát Chetiya, the "Seven Sthúpas," and Kánakhera may have some connection with Kanaka, the second of the "Four Buddhas" to whom at one time the principal Sthúpa was dedicated.

I may add, as other possible clues to the origin of the name Sánchi (*quasi* Sánti) that the sacred Swastika Cross, which is so prominent a symbol in Buddhist inscriptions and coinage, is called also Sánti, or Sánthiya; and that Sántya is one of the Vedic names of the Brahmanical fire-god Agni, with whose worship the Swastika, or Sánthiya, is so closely allied.(1)

As regards older names, there seems little doubt that this sacred hill, with its numerous Chetiyas, or Sthúpas, is the "Chetiya Giri," near Wessanagara, mentioned by Buddhist writers as the chief place in the territory of "Dakkhina Giri," between Pátaliputra, and Avanti, or Ujain. Chetiya Giri, both in signification and in position, answers to the Sánchi-Kánakhera hill; and Wessanagara has been identified as on or near the site of the adjacent town of Bhilsa. (See Turnour, "Maháwanso," 76;

(1) See on this subject Wilson's "Rig Veda Sanhitá," p 10, note c.

and "Páli Buddhistical Annals," in the "Jour. As. Soc. Beng." viii. 930; "The Bhilsa Topes," 86, 95; and Fergusson's "Tree and Serpent Worship," 1st edit., 99; and "Hist. of Ind. and Eastern Arch.," 61, 62.)

Finally, as will be seen later (Chapter XI.), the Sánchi votive inscriptions contain numerous names ending in "Giri," or "hill"; some of which, and notably Dhama Giri, or the "Hill of Dharma," may reasonably be held to represent the most ancient name of the place.

The Sánchi memorials have not, I am glad to say, been left in the neglected state in which I found them forty years ago. Colonel Cole, R.E., while Curator of Ancient Monuments in India, included Sánchi in his operations; and, as part of his work there, superintended the preparation of plaster-of-Paris moulds of many isolated sculptures, and of the entire Eastern gateway of the principal Sthúpa; casts of which are now in the Indian Museum at South Kensington.[1] And more recently, Major Keith, of the Archæological Survey Department, was busily employed at Sánchi; where he cleared the site of jungle and rubbish, cleaned the moss and other incrustations from many of the sculptures—more particularly those of No. 2 Sthúpa—and re-erected, and, as far as possible restored to their original appearance, the fallen portions of the enclosure and gateways of the principal structure.

[1] I recommended this measure in 1851, in my original Report on Sánchi.

CHAPTER II.

GENERAL DESCRIPTION OF THE ANTIQUITIES AT SANCHI.

THE celebrated ruins of Sánchi, Sátchi, or Sáchi, are situated on a low sandstone hill, close to the two adjoining villages of Sánchi and Kánakhera, in the territory of the Begam of Bhupál, in Central India, and about five miles south-west of Bhilsa, an important town belonging to the Gwáliyar State.

Previous to my explorations there, in 1849, 1850, and 1851, several cursory accounts of Sánchi and its sculptures had been published; and, as already stated, they were, soon after I had reported on and illustrated them, made the subject of a learned work by Major A. Cunningham: and as some of my measurements differ from both previous and subsequent versions, as regards the principal Sthúpa, I must preface my descriptive account by a few remarks on the subject.

Captain Fell visited Sánchi in A.D. 1819; and wrote a description of its buildings and sculptures, which was published in the third volume of the "Journal of the Asiatic Society of Bengal."

In his paper, which was evidently very hurriedly prepared, the dimensions of the principal Sthúpa, or Tope, were given very vaguely; and half of the vertical circumference, or 112 feet, was given as the height. This measurement was hence mistaken by Professor Wilson and Mr. J. Fergusson,(1) for the perpendicular height of the building; which is less than half as much. Both the above authorities, too, gave 554 feet as the base circumference of the principal Sthúpa, which is very erroneous. The largest circumference (at the ground-line) is only 380 feet, and even the outside circumference of its surrounding enclosure does not exceed 454 feet (see my Plate II., Figs. 1 and 2).

The next recorded visit to the place was in 1822; when an unsuccessful and carelessly conducted search for buried treasure did immense damage to the superstructure of the three more important Sthúpas; and hastened, if it did not originate, the dilapidation of their enclosures. I have no note as to whether any measurements were made on the occasion of this devastating visit; but an account of it is to be found in the fourth volume of the Bengal Asiatic Society's Journal.

In 1846-7, Captain J. D. Cunningham, Political Agent in Bhupál, visited Sánchi;

(1) "Ariana Antiqua," p. 39, "Magazine of Science" for June, 1848.

and his notes thereon were published in the Journal of the Bengal Asiatic Society for August, 1847. The measurements he gave were generally correct; but there was some ambiguity as to the total height of the principal Sthúpa, which in one place he represented as 56 feet and in another as only 42 feet.

His brother, Major A. Cunningham ("Bhilsa Topes," 184, and Plate VIII.), gave the total height as 56 feet; namely, 14 feet for the basement or drum, and 42 feet for the hemispherical frustum, which he described as springing from the top of the basement.

What, however, looks at first sight like a structural basement, plinth, or drum, is not really so, but is a mere adjunct to the Sthúpa, or mound proper; *against which* it has been built up, as shown in my sections;(¹) probably some time after the erection of the Sthúpa itself, the hemispherical curve of which springs from the *ground-line,* as indeed its appearance where most perfect shows.

To make the matter clear, I give in Figs. 1, 2, 3 of Plate III. three comparative sections, drawn to scale, showing the several total heights in question; viz. my own measurement, 53 feet 6 inches; Sir A. Cunningham's, 66 feet; and Captain J. D. Cunningham's, 42 feet.

In connection with this point, too, I must point out what is evidently a misprint, at page 186 of "The Bhilsa Topes," where the total height of the principal Sthúpa, when entire, is estimated as "upwards of one hundred feet."

My restored elevation, in Fig. 2 of Plate II.—which closely corresponds with that in Plate VIII. of "The Bhilsa Topes"—shows that the total height, to the summit of the top-most Tí or Chatta, cannot have exceeded seventy-two feet.

I have noticed this point thus fully, because, as is well known, the height of a Sthúpa is an important factor in judging of its age; and the relative age of the Sánchi Sthúpas and sculptures is a question of special interest, not merely in its antiquarian sense, but with reference to the origin and history of Buddhism itself (see Chapters XIII. and XIV.).

With the above exceptions, I have the great satisfaction of being able to say that Sir A. Cunningham's measurements closely, if not identically, correspond with those previously made by myself, as recorded in my original report and plates.

The Sánchi ruins occupy three separate stages or plateaux of the hill on which they are situated; the highest, to the eastward, is from 12 to 15 feet above the general level of the central, or principal plateau; and the lowest—on which stands No. 2 Sthúpa—is about 400 yards to the north-west of the principal group of buildings. These three plateaux, which were once carefully cleared spaces, partly if not entirely walled in, are marked A, B and C, respectively, in the general plan (Plate I.), the references in which are so full that but little need be said here in the way of description.

(¹) Plate II. Fig. 4; and Plate III. Fig. 1.

The central plateau (A), which contains the main portion of the Sánchi remains, was approached from the north by a staircase and sculptured portal (b), flanked by two stone "Bhairavas," or Janitors. It appears to have been connected by a small flight of steps with the upper plateau (C): and a partially paved path, with roughly made steps at one part, led from its north-west angle to No. 2 Sthúpa (E) on the lower plateau (B); passing, a little short of half-way, the remains of a building—perhaps a Sthúpa—and a broken stone basin (L), which will be described in Chapter IX.

The central object on the principal plateau is the largest, or No. 1 Sthúpa (D); to the north-east, south-east, and south-west of which are the remains of small Sthúpas, Nos. 3 to 8, marked in plan F to K. Sir A. Cunningham's plan shows ten Sthúpas in all; but of these, three are described as "merely circular foundations" ("Bhilsa Topes," pp. 180, 308, and Plate IV.), and I must have overlooked them. The remains of six small Sthúpas near the large central one are, at any rate, clearly distinguishable; and the total number, seven, indicates perhaps some original astronomical allusion. It will be seen, too, that there is a symmetrical or geometrical arrangement in the relative positions of the seven Sthúpas (Sát Chetiya); a peculiarity which both Sir A. Cunningham and I noticed in other groups of Sthúpas, and which, doubtless, has some special significance.

The other remains on the central plateau are as follows: Five Sthambhas, or isolated pillars, or portions thereof, at the spots marked M, N, O, P, Q in the plan; a large number of small models of Sthúpas, lying about in the large enclosure; and a larger one among some débris, at Z; a chaitya-hall, or temple (R), in which I found a broken steatite vase; and two small rectangular temples (S and T). I also found lying about, near S and Z, some fragments of Buddhist, Brahmanical, and Jaina sculpture. All these several remains—some of which are shown in my plates—will be described in detail later. Many of the smaller objects have, I have reason to believe, been carried off, since I was at Sánchi; and many have been shifted to safer positions, in the course of the clearance and restorations already mentioned.

The lower plateau (B) is occupied solely by No. 2 Sthúpa (E, Plate I.), round which there are traces of an open, cleared space—once walled in.

The top plateau (C), has no Sthúpas, but contains other more modern remains of interest; namely, a ruined vihára, or ranges of monasterial cells, for the attendants of the sacred buildings (U, Plate I.); a building (V), which consists of a temple and vihára combined, and a small building (W) of three cells and a verandah, which may be described as a vihára on a small scale.

There is no trace at Sánchi, or at any neighbouring place, of any large building, such as could have merited the description given in Buddhist works of the "magnificent vihára," erected at Chetiya Giri, by the wife of Asoka, and occupied by their son Mahindo, or Mahendra, during his visit to his mother, before his deputation as a missionary to Ceylon. If any such large vihára ever existed at Sánchi, it must have disappeared before the date of any of the now existing buildings on plateau (C).

At the north-west angle of this upper plateau, I found, at (f), a prostrate male figure, which had evidently once crowned a pillar; perhaps one of those at P, Q, already mentioned.

The only other building on the Sánchi ridge is a small fortified one on the north-east, not marked in my plan, but shown in Sir A. Cunningham's. It is of no importance or age. Inside it was, and I conclude still is, a fakír's cell, with an adjoining Shiwála, or temple of Mahádeva, containing the Linga and Yoni emblems of Siva and Párbati, and several fragments from the adjacent Buddhist ruins.

CHAPTER III.

THE PRINCIPAL, OR NO. I STHUPA.

THE most striking and important, as well as the most ancient of the Sánchi remains, is the large, or No. 1 Sthúpa, marked D, in Plate I.

This is a solid, truncated, hemisphere, springing from the ground-line; 110 feet in diameter at the base, and 34 feet at the summit; with a basement terrace 14 feet high, and 5½ feet wide, separately built up against the lower part of the hemispherical frustum, and following its slope. This terrace, therefore, forms a path round the Sthúpa; and was, evidently, intended for the performance of the ceremony of "parikrama" or "padakhinán," that is, a circumambulation of the building; of which there are representations among the sculptures.(¹)

The basement terrace was reached by a double staircase, on the south—almost obliterated when I saw it;—and was, originally, surrounded by a low stone coping, or balustrade, fragments of which I found lying about (Fig. 8, Plate III.).

Among the sculptures, there are several representations of terraced Sthúpas (see Plate X., and Figs. 1, 2, 3, 5, 6, of Plate XXVIII.): and there are many instances of a like construction, not only at and near Sánchi, but in other parts of India; as well as among the Topes and Tumuli of Afghánisthán, figured in Wilson's "Ariana Antiqua."

Probably, such enclosed basement terraces distinguished all Sthúpas of importance; all, that is, which were, in any sense the objects of adoration, and, therefore, circumambulated.

The construction of the mound, or Sthúpa proper, is as follows:—In centre, a shaft, or, more probably, an inner mound, of brickwork (the bricks measuring 16×10×3 inches), laid in mud, then loose stones and rubble; and, outside, a casing of dressed stones, about eight inches thick, laid one over the other, in horizontal layers.(²)

(¹) The practice of circumambulating a sacred building (or person), which the Buddhists called "padakhinán," and the Bráhmans "parkarma," or "parikrama," was by no means peculiar to Indian cults: but is known to have formed part of the worship of many ancient, and widely-separated nations. There can be little doubt that it is one of many relics of the old Mithraic rites, which, in India, preceded, and were largely adopted by, both Bráhmanism and Buddhism.

(²) In Captain Cunningham's section (see Fig. 3, Plate III.) these outer stones are, erroneously, represented, as pointing centre-wards.

The exterior was, once, coated with plaster, about four inches thick; portions of which I found still adhering to the building.(¹)

No interior cement was used; nor are there any traces of exterior ornamentation, such as appears in some of the Sthúpas represented in the sculptures. The material used is the laminated limestone of the hill; whereas, in the construction of the enclosure and gateways, large blocks of sandstone were used, which must have been brought from a distance; possibly from Udaya Giri, a few miles off, where there are old quarries.

The most noteworthy feature of this Sthúpa is its curious palisaded enclosure; which calls for a somewhat lengthy description. Enclosures of like character, as will be seen, also surrounded Nos. 2 and 3 Sthúpas.

The enclosure is semi-circular on the north-east and north-west; and semi-elliptical on the south side; where the staircase necessitated a gradual enlargement of the curve: and, as will be seen from the plan (Plate II., Fig. 1), it leaves a free passage all round the Sthúpa, at the ground level, 9½ feet wide, save opposite the double staircase.(²)

There are four entrances to the enclosure, one at, or strictly speaking, nearly at, each cardinal point. These were, originally, like those of No. 2 Sthúpa, shaped as shown by the letters *a* to *e*, in Fig. 4 of Plate III.; the portions of enclosure marked Y, Z, and the sculptured gateways (*h*, *h*,) having, as I shall show, been added at a later date.

At the time of my visit, most of the western portion of this enclosure was prostrate, or nearly so: but, when complete, the original enclosure consisted of 120 stone uprights, of irregular octagonal section (2 feet 1 inch × 1 foot 10 inches), and 8 feet 8 inches high, above ground. These uprights are 2 feet 4 inches apart; and are connected by three rails, or cross-bars of double convex section, 2 feet 4 inches wide, and 4¼ inches apart. These cross-bars were, we learn from the Bharhut inscriptions, called "suchi," or needles, in Páli. A coping stone, 2 feet 4 inches high, slightly rounded at top, crowns the railing; and binds the whole together; no cement being used, anywhere. The total height of the enclosing railing is, thus, eleven feet. (See, for details, Figs. 6, 7, of Plate III.)

At each of the four entrances once stood a fine sculptured "Torana," or gateway;

(¹) The mode of construction above described, resembles that of the comparatively modern Topes and Tumuli of Afghánisthán, as described by Masson, and Professor Wilson ("Ariana Antiqua," 39, 55, 56): and, in some of these, a complete inner relic Tope was found to have been encased in another structure (see, for instance, the Sultánpur Tope, figured at page 78 of Fergusson's "History of Indian and Eastern Architecture"). A similar successive construction is said to have been noticed, in the well-known Tope of Mánikyála, in the Panjáb, but I failed to discover any traces of it, myself. According to the Burmese, the famous Shuedagon pagoda at Rangoon, was, originally, a small relic-shrine; and has been repeatedly built over, until it reached its present dimensions. The practice of so building and enlarging, is mentioned in Buddhist works; and was doubtless of foreign origin. It is known, for instance, to have obtained among the pyramid builders of Egypt: and is supposed to have existed in Assyria, also.

(²) Sir A. Cunningham's careful measurements, made with the aid of instruments, proved that the Sthúpa is a perfect circle in plan: and the enclosure, half semi-circular, and half semi-elliptic.

of which two only, the Northern and the Eastern, were standing in 1850. The Southern gateway had long been prostrate, when Captain Fell visited Sánchi in A.D. 1819; and the Western gateway fell down some few years before I visited the place.

All four gateways were of the same general style; and similarly constructed: that is, like the enclosure, without cement, and on the "mortice and tenon" principle. Mr. Fergusson considered the mode of construction, which he characterized as "more like carpentering than stone-work," a proof of his theory that prior to the reign of Asoka, Indian buildings were, for the most part, of wood.

It will be seen, from Plates II. and III., that these gateways, and the portions of railing Y, Z, which connect them with the main enclosure, are quite detached: and this alone would have shown that they are of later date than the enclosure itself: but there is further proof of this, in the comparatively recent character of the gateway inscriptions (¹): and all doubt on the subject is removed, by the fact, which I pointed out in my first report on Sánchi, that, at the western entrance, where the portion of railing Y, Z, had fallen inwards, an inscription in the oldest form of Páli was exposed, on the upright X, which was entirely concealed by Y, Z, when erect.

The name given to this style of palisade, by Sir A. Cunningham, is "the Buddhist railing:" a designation which I shall adhere to, in this book: though I consider, for reasons elsewhere given, that it is by no means peculiar to *Buddhism.*

The several modes in which it is used, in connection with sacred buildings, are as follows:

1. As the basement, and upper enclosures of structural Sthúpas, not only at Sánchi itself, but at other neighbouring places: and, also, at Buddha Gaya, Bharhut, and Amarávati (see Plates II., III., XXIX., and XXX.). In these instances, there is a *triple* row of rails, or cross-bars—doubtless allusive to the triad worshipped, one of whose meanings was the three-fold division of "time:"—and in the large Sánchi enclosure, the total number of these cross-bars was exactly 360, the old diurnal subdivision of the "circling year." (²)

A further illustration of Mithraic allusion is afforded by the ground-plan of the enclosure; which, with its four angular entrances, represents a combination of the

(¹) Sir A. Cunningham gives the inscriptions on the four gateways of the large Sthúpa, separately, because of the comparatively recent form of their characters. (See "The Bhilsa Topes," 262 to 267, and 272, and Plate XIX., Nos. 178 to 196.)

(²) See, in Chapter XIV., further remarks on the analogy between this mystical ring, round the structural emblem of the Supreme, or Adi Buddha, or Iswara, and such solar impersonations as Siva, in the Linga form, encircled by his Sakti, Párbati, as the Yoni: Súrya, or Mitra, the Græco-Persian Mithras, with his Sakti, Pradhá, or brightness, in the shape of his surrounding halo, or aureole: and—the prototype of both—the ring-encircled figures, crosses and discs, which, in Assyria, Egypt, and Persia, symbolized the Supreme Deity.

"Swástika" cross with a circle (¹): a conjunction of the cross and disc, which is not only Bráhmanical, as well as Buddhist; but is a well-known feature in the far more ancient symbolism of Greece, Persia, Egypt, and Assyria.

Structural railings of this same kind, were found, by Sir A. Cunningham, at Mathura; but with what building connected, I am not aware: and in further illustration of the wide prevalence of its use, I may mention that, at Kyángain, in Lower Burmah, there is a perfect specimen of a square wooden enclosure, round a triple shrine; which consists of cylindrical posts, and a triple row of cross-bars, exactly analogous to this "Buddhist railing." I was told that such wooden railings are common in Burmah, and generally enclose funereal structures.(²)

2. As the basement and upper enclosures of Sthúpas, represented in the sculptures (Plates IV., X., XIII. Fig. 1., and XXVIII.).

3. As the enclosure of a forest shrine, or ascetic's hut (Plate V.).

4. As the balustrade of triple pavilions, round sacred trees, and overshadowing the disc-and-crescent symbol (Plates XII. Fig. 2; and XVIII., top compart.).

5. As the balustrade of a fire temple (Plate XIII., Fig. 2).

6. As the enclosure round sacred trees (Plate XVI.). This is frequent; though my Plates include only one specimen from the sculptures. It occurs, also, on many coins. (See my Plate XXXIX., Figs. 8, 13, and "Bhilsa Topes," Plate XXXI.)

7. As the balustrade of a relic pavilion (Plate XVIII., bottom compart.).

8. As the lower, and roof balustrade of a pavilion in a sacred barge (Plate XXI., Fig. 2).

9. As the plinth which supported the central wheel over the West gateway, and as the enclosure of a "Chakra-Sthambha," or wheel-pillar (Plate XXXI., Fig. 2).

10. As the abacus of the láth, which once stood near the North gateway (Plates XXXII., Fig. 2, and XXXIII., Fig. 1). Probably, all such isolated pillars were so *enclosed*, also: (see above, and the pillar in Fig. 13, Plate XXXII., of "The Bhilsa Topes").

The Buddhist railing also forms a common moulding and ornament, throughout the Sánchi sculptures. It divides all the sculptured compartments; and forms the abacus of eight out of ten gateway pillars; and the bottom moulding of each of the lintels and their supporting props (see Plates IV., V., XVII., XVIII., XX., XXI. Fig. 1, XXV. and XXVIII.).

Finally, it was used in secular as well as in sacred architecture; as shown in the sculptured representations of gateways, balconies, pavilions, raised terraces,

(¹) See Plate III., Fig. 5. The great Sthúpa at Sánchi, resembles in shape the "tumulus," rather than the "Tope," as classified by Masson: according to whom, a "perfect tumulus" had four interior passages, meeting in its centre. I found no trace of such passages, at Sánchi: but, supposing them to exist, they would complete the form of the ordinary Swástika, as shown in my figure. Many of the relic chambers opened at Sánchi, and other places, were Swástika-shaped in plan: as, also, were the funereal chambers found in some of the kist-vaens of Southern India. And, in the centre of a Sthúpa, lately opened, in the Madras Presidency, this form of cross was found, marked in masonry, at the central place of deposit for relics.

(²) This Burmese quadrangular enclosure, has entrances on the east, south, and west; but none on the "fateful north." I could not learn why.

garden enclosures, etc. (See Plates IV., VI., Fig. 2; VII., Fig. 1; IX., Fig. 2; XVI., XX., XXII., Fig. 1; and XXVII.)

Corresponding illustrations of its use in secular architecture are found in the sculptures of Bharhut, Buddha Gaya, and Amarávati; and also in the Yusufzai, and other far north-west districts of the Panjáb, whence, apparently, the style of building shown at Sánchi was derived; and doubtless Indian explorers could cite many another instance of its use, in both sacred and secular art.

It is noteworthy that the characteristic idea in this curious railed enclosure, that is, the combination of a circle with rails, or cross-bars, in single, double, or triple lines, is embodied in the symbolism of both the Bráhmans and the Assyrians. Among the "lakshanas," or sacred sectarial marks of the Bráhmanical Vishnu—whose latest Avatára was Buddha—are single, double, and treble horizontal bars, in combination with a disc or circle: and the "sacred horned cap," of the Assyrian deities, has three fillets, or bars, encircling its Sthúpa shaped crown. (See Fig. 38, 39, 40 of Plate XXXIX.; and Fig. 1 of Plate XL.)

The construction of each gateway was the same; and is sufficiently explained by Plate IV.; and each gateway pillar and lintel consisted of a single block of sandstone; the whole being put together, like the circular enclosures, by mortice and tenon, and without any cement.

The entire surface of the gateways, pillars, entablature, and supporting props, is covered by sculpture in bold relief; and small figures once occupied each of the spaces between the props.

The subjects represented give a very striking picture of the religious and domestic life of the period; and of the buildings, costumes, chariots, arms, instruments, utensils, and ornaments then in use: and many of the scenes, symbols, and supernatural forms represented indicate that, at the time the gateways were erected—the first century A.D.—the prevailing religion was still largely mingled with sun, fire, and elemental worship, and was entirely devoid of any representations of Buddha himself!

Scattered about, on the summit and slope of the breach, and in and near the enclosing railing, I found numerous entire and broken pillars, cross-bars and portions of coping, which I was able to identify as the remains of a balustrade round the lower terrace (Fig. 8, Plate III.); a circular enclosure round the summit of the Sthúpa (Figs. 9, 10, Plate III.); and a square enclosure for the crowning Tí or Chatta (Figs. 11 to 13, Plate III.). I also found, at the spot indicated in my plan, fragments of the Tí itself; which was evidently double, if not treble; the socket for an upper one being cut in the upper surface of the lower portion.

I have shown the restored plan and elevation, complete, in Figs. 1, 2 of my Plate II. [1];

[1] It is evident from Captain Fell's description ("Journ. As. Soc. Beng." III. 490), that the Tí, and its square enclosure, were already prostrate in A.D. 1819: and were not thrown down by the reckless explorers of three years later. I was told, by an old inhabitant of Sánchi, that there was once an outer ascent to the enclosure at the summit of the Sthúpa: but he could not explain its nature. No traces of any such outer

and have therein imitated the spreading cymatium which crowns most of the superstructures represented in the sculptures.

Resting against the basement wall, opposite each entrance, there was, once, an alto-relievo image of Buddha, under a carved niche, or canopy; many fragments of which I found lying about. The northern image was still in its place, in 1851; but the other three figures had been displaced. Those at the northern, eastern and western entrances are seated Buddhas, with the usual two attendants; and small flying figures, and there is nothing of special importance about them. The head of the northern figure, however, is of somewhat unusual character, and I, therefore, give a sketch of it (Fig. 10, Plate XV.). It was lying, broken off, near the figure.

The figure at the southern entrance is standing; and is on a smaller scale, and different in appearnace. It is shown in Plate XIV., Fig 1. I could not find the head, which is unfortunate, as the head-gear is often of importance.

The elephant, on which the right hand of the figure rests, is, as elsewhere shown, an important animal in Buddhism; and is often used as a symbol of the Buddhist faith; which is called, by some Buddhist writers, "the religion of the elephant."

Neither of these images has any inscription; but they are, evidently, the "four Buddhas" referred to in one of the Gupta inscriptions at the eastern entrance; which mentions the "shrines of the four Buddhas" (see Chapter XI.).

Within the enclosure, lying about, or ranged against the basement wall, were a number of miniature stone Sthúpas, of various sizes and shapes, some with, and some without capitals, as shown in Figs. 1 to 5, 7, 8, 9 of Plate XV. Some of them have single, and some four figures; and one, three, five, or seven encircling plat-bands, or "belts of mouldings," to use Masson's expression.(¹) Outside the Eastern gateway, at Z, there was a large model Sthúpa, quite plain in shape, but covered with like-shaped objects, in twelve rows. This exactly resembles what the modern Hindús still worship, as the multiform, or Sás-Mukhti Linga of Mahádeva—the Great God—Siva: while others, in their simpler form, are identical in form and appearance with the ordinary "linga," which is shown, for purposes of comparison, in Fig. 6, Plate XV.

In a purely Buddhist point of view, the multiplication of symbols in a single

ascent remain; and none of the Sthúpas represented in the sculptures show any indication of any such exterior access. If anything of the kind ever existed, it was, perhaps, a wooden construction, on the south side. But most probably, my old informant alluded to some kind of scaffolding erected by the visitors who ascended, and destroyed, the Sthúpa, in A.D. 1822.

(¹) Masson said, regarding structural Topes, of which these miniature Sthúpas are models, "belts of mouldings, round the superior portion of the Tope, sometimes containing arches and pilasters, sometimes pilasters only, and sometimes plain, in relief, seem peculiar to the more ancient Topes, and render them easily recognisable." ("Ariana Antiqua," 55.) On the other hand, Mr. J. Fergusson, derives this kind of ornamentation from the more ancient plain Sthúpa, with its surrounding palisade or railing. The detached railing, he considers, merged, in process of time, into encircling rows of pilasters round the base, and upper portions of the structure; as seen at Mánikyála and Sárnáth; and, ultimately, came to be represented by one or more simple mouldings. Such a gradation may, perhaps, be traced, by comparing, successively, the representations of structural Sthúpas in my Plates II., Fig. 2; X.; XVIII., Fig. 6; XXVIII., Figs. 1 to 5; and the models of Sthúpas shown in Plate XV., Figs 1 to 5, and 7 to 9.

figure, would represent either the numerous pre-existences of Buddha, or the many events, discourses, or doctrines, in honour of which Sthúpas are supposed to have been erected: while in a Bráhmanical sense, such multiform objects would represent the Sás-Mukhti, or Sahasrarúpa Siva, or Mahádeva, whose thousand-fold forms, energies, and attributes were indicated by either such symbols as the single, triple, chau-mukhti, panch-mukhti, or Sásmukhti Linga, with its encircling Yoni; or by a human figure, in a halo, or aureole; and with numerous heads, arms, weapons, and symbols.(¹)

With one exception (Fig 9, Plate XV.), which has illegible inscriptions in the "Kutila" character, none of these model Sthúpas have any inscriptions, to show whether they are of a funereal character, or are votive symbolical offerings, and such as were used in domestic worship. They have been regarded in both lights: Major Kittoe considering such Sthúpas funereal; and Sir A. Cunningham calling them "small dedicatory topes" ("Jour. As. Soc. Beng." XVI. 276, "The Bhilsa Topes," 178): but perhaps the simplest explanation is to be found in M. Rémusat's notes to the "Foe-Koue-Ki" (Chapters III., note 3, and XIII., note 6), regarding the "towers of deliverance," described by Fa Hian. He says, "these little structures are built of stone or brick, in the form of a tower, without capital. They are of one, two, three, or four storeys, for the Srávakas, or auditors of Buddha, of the first four ranks." A description which very closely answers to the appearance of these miniature Sthúpas, with their dividing mouldings.(²)

Finally, as showing the votive character of miniature Sthúpas, at any rate among Buddhists, I may instance the small terra-cotta models dug up in such numbers near Benares, and other Buddhist sites; each containing a disc-shaped tablet or seal, bearing the well-known formula "Ye dharmma hetuprabhava," etc.

Some of the small Sthúpas, particularly those with four figures on them, are unquestionably purely Buddhist: but others look more Jaina than Buddhist; and are, probably, later Jaina offerings: at any rate, the presence of any figures at all seems conclusive as to the emblematic, and dedicatory character of the models.

I shall endeavour to prove, elsewhere, that large and small Sthúpas alike; the pyramid and the pagoda; the pillars near caves, temples and shrines; the linga of Siva; the ring-encircled figures and emblems of Assyria, Persia and Greece; and the "pillars of Baal;" are, one and all, analogous, and of the same origin and significance.(³)

The custom of grouping round the main building—whether temple or tomb—small models resembling it in shape, was, there can be little doubt, structurally

(¹) Many writers have ridiculed the redundancies and extravagance of Indian mythological figures: but they are scarcely, if at all, more unnatural and extravagant than the strikingly analogous figures of the Assyrian, Egyptian, and Greek pantheon; and all, alike, were, in their earlier forms, the expression of the universal power and attributes of one supreme deity.

(²) Colonel Sykes considered dedicatory Sthúpas of this kind analogous to the isolated votive pillars, in front of temples; particularly cave temples ("Jour. R. A. Soc." VII. 274).

(³) See on this subject, Chapter XIV.

adopted in the open temples which succeeded the more ancient solid Sthúpa. The clustered towers, or "Sikharas," of Buddhist, Jaina, and Bráhmanical temples, have, usually, rows of miniature Sikharas, at their four angles; ordinarily seven in each vertical row: which represent the encircling model Sthúpas, now under notice. The shape of the Egyptian pyramid, and the Burmese pagoda, which are analogous structures to the Indian Sthúpa, precluded the addition of such structural imitations; but in both countries, as in India, the practice obtained, of surrounding the principal building with numerous small "replicas" of its shape.

The villagers of Sánchi and its vicinity, albeit unaware of the justness of the appropriation, have "canonized" many of the miniature Sthúpas; which may be seen, daubed with the sacred vermillion, and set up, for worship, as the "linga" form of Mahádeva.(¹)

Scattered about, in the enclosure, particularly near the eastern entrance, I found several mutilated figures, between three and four feet high; which, though clothed in long robes, which is usually considered to be a Buddhist characteristic, have otherwise a Jaina character.

They are probably imitations of Buddhist figures, added, at a comparatively recent period, by the Jainas, and one of them has a short inscription in the "Kutila" character, of the 8th to 10th century A.D.(²)

Other figures of Buddha, with "Kutila" inscriptions, will be mentioned later; and we have thus three epochs of sculpture represented at Sánchi: that of the gateways, which are of about the first century of the Christian Era, and which, like the sculptures of Buddha Gaya and Bharhut, have no representations of Buddha in human shape; that of about the fifth century A.D., which is the date of the four Buddhas" at the entrances of the enclosure; and that of the figures with "Kutila" inscriptions, which are of the 8th to 10th century.

The fifth century A.D. would seem, from other evidence, to have been the period when images of Sákya or Gautama in deified human form, were first used in India proper. No such images, bearing any earlier date, have, so far as I am aware, been there discovered; while those of much later date abound (³): and the Chinese travellers in India, though they quote traditional statements, current in their time, as to the

(¹) Several European writers have remarked upon the identity between the Buddhist Chaitya, and the Saiva Linga: among others Maurice, in his "Indian Antiquities," and Sykes, in his account of the Ellora caves. The general subject of Indian Phallic worship will be found treated in Tod's "Rájasthán, I. 604, and the "Jour. Roy. As. Soc." VI., 240, 241.

(²) The Jainas of Bhilsa, though they pay no reverence to the Sánchi Sthúpas, attribute their erection to a Jaina Rája Chandragupta, of Pátálpura, 162 years after the date of Mahávira (equivalent to B.C. 575). They gave me, from the Jaina "Bhadrawá Cheritra," the succession of Rájas, as Vindusára, Asoka, Kunála, Chandragupta, and Sinhasena; which is, evidently, a garbled version of the Pauránik genealogy of the Maurya dynasty of Pátaliputra. (See Chapters X. and XI.)

(³) See, for example, the Amarávati sculptures, which are said to be of about 450 A.D. Sir A. Cunningham unearthed at Mathura, sculptured figures, which he attributed to the Jainas, and dated between 80 and 180 A.D. The Jainas were an offshoot from Buddhism, and, according to Tod, were not idolaters until after the death of Krishna—that is, as late as the 7th century A.D.—when images of Nem-Náth, commonly called "Arishta Nemi," or the dark Nemi, were introduced, to rival those of the blue-hued

ancient use of "statues of Fo," do not mention having *seen* any! On the contrary, Fa Hian, the earliest of these travellers, who visited a great part of India, between 404 and 412 A.D., tells us, in effect, that up to his time, Buddha was represented by symbols only; namely, the wheel, and the bull's head, which, as I shall elsewhere show, is a form of the "disc-and-crescent" symbol. He says ("Foe-Koue-Ki," Chapter XX.), that the first representation of Fo—made by Rája Prasenajit, and sanctioned by Buddha himself—was "the head of an ox, carved in sandal-wood"; the approved "model for imitation by the four classes" . . . . It was the first of all the "statues of Fo, and that which men of subsequent times have copied."

This, according to the usual Buddhist computation, gives the 6th century B.C. as the date of the first sculptured representation of Sákya Buddha; but it has no reference to a ***human-shaped*** image.

In another place, however, Fa Hian dates the introduction of Buddhism into China, and the first use of images, from the erection of a statue of the Bodhisatwa Maitreya, 300 years after the Nirvána, or B.C. 243 ("Foe-Koue-Ki," Chapter VII.).

According to other Chinese writers quoted in M. Rémusat's notes to the "Foe-Koue-Ki" (Chapter VII., note 5), the Chinese statues of Fo, or Buddha, were imitated from a golden image, worshipped by the King of Hieou-thou (Afghánisthán, or Bactria), and brought thence, in 121 B.C., by the conquering General Hou-Khin-Ping.

The generally accepted date of the introduction of the Buddhism of Sákya into China, is A.D. 61 to 64; and the religion was not actually adopted there until a much later date: so that the above mutually discrepant dates are contradicted by Chinese history itself; and there is no other proof that Chinese images are any older than authentic Indian specimens. (See "Jour. Roy. As. Soc." VI. 250, 251, 277, and Murray's "Hist. of China," II. 142.)

The only safe conclusion, on the above data, appears to be that at some time between the end of the first and the middle of the fifth century of the Christian Era, the Buddhists of Central and Southern India began to use human-shaped images of Buddha, in lieu of, or, rather, in addition to the older *symbols:* the custom having originated, at an earlier date, in Afghánisthán and Bactria, where it was directly due to Greek influence.

Krishna, in popular veneration ("Rájasthán," I. 535). I have never myself met with any Jaina figures which could, unhesitatingly, be dated earlier than the 10th century A.D.: but if Sir A. Cunningham's date is correct, they must have seceded from the Buddhism of Sákya, soon after its first institution, about the commencement of the Christian Era. Some writers think the Jainas are an *older* sect than the Buddhists.

CHAPTER IV.

THE NORTHERN GATEWAY OF NO. I STHUPA; AND ITS SCULPTURES.

In my original report, I commenced my description of the sculptures with those of the North Gateway; as it is the first seen as you approach from below; and I took the subjects from left to right, and from bottom to top. Sir A. Cunningham, in his description ("The Bhilsa Topes," 201), adopted a different order: but I have found it more convenient to adhere to my previous plan.(1)

Plate IV. shows the rear of the gateway, exactly as I found it in 1850: and Plate V. shows the three sculptured faces of the left pillar; the blank compartments being those which are represented in separate Plates.

The left, or outer face of the left gateway pillar shows a votive "sthambha," supporting a chatta-shaded symbol, which I have called the "disc-and-crescent" symbol (see Chapter X.): and which, as well as its triple Ti or chatta, evidently refers to the triad worshipped at the date of the sculpture. At the foot of the pillar is the "padma," "charna," or "sripáda;" that is, the sacred foot-prints; each marked by the rayed disc, or "chakra," the mark of sanctity, and universal sovereignty, both celestial and terrestrial.(2)

Both pillar and symbol are covered with floral ornamentation, in which the lotus, and a kind of honeysuckle predominate: and on eight projecting pegs, on either side of the pillar, hang jewelled belts and necklaces, like those worn by men represented in the sculptures; and two strings of emblems, which call for separate notice.

Part of the ornamentation of the "disc-and-crescent" is a long serpentine scroll; which, judging from its prominent use at Bharhut and Amarávati, evidently had some symbolic meaning. In the centre of the crescent, this scroll is combined

(1) To obviate confusion between our two versions, I shall, in each instance, quote Sir A. Cunningham's page, and compartment.

(2) The oldest representations of the sacred foot-print were marked, as in this instance, by the "chakra" only: but eventually, as is well known, the symbols on such objects became very numerous. The "chakra" was the distinguishing, and predictive, sign, alike of the Bráhmanical god, the Buddhist deified saint, and the Jaina Tirthankara; and, also, among all three sects, the symbol of supreme earthly sovereignty. Among the Bráhmanical Hindus, it is the especial weapon and symbol of Vishnu (who in his last Avatára, is Buddha): among the Buddhists it was called the "dharma chakra," or sacred circle of the law of Buddha; and was at one time his only symbol: and, in fact, it has a multiplicity of meanings. In its oldest form, a simple cross in a circle; it occurs in the ancient symbolism of Assyria, Egypt, and Greece; and it ultimately became the many-rayed disc, or wheel, which will be more fully noticed later (see pages 39, 40).

with a curved cruciform figure, which seems to me to be a variety of the symbol shown in Figs. 8 and 12 of Plate XXXIX., called by Fergusson "two serpents."(¹)

The flower which I have called the "honeysuckle," is separately represented in numerous other sculptures (see Plates IV., XVII., XIX., and XXXIII., Figs. 2, 4); and was evidently sacred. It resembles, and was, probably, copied from, the Greek honeysuckle; which was derived, through the Phœnicians, from Assyria.

The two necklaces of sacred symbols (shown, enlarged, in Figs. 15, 16, of Plate XXXIX.) have never, I believe, been much noticed, hitherto: but they seem to me to be of considerable interest and importance. They probably represent symbolical ornaments worn, perhaps as charms, by the local monarch, who, we may suppose, made offerings to the deity worshipped, of his personal ornaments; an old custom, still followed in Buddhist countries.(²)

Some of them, marked *a, b, c, d, g, h*, are component parts of the disc-and-crescent symbol itself.

a.a. (See, also, *a*, in Fig. 1, Plate XXXIX.) are the blade-shaped object, which, as a sword, or spear or arrow-head, symbolized the solar ray, or fire, in other countries, as well as in India. In Assyria, for instance, the arrow-head—the radix of the cruciform character—was sacred to Nebo: and, in Egypt, the hieroglyph of an arrow-head, or arrow-shaped sword, represented the sacred syllable or letter "nun"; which letter, in ancient Arabic, also signified both a "sword" and a "fish."(³)

b.b. Is the disc-and-crescent symbol itself; without some of its details, and with six branched supports.

These two symbols, *a* and *b*, as well as the "bhalli," another form of the sacred arrow-head, occur frequently in the sculptures; sometimes as ornaments and trappings, and sometimes as sacred objects, round rayed discs, or wheels (see Plates XXI., Fig. 1; and XXXI., Figs, 2, 4, 5; and Chapter X.).

c.c. Is the central symbol, within the crescent, shown in Plates IV. and XXXIX., Fig. 1. In Plate IV. (bottom lintel) it is seen held aloft by one of two (? twin) children (see description of the lintel). It occurs among the sculptures at Karli and Khandgiri: and is one of the symbolic figures of Burmese sacred art.

(¹) I cannot, myself, see much resemblance to serpents, in this (coin) device; but figures just like this double cruciform symbol, are called by some writers, the "Sun-snake"; and a variety of the Swastika cross. It is possible that the long scroll-shaped ornament may merely denote that the disc-and-crescent symbol, among its other meanings, represents the element water, which was specially sacred, in both Bráhmanism and Buddhism (see Chapter X.); and was, I may add, typified by the Nága, or serpent: whence, probably, the custom, common to the ancient Egyptians, and the Buddhists and Bráhmans of India, of representing water by a simple wavy line.

(²) These symbolic necklaces may be compared with those in the Assyrian sculptures; to which Sir A. Layard attributed a Mithraic or Saiva character (see my Plate XL., Fig. 1).

(³) Sir A. Cunningham, in his interpretation of the disc-and-crescent symbol ("The Bhilsa Topes," 356), also connects the bladed projections, *a*, with the letter or syllable Na, or N; but in a different sense.

In the elemental interpretation of the disc-and-crescent, it represents "ákás," or ether (see Chapter X.).

d. Is the eight-petalled lotus, or rosette, which sometimes replaces, and sometimes forms the centre of, the simple disc, as seen in Plates IV.; V.; XII., Fig. 2; XVIII.; XXXI., Fig. 4; XXXV., Fig. 7; and XXXIX., Figs. 1 and 2.(¹)

g.g.g. Are other varieties of the disc; the curved lines of which are supposed, in the Indian symbols, as they are in the "whorls" and other emblems lately excavated by Dr. Schliemann, at Troy, to indicate the rapid apparent motion of the sun.

h.h. Are two forms of the sacred axe; the blade of which, like the "bhalli" or sacred arrow-head, elsewhere mentioned, resembles the crescent portion of the disc-and-crescent symbol. Axes of this shape are among the arms of giants, represented at Sánchi; and are seen in Indo-Scythic coins. They are met with, also, in the symbolism of other nations, as will be noticed later.

The symbols marked *e, f, i, k, l* and *m*, are unconnected with the disc-and-crescent.

e.e. Are two forms of a symbol, which, in various shapes, is very common in Buddhist sculpture, inscriptions, and coins. It looks like a combination of several Páli letters, or syllables; but has not, as yet, been satisfactorily explained (see "The Bhilsa Topes," 354, 355). It is No. 166 of Professor Wilson's list of coin-monograms (see my Plate XXXIX., Fig. 14).

Whatever the interpretation of its more complex forms, there can be little doubt that, in its simpler shape ♀ it is analogous to, if not identical with, the "crux ansata," or "symbol of life," carried by most Egyptian deities (see Chapter X.).

f. Which is No. 164, *a*, of Wilson's list of monograms, is the symbol seen on the coins shown in Fig. 8 of my Plate XXXIX., and Fig. 11, Plate XXXI. of "The Bhilsa Topes." It represents, either the sacred tree, or the Tí or chatta, in an enclosure; or it may, possibly, be meant for some kind of lustral vessel, with a handle; in which case it would be analogous to that carried by the Assyrian deities and priests.

i.i. Are clusters of jewels; represented in the conventional mode common to Brahmans, Buddhists, and Jainas. The last-named sect include it as one of the sixteen dream-portents which herald the birth of each of their twenty-four Tirthankaras: the "four-and-twenty elders" of the Jaina phase of Buddhism.

k.k. A pair of fish, is not only one of the twelve zodiacal signs, in many systems of astronomy; but occurs, in conjunction with the crook, on Egyptian scarabæi.

(¹) The disc and the crescent both occur among the sacred symbols in the Assyrian necklace alluded to in Note 2, p. 19. The disc there encloses an eight-rayed star; which is an earlier form of the eight-petalled lotus.

Like the jewel cluster, it is one of the Jaina dream-portents: and as a purely Buddhist symbol, the single fish is typical of Sákya Buddha himself; who, in Buddhist works, is represented as having—like the Bráhmanical Vishnu—been once incarnate as a fish: the Makara, and Matsya of Sanskrit.

l.l. Are varieties of the "Kalasa," or water-vase; which was not only part of the paraphernalia of Buddha himself, and of every Buddhist priest; but is, itself, a sacred symbol of high antiquity. A water-vase and goat, for instance, form the hieroglyph of the Egyptian god "Num," or "Nub," the Nebo of Assyria.(1)

m.m. The "Ankus," or elephant-goad, owes its significance, as a purely Buddhist symbol, to its connection with the elephant, which is, itself, a symbol, both of the religion, and of its founder Gautama or Sákya. But it has, also, a much more extended import. It represents the "crook"; the pastoral symbol which, in some shape or other, is carried by so many of the male deities of Egypt; between whom, and the earlier or Mithraic "Buddha," there are so many points of resemblance. It also formed the "lituus," or divining staff, of the Roman Augurs; and there would seem to be some combination of it in the so-called coin-monogram shown in Fig. 14 of my Plate XXXIX.

It will be seen that these symbols are, in several cases, marked by cross-lines, or chequers; while others are plain: a distinction which has, doubtless, a special significance. I can suggest no satisfactory explanation, from a purely Buddhist point of view; but I would remark that this cross-bar or chequer-marking, is met with in the sculptures of Mexico, Egypt, and Ireland; and is supposed, at any rate in some cases, to represent the alternations of day and night. Such was, certainly, its meaning in the figures of the Bráhmanical Súrya, shown in Figs. 4, 5, of my Plate XL.(2)

The front face of the left pillar has five compartments, separated, as they are throughout the sculptures, by a "railing" moulding.(3)

The first, or lowest compartment ("Bhilsa Topes," V. pp. 232, 233), which is

(1) The Bráhmanical fire-god, Agni, one of the three primitive Vedic deities, has the water-vase, and goat, as his symbols; like the Egyptian "Num": and the same two symbols form the Indian zodiacal sign of the Makara; commonly called the "Sea-goat." Other curious coincidences might be cited; but they will be more conveniently noticed elsewhere.

(2) The well-known modern sign of "the chequers," for places of public entertainment, still indicates that they are open "day and night": and it is curious, to say the least, that a like sign was used, doubtless with like meaning, for the wine taverns of Pompeii nearly 1900 years ago.

(3) Many of the representations of this "Buddhist railing" have rows of projections below, and along the front, which are evidently the lower tenons of the uprights and the ends of cross-beams. (See Plates XVII., XVIII., and XXVII.) In the bottom compartment of Plate XVIII., the beams of which these projections are the ends, are clearly shown in perspective. The analogous projections in the Doric style of architecture are held to prove that it originated in wooden constructions; and this peculiarity at Sánchi, seems to justify a similar conclusion. The late Mr. J. Fergusson had no doubt on the subject.

shown in Plate VI., Fig. 1, represents an aquatic scene; with men, in Indian dress, and nude women, carousing, in amatory fashion, near a pool, or stream of water, in which are mounted elephants, and more nude women.(1)

The water is represented by wavy lines; amid which are plants and shells (2); and the action of the figures in it is very spirited and natural: the elephants being particularly well carved.(3)

The peacock, represented on the rocks to left, was a favourite and sacred bird, among both Buddhists and Bráhmans, as well as among many other ancient races; and it figures in many Buddhist legends (4); though here, most likely, it is a mere ornamental addition.

The tree represented is perhaps a highly conventional mango; but may possibly be meant for the "Kalpa darm," the mythical Buddhist tree which answers to the "Kalpa vriksha," or "Párijata" of Indra's paradise.

As the Buddhists considered the elephant a type of their religion, and called human life "a waste of waters," it would be easy to view the sculpture as an allegorical representation of emancipation through religion, and the attainment of paradise; but such a construction would be utterly antagonistic to the Buddhism of Sákya; the final bliss, or Nirvána, promised by which, is quite inconsistent with the action of the convivial couples in the upper part of the sculpture.

I am inclined to regard it as representing the king and his son, or minister, with their wives, enjoying themselves, while watching the aquatic sports of the women of the palace: a well-known Indian pastime, both in ancient and modern times.

The second compartment ("The Bhilsa Topes," IV. p. 232; and my Plate VI., Fig. 2), represents a horseman, numerously attended, leaving the gateway of a city or palace; watched by spectators on the walls and in the gateway alcoves. Two of these hold their right hands up to their mouths, as if out of respect.(5)

(1) There is no question as to the nudity of the women in this sculpture; but it is quite a mistake to suppose that nudity is the rule among the female figures at Sánchi. Some who appear, on a cursory glance, to be totally nude, only appear so because the sculptor, like the early Greek artists, represented thin drapery, over the lower limbs, by simple lines. In figures, however, whose attitudes necessitate it, the drapery is fully shown (see, for instance, Plates IV.; IX., Fig. 2; XVIII.; XXII., Fig. 1; XXIII., Fig. 1; and XXIV).

(2) Throughout the Sánchi sculptures, water is thus represented; the wavy lines encircling lotus flowers, buds, and leaves; shells; fish; turtle; alligators; and various birds; all fresh-water objects, and, therefore, precluding the idea entertained by some writers, that the Sánchi sculptures represent a maritime race.

(3) At Sánchi, and, I may add, in all the Indian sculptures I have seen, elephants are exceptionally well carved; and, as a rule, animals of all kinds are better executed than the human figures, though the latter, too, are often very spirited, and even graceful; and are devoid, for the most part, of the mannerism which so often characterizes Hindu sculpture. Indeed in many of the figures and animals represented at Sánchi, one almost fancies Greek influence, if not Greek workmanship.

(4) See, for instance, the legend quoted, in Rémusat's Notes to the "Foe-Koue-Ki," (Chapter VIII., Note 1); which relates how Buddha, when formerly "King of the Peacocks," struck a rock with his beak, to supply water for his followers; and thus produced a lake, whose waters cured diseases.

(5) Among the sculptures of Bharhut there are representations of men worshipping the sacred pipal tree of Sákya Muni, who are holding their left hands up to their mouths (see "Stupa of Bharhut," p. 114, and Plates XIII., Fig. 1; XVII., Fig. 3; and XXX., Fig. 3). I am not aware of any corresponding gesture in the modern worship of the Buddhists; but these attitudes remind one of the reverential ceremonies of the

Inside the city are two groups, each of a male and two female figures, carrying refreshments, or some kind of offering; to a third female on the left, and, on the right, to a male figure near a peacock-standard; curiously like what a Hindu would call the monkey-god Hanumán.(¹)

All the figures, save four, are in the ordinary Indian costume; but the two attendants nearest the horseman, and two spearmen, appear to represent foreigners; perhaps of Greek origin; though the dhotis show that, if foreigners, they had been partly Indianized.(²)

The principal figure, who carries a "Vajra," or thunderbolt-mace, and is shaded by an umbrella—both marks of sanctity, or of kingly rank—doubtless represents the king, proceeding, with his escort and musicians, on some state or religious expedition; or it may represent the prince Siddhártha, starting on one of the four excursions which are said to have led him to asceticism, and the final attainment of Buddhahood.

I know of no existing style of building, in India, with which to compare those shown in this sculpture, and so many other sculptures at Sánchi. Their pinnacled roofs, and peculiar gables, remind one of the structures of China, Japan, Burmah, and Nepál, in which wood is so largely used; and there are many indications that wood was a principal material in their construction; at any rate, as regards roofing.

Whatever their material or origin, however, it is quite clear that, at the date of these sculptures, buildings of this kind were in common use throughout India, for both religious and secular purposes: for we find the style represented in the older cave temples of the south; in Yusufzai on the far north-west; here, at Sánchi, in the heart of Central India; at Buddha Gayá, in Bahár; at Bharhut, in Bhagelkhand; and at Amarávati, in the Deccan.

As regards the peculiar recessed and chambered gateways, we have a proof of their use, in Tartary, in the "Foe-Koue-Ki" (chap. III.); where Fa Hian speaks of "the pavilion over the gate, whence the ladies and young damsels" (of Yu-thian or Khotan) "scattered flowers over the car, which contained the sacred image," or symbol. Gateways with side guard-rooms, upper chambers, and open "Naubut Khánas," or music galleries, are still common in India; but the style of building

Bráhmans (and Jainas also, I believe), who are directed to make their daily invocations to the mystical "Om," and the triad "Bhuh, Bhuvah, Swar," while the breath is suspended, by closing the mouth and nostrils ("Vish. Purán." 274, Note 5).

(¹) I shall have to describe several sculptures in which the ape is prominently introduced (see more particularly Plates IX., Fig. 1; and XXI., Fig. 2). The ape is also frequently represented at Bharhut; but in a less striking manner than at Sánchi. The Bráhmanical Hanumán, and his army of apes, the allies of Rámachandra in the conquest of Ceylon, were, most probably, Indo-Scythians. Scythia, the country of the Huns, Sáka, or Sacæ, and the nidus of the race to which Sáka Muni, or Sákya Sinha belonged, was known as "the land of apes"; and the Indo-Scythians gave the name of their own country to Sindh, the part of India which they and the Buddhists first occupied.

(²) For other representations of foreigners, see Plates VII., Fig. 1; X.; XVI.; XX.; XXII., Fig. 2; XXVII.; and XXXV.

here represented, does not exist; and was, we may suppose, discontinued when, owing doubtless to the increasing scarcity of timber, stone or brick replaced wood as the staple material for architecture.(1)

The third compartment ("Bhilsa Topes," III. p. 232), represents the worship, by six men and a child, of three trees; see Plate V.

The fourth compartment ("Bhilsa Topes," II. p. 232, and my Plate V.), has three hut-shaped buildings, apparently sacred, among five trees; which, as well as the central tree, are being worshipped by six men, in Indian costume. One of the three shrines, (2) which we may assume to be sacred to the triad, stands in a railed enclosure; and seems, therefore, of more importance than the others. Probably it is dedicated to the principal personage of the triad.

I can suggest no explanation of the small plumed figure between the two lower shrines. It may represent a child; or the attendant on one of the buildings, shown on a small scale.(3)

The fifth, or top compartment (Plate V.), represents twenty-one men, in Indian costume, worshipping a chatta-shaded tree (perhaps a mango), with an altar in front of it. Over all hover two "Kinnara;" supernatural beings which will be noticed later. With the exception of two drummers, and the two central seated figures, all wear jewelled necklaces; but the two above excepted have light scarves, so worn as to leave the "right shoulder bare," a ceremonial custom much quoted in Buddhist works, and of great antiquity.

The right, or inner face of the left pillar has four compartments, and forms one side of the entrance.

The first, or lowest compartment (Plate V.), has a large figure of a man richly dressed in the costume which I have called Indian, and which was evidently that of the principal, and ruling race represented in the sculptures. He wears a short "dhoti," with an embroidered girdle; a large turban with the hair twisted up with its folds; (4) very large ear-ornaments; and, round his neck, a jewelled necklace. He is unarmed, bare-footed, and nude from the waist upwards, save a light scarf which leaves the right shoulder bare.(5)

(1) See Note 3, p. 21, as to the indications of a wooden original in the buildings represented at Sánchi.

(2) This right-hand shrine, save that it has, like the others, an altar in front of it, exactly resembles the leaf-thatched huts which are represented in other sculptures, as the habitual abode of Buddhist recluses (see Plates XIII., Fig. 2; and XXIII., Fig. 2). The use of this particular "hut" shape, for a sacred building, may be explained by the tradition, that Sákya Buddha, himself, was once a "Jhayaka," and dwelt "in a leafy hut by the side of the monkey-tank," at Vaisáli (Beal's "Romantic Legend of Sákya Buddha," p. 270).

(3) It seems probable that some of the small figures in the sculptures, really represent adults, shown on a smaller scale, as a convenience to the sculptor; and such may have been the case in this instance. Many of the subjects at Sánchi, however, and also at Bharhut, unquestionably include children; and notably, children wearing tufts or plumes, and looking like twins.

(4) While in Burmah, I was reminded of the Sánchi sculptures by the huge turbans, with intertwined hair, worn by the better-dressed men; and the large ear-ornaments of both sexes. The same thing is observable in the Ajanta paintings; and Sir H. Durand told me that he had noticed similar headgear and ornaments in Tenasserim.

(5) Many of the worshippers in Indian costume have their long scarves thus arranged: and the upper

The figure stands between two trees, of the kinds most common in the sculptures: one, to the right of the figure, resembles the tree among the sculptures of Bharhut, which Sir A. Cunningham identified with the Pátali, or trumpet-flower tree (Bignonia suaveolens); the "bodhi," or sacred tree of "Vipaswi," the first of the "seven Buddhas" of Buddhist writers: and which is inscribed in Páli, as the bodhi of the Bhagavata Vipaswi (see "Stupa of Bharhut," 10, 45, 46, 113; and Plates XXIX., Fig. 1; and LIV., No. 68). The other tree is of the species elsewhere compared to the mango.

Similar large janitor-figures occupy the bottom compartments of the inner faces of all the gate-pillars: so that each entrance was guarded by two of them. At Sánchi all are male figures; and all without inscriptions: but, at Bharhut, the entrances are guarded by both male and female figures; with their names inscribed, in some cases; showing that they represent the Yakshas, Yakshinis, Devatas, and Nágas, who guard the four quarters of the central mount of the universe; and who, therefore, are appropriate guardians of the four approaches to the sacred structures which, both in Bráhmanical and Buddhist mythology, symbolize, among other meanings, the sacred Mount Meru.(¹)

There is nothing in these Sánchi janitors to indicate, with certainty, whether they represent the class of divinity or demi-god which guards the entrances at Bharhut; or whether they belong to a phase of religion, anterior to such adaptations from Bráhmanism: but be this as it may, the Sánchi gate-guardians are analogous to the two supporters, or attendants, which accompany most Buddhist, Bráhmanical, and Jaina images; and which flank the carved portals of the temples of all three sects: the attendant figures being sometimes male, sometimes female, and sometimes of both sexes. Such triple groups, however, are not indigenous to India, but are of foreign origin; and analogous triads are found in the mythological representations of most ancient countries.(²)

In India, these attendant, or guardian, figures, had other names besides those above mentioned. Among Buddhists, they represented the acolytes, genii-pedes, or principal Bodhi-Satwas of a mortal Buddha; or the two minor members, "Dharma," and "Sangha" of the mystical, as distinguished from the personal triad. The Jainas, who, in imitation of the Buddhists, assigned two companions to each of their twenty-four deified saints, or Tirthankaras, called them "Bhairava"; or, particularly when placed at the portals of temples, Ajaya and Vijaya. And, among the Bráhmanical

garment, or scarf (Uttara Sangháti), of the ascetic or priestly class, is invariably so worn; as, also, is the long light robe which is the usual upper garment of figures of Buddha. The arrangement of the dress so as to leave "the right shoulder bare," was an important feature of Buddhist ceremonial; but seems to be traceable to a foreign source (see "Jour. As. Soc. Beng.," VI. 517, 519: Laidlay's "Fa Hian," Chapter XXIV., note 4; and "The Bhilsa Topes," 28, 58, 61). In some of the Sánchi sculptures, however, the scarves of worshippers cover *both* shoulders.

(¹) See "Stupa of Bharhut," pp. 10, 11, 18 to 27, 29, 39, 40, 41; and Plates XXI., XXII., XXIII., LIII., LIV., and LV.

(²) Compare, for example, the temple entrances, figures, trees, and other symbols, guarded by Sphinxes, human and animal hybrid figures, and cherubs, among the Assyrians, Egyptians, and ancient Hebrews.

Hindús, they were variously named, according to the deity to whose image or shrine they are attached; and when, as is very often the case, represented in female form, they are the Saktis, or energies—hence considered as the wives—of the central divinity.(1)

The second compartment ("Bhilsa Topes," III. pp. 233, 234; and my Plate V.), represents the worship of the sacred (mango) tree, with its altar, by a man and eleven women, all in Indian dress. The only noticeable peculiarity is that the man is bare-headed, and has his head dressed in a large top-knot on the right side of the head.(2) All the figures are in reverential attitudes; save one of the women, who is presenting a garland for the tree.(3)

There are seven trees in all; including, apparently, two mango-trees; two plantains; two of the kind elsewhere called the bodhi of Vipaswi; and one a jewel-bearing tree, evidently the kalpa darma, of Buddhist literature; which is analogous to the kalpa vriksha, or Párijáta, the tree of life and plenty, in the paradise of the Bráhmanical Indra.

The trees reverenced by the followers of Gautama, or Sákya, were, at any rate among his later followers, very numerous; as, not only was one particular tree, the pipal, or Ficus religiosa, his special "bodhi," and the type both of himself and of his doctrine, or law (dharma); but some kind of tree was connected with most of the leading incidents in the career, not only of Sákya Muni himself, but of his principal disciples.

The following, among other, trees are connected, in various Buddhist works, with the history of Sákya, both as Prince and Saint.

1. The Asoka (Jonesia Asoka): under which his mother, Máya Devi, or Mahá Máya, gave him birth ("Foe-Koue-Ki," Chap. XXI., and Note 19). According to some authorities, this event occurred under a Sála, or Sál tree; a tree which, as will be seen, has also other claims to sanctity (see "Stupa of Bharhut," p. 46).

(1) One of the best-known triple groups of the Bráhmanical pantheon is that of Jagannáth, or the supreme Vishnu (whose last Avatára or incarnation was Budha), with his male and female attendants, Balaráma, and Subhadrá; a group which—as I pointed out in my original report—was directly copied, as were, also, the Jaina Tirthankaras and their two Bhairavas, from the older Buddhist triad. (See my remarks on Plate XVIII.; and Chapter X.)

The two companions of Buddha are, sometimes, held to represent his "right and left hand disciples," Sáriputra and Mogalána: in fact, almost endless explanations have been given—and the more fanciful, as they are more modern,—of this nearly universal junction of three figures or symbols; which, as will be more fully shown later, is, primarily, traceable to Egypt and Assyria.

(2) This is, so far as I noticed, the only figure in Indian lay-costume, which has a top-knot on the right side of the head: a peculiarity which, according to Sir A. Cunningham, distinguished the prince Siddhártha, before he became Buddha. A precisely similar figure, in Plate XIII., Fig. 2, has the top-knot on the top of the head; and the ascetic or priestly class wear their hair either hanging loose, or in matted locks, like the modern Bairági; or knotted, indifferently, on the top, or either side, of the head. (See "Stupa of Bharhut," 30, 31, on this subject.)

(3) The attitudes in this sculpture, and other representations of worshippers, show that prayer was offered sitting, and standing, as well as kneeling; and the position of the hands is precisely that adopted, in prayer, at the present day.

2. The Jambu (Eugenia Jambu): under which the Prince Siddhártha, after one of the four excursions which led to his becoming a Buddha, watched labourers at work, and attained "the first degree of contemplation" ("Foe-Koue-Ki," Chap. XXII., and Note 16).
3. The Pippala (Ficus religiosa) or Pípal; under which Sákya sat, for six years, in penance; attained "the third contemplation," thus becoming Buddha; and, thenceforward, habitually preached, or "turned the wheel of the law" ("Foe-Koue-Ki," Chapters X., Note 4, and XXII., Note 20). The Pippala, or Pípal, hence became the special "Bodhi," or sacred tree, of Sákya Muni, and Sir A. Cunningham's discoveries at Bharhut, have furnished sculptural and inscribed proof that such was the case (see "Stupa of Bharhut," pp. 45, 114 and 115). This determination of the nature of the special "bodhi" of Sákya is of the more importance, because, in Buddhist works, several other trees, viz., the Phou-thi, or Bauhinia scandens, the So-lo, Sála, or Sál (Shorea robusta), the Tála, or Toddy (Borassus flabelliformis), and the Nyagrodha, or Banian (Ficus indica), have been mentioned as the tree under whose shadow Sákya obtained the rank of Tathágata, Buddha, or Bhagavata. (See "Foe-Koue-Ki," Chapter XXII., Note 8; Chapter XXXI., Notes 3 D, and 6; and Laidlay's addition to the last note, at p. 294 of his English version of Fa Hian.)
4. The So-lo, Sála, or Sál (Shorea robusta), besides its claims to sanctity, as above noticed, is also sacred because it was between two of such trees that Sákya Buddha attained "Nirvána"; that is, ended his human life ("Foe-Koue-Ki," Chapter XXXIV., Note 3).
5. The Ám, or mango (Mangifera indica), though not invested, in Buddhist works, with the same sanctity as those above mentioned, was reverenced as connected with incidents in the life of Sákya; and, as already shown, it appears as the object of worship at Sánchi (see my Plate V.; top compartment, centre face, and second compartment, right face). It is, also, an object of worship at Bharhut (see "Stupa of Bharhut," Plates XVI., Fig. 3; XVIII., Fig. 3; and LVII.).

This Buddhist tree-worship, however, did not, even according to Buddhist writers themselves, *originate* with the Buddhism of Sákya; but was, with some other popular rites and customs, adopted from the earlier cult, of which Krakuchanda, Kanaka, and Kásyapa, were the presiding deities or saints. Each of those acknowledged predecessors of Sákya, as "former Buddhas" of the present age or "kalpa," as well as the three still earlier Buddhas of the previous kalpa, "Vipaswi," "Sikhin," and "Viswabhu," (¹) had, according to Buddhist authors, his

(¹) There is an evident connection between the Buddhist belief in successive "játakas," or incarnations of Buddha; and the successive avatáras, or manifestations of Vishnu; both comparatively modern myths; one copied from the other. The ninth or last avatára of Vishnu, as Budha, appears to have been invented in order to appropriate the Buddhist reformer as a member of the Bráhmanical pantheon: and, in both systems, there is a final incarnation yet to appear; Maitreya according to the Buddhists, and Kalki according to the

special "bodhi," or sacred tree; under which he is supposed to have preached his doctrine: and Sir A. Cunningham found, at Bharhut, six, out of the seven "bodhi" trees above mentioned; each with the name of its deity or saint inscribed in Páli; the designation, however, being, not Budha, or Buddha, but "Bhagavata." (See "Stupa of Bharhut," 45, 46, 107, 108, 113 to 116, 132, 134, 137, and Plates.)

Some, at any rate, of these sacred trees, are represented at Sánchi; but, unfortunately, they have no Páli designations.

Even this *pre-Sákyan* tree-worship was not of indigenous origin. It was, there can be little doubt, first introduced into the countries north-west of India by the Persian invaders of the sixth century B.C. (the epoch long afterwards assigned, in Buddhist chronology, to Sákya). And the sacred "Homa" tree of the ancient Persians (the "Soma" of the Vedas and Puránas) was, as is well known, derived from the "Ashira," or sacred tree of Assyria; which has been supposed, among other interpretations, to be traditionally connected with the Biblical tree of knowledge and life. With reference to the Assyrian representations of the king worshipping the sacred tree, Layard ascribed to a common origin, the trees of life, or knowledge, of various systems of religion; and said, "We have the tree of life of Genesis; and the sacred tree of the Hindús with its accompanying figures, a group almost identical with the illustrations of the Fall in our old Bibles. The Zoroastrian 'Homa,' or sacred tree, was preserved by the Persians, almost as represented in the Assyrian monuments, until the Arab invasion. M. Lajard has collected all the authorities on the probable connection of this object with the worship of Venus; and its introduction, from Assyria, into Asia Minor, Persia, and Central Asia on one side, and into Arabia on the other." ("Nineveh and its Remains," II. 472.) In Egypt, as well as among the ancient Arabs, the tree was an object of worship; and was in some way connected with the generative or productive powers of nature (see Wilkinson's "Man. and Cust. of the Anc. Egyp.," III. 185; and Conder's "Syrian Stone Lore," 324, 325): and, in both cases, we can trace the worship to Assyria, where, from the earliest times, it was customary to dance round the sacred tree; a custom preserved to modern times in the now obsolete May-pole dances.

As regards India, the earliest known allusion to tree-worship is, I believe, the statement of Quintus Curtius, to the effect that the Indians of Alexander's time, like their ancestors, paid special reverence to trees (see quotations in "The Bhilsa Topes," 66, 222, 223). And next, in order of date, is the mention of the holy aswattha, or pípal, in some of the Piyadasi edicts (Spence Hardy's "Eastern Monachism," 215; and Cunningham's "Stupa of Bharhut," 106). There is nothing, however, in either case, to connect the tree-worship with the Buddhism of Sákya;

Bráhmans. As regards the Buddhist name "Viswabhu"; it is analogous to, if not identical with, the second of the many names of Vishnu, "Vishwabhavana"; which signifies "the creator of the universe; or the centre of the existence of all things"; which is also one of the definitions of the Buddhist Adi Buddha. (See "Vishnu Purána," p. 2, Note 2.)

and though the "aswattha" was made the special "bodhi" of Sákya Muni, the same tree is, in the Vedas, connected with the rites of fire-worship.

In Greek mythology, which was so largely based on that of Egypt and Assyria, a tree was dedicated to, or symbolical of, almost every deity or demi-god: and among the Hebrews, the traditions of the cherub-guarded tree of life, in Eden, which were preserved, for all time, in the writings of Moses, were, also, embodied in sculptured form; a leading feature in the ornamentation of Solomon's temple having been palm-trees guarded by two cherubic figures (see 1 Kings vi. 39; and Ezekiel xli. 18; and compare the Kinnara-guarded trees of the Sánchi sculptures with the genii-guarded "Ashira" of Assyria).

In course of time, the tree, originally a pure symbol of God, and of the "knowledge" of his word, or law, became a symbol of the Sun-god, whose worship replaced that of the supreme spiritual deity. "Tree," "Knowledge," and "Sun," were in the oldest known languages, represented by one and the same word.(1) And the junction of the moon, with the sun, as objects of worship, led to the connection of the tree with the worship of Venus, and the productive forces in nature, just noticed. (See on this subject, O'Brien's "Round Towers of Ireland," Chap. VIII.)

The Scythian invaders, hordes of whom overran parts of Europe at the same time as others entered India, that is, shortly before the Christian era, carried with them, into Scandinavia, the tree-worship, and traditions of the tree of paradise, which they had, originally, received from Assyria: and hence we derive the reverence for the oak and mistletoe among the Druids of Britain, and the tree-worship of the "hardy Norsemen"; whose "Ygg drasill," or mystic ash-tree of life, with its eagle and serpent in conflict, is manifestly the embodiment of a confused tradition of the trees of "life," and of "the knowledge of good and evil," and the conflict between the good and the evil principle, in our own Bible story.(2)

That the tree, in the Sánchi sculptures, is, apart from any mystical or metaphysical interpretation, intended to represent the supreme divinity worshipped,

(1) This is the case, also, in both the ancient languages of India. In both Páli and Sanskrit, "bodhi" signifies, not only a "Buddha" himself, the embodiment of light, and intelligence; but, also, his sacred tree; and the doctrine, or law ("Dharmma") which he preached: the junction of which ("Sangha") constituted the "three precious ones," or "three precious gems" of Buddhism, as now known to us. In the earlier cult, which preceded Sákya's system, and was adopted in it, the conjunction ("Sangha") of "Budha," and "Dharma," that is, of the sun and moon; mind and matter; the all-creating spirit, and passive matter or concrete nature; produced the five elements, and mankind, formed out of those elements. Various modes of representing the triple form of the supreme divinity, will be found described in this book; and the constructions put upon the triad, in both its esoteric and its exoteric sense, are very varied and numerous. But, whatever the symbolism employed, and whatever its fanciful interpretation, the *original* idea is foreign to India, and, certainly, in no sense peculiar to the Buddhism of Sákya.

(2) The allegory of the perpetual conflict between the good and evil principles—the latter commonly represented by a serpent, dragon, or other analogous symbol—is common to the mythology of Assyria, Egypt, Persia, Greece, India, and Scandinavia; and its varieties could easily be amplified into a separate volume. As regards my present subject, however, its importance lies, chiefly, in the collateral evidence which it affords, of the foreign derivation of Indian Buddhism. (See, among others, Mallett's "Northern Antiquities"; Fergusson's "Tree and Serpent Worship"; and Cunningham's "Bhilsa Topes," Preface, v., and page 24.)

howsoever designated, is sufficiently evident from its parallel use with other symbols which, unquestionably, typified the deity. We find the "bodhi," and the "Sthúpa," alternating with each other; standing in similar railed enclosures; shaded, alike, by the Tí, or umbrella, and decorated with pennons, wreaths, and streamers; guarded, alike, by hovering "Kinnara," and attended and worshipped, both by human beings and animals, with precisely similar state and ceremony. Moreover, the tree, like the "Sthúpa," the symbol which I have called the disc-and-crescent, and the Tí or umbrella, is represented sometimes singly, sometimes in triple form, and sometimes, in groups of three; showing that all, alike, are parallel, and interchangeable symbols; with one and the same meaning in Buddhism, and a common derivation from sources foreign to Buddhism. (See remarks at page 61, as to the connection between the tree, and the Nága, and other quasi-Buddhist symbols.)

The third compartment of the right or inner face ("Bhilsa Topes," II. 233; and my Plate VII., Fig. 1) shows a procession leaving a city or palace; watched by numerous spectators. The principal occupant of the chariot represented, is bare-headed, with a top-knot on the *left* side (see Note 2, p. 26); and may be supposed to represent the prince Siddhártha on one of the excursions which led to his becoming an ascetic.

The fourth, or top compartment ("Bhilsa Topes," I. 233), is shown in my Plate VIII.; and is very curious and interesting. Ten men, in Indian costume, one of whom has a lyre, or "khin," are worshipping before the entrance to a cave, among flaming rocks. The style of the entrance exactly resembles the façade of existing cave temples in India: and the sacred character of the cave is evident, not only from the worshippers in front of it, but from the altar at the entrance; on either side of which, emerging from cavities in the fiery rocks, are lions, and human-faced rams. Similar animals are seen, among rocks, in one of the Bharhut sculptures, ("Stupa of Bharhut," Plate XXI., Fig. 3); which represents "Chakawako," one of the race of Nágas; who, according to Tod ("Rájasthán," I. 107), were fire-worshippers.

We have, in this sculpture, evidently, a cave temple, dedicated to Fire; a structural temple to which will be noticed later. Maurice, in his "Indian Antiquities," says that caves were specially connected with the Sun, and fire-worship: and such was, apparently, the original dedicature of the older cave temples of India; the peculiar emblem in which was adopted, successively, by the Buddhists as their "Chaitya," and by the Saivas as their "Linga."

The introduction of the lion, the ram, and the Nága or serpent, in connection with the fire-cave, and fire-temple above alluded to, is an additional proof that, at the date of the Sánchi sculptures, the old worship of fire was still practised; and we have the evidence both of inscriptions and books that it remained part of Buddhist ritual even as late as the 5th century A.D.(1)

(1) The connection of the lion, ram, and serpent, with the Sun, and with fire, as a type of the sun, is a generally accepted fact. The Egyptian God Noub, or Noum, and many other Egyptian deities, of a marked solar type, were ram-headed; and in India, the fire-god Agni—whose symbols are identical with those of

The left, or inner face of the right pillar has five compartments; the lowest containing the companion janitor figure to that described at page 24.

The second compartment ("Bhilsa Topes," II. 231; and my Plate VII., Fig. 2) represents the worship of a tree and altar, by a royal personage, attended by two men, and five women; all in Indian costume. Over the group hover two male "Kinnara," with wreaths and offerings (¹); and another male personage, with offering, riding on a winged monster, with the head and fore-paws of a lion, and the tail of a fish, or dragon; like the form of the sacred barge in Plate XXI., Fig. 2.

The tree in this sculpture appears to be of the same species as that in the Bharhut sculptures, which is inscribed as the "bodhi" of the Bhagavata Kanaka Muni (see "Stupa of Bharhut," 45, 46, 114, 132). A similar tree will be seen in my Plate XXIX., Fig. 4.

The third compartment (Plate IX., Fig. 1) shows two men, four women, and a child, in Indian dress, and two large apes, offering worship to a tree and altar, between two other trees. Two of these trees resemble those at Bharhut which bear the names of the Bhagavatas Krakuchanda and Vipaswi: and the third is of the same species as that shown in the third compartment, front face, of Plate V.

The fourth, or top compartment ("Bhilsa Topes," I. 230, 231) is shown in my Plate X. It represents the worship of a three-terraced Sthúpa, crowned by three Tís or chattas, and two pennons; and with an entrance gateway of the same style as those of Nos. 1 and 3 Sthúpas. The domical portion of the structure is decorated with a string of lotus flowers, and a serpentine scroll, probably an offering, of the kind still used by the Buddhists of Burmah.(²)

Four male Kinnara, with garlands, hover near the Sthúpa; which is worshipped by eighteen men. Four, with offerings and garlands, are circumambulating the building, both to right and left; three are in the attitude of prayer; three present

Noum—has the ram as his Vahana, or sacred animal. Fa Hian saw, at Seng-Kia-Shi (Samkassa), a temple called "the limit or boundary of fire"; which, it is supposed, may allude to an old legend, or to a volcanic eruption, or thermal spring. ("Foe-Koue-Ki," Chapter XVII., Note 30.)

(¹) The descriptions of "Kinnara," in Wilson's "Vishnu Purána" and Sanskrit Dictionary, do not tally with the Sánchi representations (see "Vish. Purán." 42, 43): but figures of this kind are among the symbols on the "Srípáda," or sacred footprint of Buddha: and in ancient Egyptian sculptures and paintings, the souls of deceased persons are represented by figures just like those at Sánchi (see Coleman's "Hind. Myth.," 211; and Rawlinson's "Rel. of the Anc. World," 40).

The Assyrian sculptures have, also, similar figures; which Layard describes as follows ("Mons. of Nin." XLVI., Fig. 2):—"Two winged human figures, with tails, and with the legs and feet of a bird, standing before the sacred tree"; a description which, like these Buddhist "Kinnara," reminds one of the Jewish Temple, with its ornamental representation of the cherub-guarded tree of Eden. (See 1 Kings vi. 29; and Ezekiel xli. 18.) In Layard's "Nineveh and its Remains" (II. 449), there is the following note on these cherubic figures, and the "harpies," to which they are akin:—"M. Scharf is inclined to trace, in the oval form of the Harpies of the Xanthian monuments, some connection with the winged globe. The Persian origin of these figures renders the conjecture not improbable."

(²) Similar, but far larger, and more elaborate, scrolls, are a very prominent feature in the sculptures of Bharhut, and Amarávati (see "Stupa of Bharhut," Plates IX., XI., XII., and XXXIX. to XLVIII.: and Fergusson's "Tree and Serpent Worship").

offerings (1); one carries a standard emblazoned with a crescent, and seven small discs, and crowned by the disc-and-crescent symbol; and seven are playing musical instruments.(2)

The costume is quite un-Indian; and in several respects looks very Grecian. All the men wear sandals (shown, on a larger scale, in Fig. 2, Plate XIV.), and kilt-shaped skirts; close fitting, short-sleeved jerkins; and short cloaks, or capes, fastened at the throat.

Two of them wear conical caps, something like the Persian Kuzzilbásh cap; and the rest are bare-headed; some with short hair, either curly or straight, and in some cases partly shaven; and some with their hair confined by fillets, with long ends.

The custom of shaving the front part of the head obtained both among the Greeks and the Scythians: and the Hindu Puránas represent it as having been imposed upon the "Yavanas" (Greeks) and "Sákas" (Scythians), as a mark of their subjection, by the celebrated monarch "Sagara" ("Vishnu Purána," 373 to 375).

Whether the men here represented are Greeks or Scythians, or the descendants of either, can only be conjectured; they were, at any rate, followers of the local religion, whatever their original nationality: and that Græco-Bactrian, and Scythian colonists and adventurers penetrated far into India proper, and became mixed up with the local population, there are many independent proofs.

The front face has four compartments; the first or lowest of which is obliterated. The second compartment represents twenty-nine men, in Indian dress, worshipping a tree, before which is the small flat altar, called, in Buddhist works, the Vajrásana, or bodhi manda; and answering to the small chabutras commonly seen, at the present day, before the pennon-crowned banyan, pípal, and aonla trees; and used for depositing offerings. At Bharhut, many of these tree-altars have floral and other offerings shown on them; but this is not the case at Sánchi.

The third compartment (Plate IX., Fig. 2), shows a city or palace; inside which, seated in a raised pavilion, is a male personage of distinction, holding a vase or goblet, and attended by eight women; all watching a procession, which is leaving the gateway. This consists of an empty, chatta-shaded chariot, preceded by a loose horse, bridled and saddled; and accompanied by seven men, in Indian dress, two of whom are, apparently, worshipping the chariot.

This scene appears to represent a horse and chariot which have been dedicated to the deity; and have therefore, themselves, become sacred. There are other subjects, at Sánchi, which seem to have a like meaning; and we learn from the

(1) Two carry their offerings in boat-shaped vessels, marked with the double-cross device seen on some of the shields and standards. The boat, or ark-shaped receptacles for offerings are the "Argha-patra" of Sanskrit: and are supposed, by some writers on mythology, to be emblematic of the ark of Noah.

(2) The double pipe, here represented, reminds one of Greek sculptures; and the "khin" or lyre, also, has an un-Indian look; and differs from other lyres shown in the sculptures. The "khin," according to M. Klaproth ("Foe-Koue-Ki," Chapter XXVIII., Notes 3, 4), was "a species of horizontal lyre, with seven strings," used by the celestial musicians of "Shi," or Indra: that is, the Khinnara or Kinnara, whose name may be derived from "khin."

Bráhmanical Puránas, that such dedications, and, also, the sacrifice of horses, to the sun, were Indian customs; derived, doubtless, from the Scythians and Persians. The sacrifice of a horse to the sun was a well-known Scythian rite: and the dedication of chariots and horses to the sun, was not only (according to Herodotus) a custom among the ancient Persians; but was an old rite, in Asia Minor, before the Persian rule; and is mentioned in 2 Kings xxiii. 11 (see Layard's "Nineveh and its Remains," II. 364, 365).

In India, the horse-sacrifice, or "Aswamedha," besides its religious significance, was one of the signs of kingly supremacy; and though, probably, the Buddhists, with their peculiar tenets, soon abandoned, even if they ever practised, the *sacrifice* of the animal, we can easily understand the adoption, by a Buddhist monarch, from his Bráhmanical predecessors, of the dedicatory rites, which were a part of royal ceremonial.(¹)

The fourth, or top compartment ("Bhilsa Topes," I. 230) is shown in my Plate XI., Fig. 1. It represents two trees, with altars, connected by a kind of ladder, or flight of steps, enclosed by a plain, and a "Buddhist" railing.

The lower tree resembles that in Plate VI., Fig. 2, identified with the "bodhi" of Kanaka Muni; and, on either side of it, stand a man, woman, and child praying; and two other trees; the mango, and the tree already compared to the Kalpadarm or párijáta.

On each side of the connecting ladder, stand six men, in Indian dress; two playing large drums; nine worshipping the ladder; and one (evidently the principal personage) holding up a fan-shaped object; which is either a kind of sceptre, or the fan, or broom which was part of the paraphernalia of Buddhist, and Magian, priests.

The upper tree is like the "Ging-Ko," the principal sacred tree of Japanese Buddhism; and resembles, also, the "Kachnár," or Bauhinia variegata.(²)

This subject admits of a Mithraic, as well as a purely Buddhist explanation: the ladder being a symbol common to both faiths; and, I may add, one of the symbols found on Assyrian gems.

In the Mithraic worship of the ancient Persians, who derived much of its symbolism from Assyria, and, doubtless, introduced it into India, the passage of the soul, from earth to heaven, was symbolized by "a high ladder, on the ascent to which

(¹) It was not only in the countries above indicated, that horse sacrifices, and the dedication of horses and chariots, to the sun were customary. Such rites existed among the Phœnicians, for instance, at a period long anterior to any traces of them among the Rájput, or other races of India. I cannot do more than refer to the subject here; but full information can be found in the "Journal of the Asiatic Society of Bengal," Vol. III.; Tod's "Rájasthán," I. 24, and 563 to 565; and Rawlinson's "Religions of the Ancient World," pp. 107, 142, 166 and 244.

(²) As elsewhere mentioned (p. 27), another variety of the Bauhinia, or mountain ebony, the "Phouthi," or Bauhinia scandens, was, according to some authorities, the tree under which Siddhártha, or Sákya Muni, became Buddha. Apparently "phouthi," "pieto," and "bodhi," are the same word, and mean *any* sacred tree; and the tree specially sacred to Sákya Buddha, seems to have varied, according to the species most prevalent, and useful, in different localities.

were seved gates, according to the number of the planets." (Maurice's "Ind. Ant.," II. 279.)

The same idea is traceable in other ancient systems of mythology: and, in Buddhism, is found in the sacred ladder, adorned with "the seven precious things," so often mentioned in Buddhist works. It was by such a ladder that Sákya Buddha, attended by gods and demi-gods, descended to earth, at Samkassa, from the heaven called "Trayastrinsha," or the abode of Indra and his thirty-two attendant deities—itself an indication of a Persian source for the legend (see note 2, p. 37): and of this celestial ladder, after Sákya's descent, only "seven steps" remained visible; over which, according to Fa Hian, a shrine was built. ("Foe-Koue-Ki," Chapter XVII.)

The Persians, at any rate, if not their later imitators, the Buddhists, were acquainted with the Mosaic writings: and this myth of a sacred ladder, reaching from earth to heaven, was, most probably, based upon the ladder which Jacob saw in his vision, at Bethel (Genesis xxviii. 12).

According to Buddhist writers, the Samkassa ladder was triple; Buddha having descended by the central portion; and Brahma and Indra, on his right and left: and there is a representation of a triple ladder, at Bharhut, which illustrates this (? later) form of the legend (see "Stupa of Bharhut," 91 to 93, and Plate XVII. centre figure). The single ladder represented at Sánchi, if held to represent this Samkassa ladder, points to a simpler and earlier phase of the story.

Whatever its original meaning and derivation, the ladder became, among the Buddhists, a common type of progressive spiritual knowledge; which was metaphorically described as "mounting the steps of the doctrine" (dharma, and bodhi); and the sculpture may, therefore, merely represent, either spiritual advancement in general, or Sákya Muni's own gradual progress in holiness; culminating in his final absorption into the divine Essence, or Nirvána.

On the abacus, just above this sculpture, is a much-worn inscription, in later Páli: but it only records the gift of the "thabho," or pillar, by Nágapriya, son of Sethi, and Sangha.(1)

The right, or outer face, is covered with scroll work, and floral ornamentation; and calls for no description.

The rear face of each pillar has a small sculptured compartment, on the portion visible over the enclosure railing. These represent, respectively, Sthúpa and tree-worship, by men and women in Indian dress.

The capitals are formed by four caparisoned elephants, with male and female maháwats (drivers); surmounted by large honeysuckle flowers, like those on the votive pillar in Plate V.

On these rests the lowest lintel: the projecting, voluted, ends of which are

(1) Sir A. Cunningham does not give this particular inscription; but he gives others, from the Eastern and Western Gateways, which correspond with the first part of it: and we thus see that these three gateways were the joint gift of the same donors; and, therefore, coeval in date. (See "The Bhilsa Topes," pp. 263, 267; and Plate XIX., Nos. 182, 192.)

supported by the curved stems of trees, overshadowing female dancers (see Plate IV.; and Fig. 3, Plate XIV.).

The costume of these dancers—though of exceptional richness—is that of the majority of women represented in the sculptures; and evidently was the ordinary Indian dress of the period: a dhoti or petticoat, supported by a waist-belt, and gathered up between the legs: ornamental girdles round the hips; and rows of bangles on the arms and legs: and bead, or jewelled, necklaces. The upper part of the person, in these dancing figures, is nude; which, indeed, seems to have been the case universally: and in fact, the only noticeable variety in the costume of women, seems to have been in the head-gear.

The hair is, as a rule, represented as worn in two long thick plaits, hanging below the waist, and joined at the ends. Over it hang strings of jewels or beads, and cords of some worked material, which pass round the forehead: and the whole is, in some cases, confined by a band, or fillet (Fig. 4, Plate XIV.); while in others (Figs. 5, 6, 7), the head is decorated by a tuft, or plume; or the hair is gathered into a pendent knot, either plain, or more or less ornamented.(¹) Other varieties of head-gear will be noticed as they occur.

On each end of the lowest lintel is a winged garland-bearer; and its slightly arched under-surface is decorated with rosettes, foliage, and lotus buds. The cubical portions, over the pillars, have, in front, two kneeling, winged, bulls, with riders; and, in rear, two kneeling, mounted, horses.

The whole surface of this lintel, front and rear, is covered with elaborate sculpture, representing successive incidents of one story; apparently that of the "Wessentara," or "alms-giving" Játaka, of Sákya's former history. The front face is much obliterated; and so constantly in shadow, that I could not make a drawing of it: the rear face is shown in Plate IV.: and both are so crowded with figures that a detailed verbal description would be more confusing than explanatory.

Among the principal features is the presence of numerous members, of both sexes, of the ascetic, or priestly class; and the repeated representations of plumed children, who, as well as a woman, a four-horsed chariot, and elephants, are evidently being presented to the ascetics, by the king. In one place, an ascetic is about to re-harness, and drive away, the royal chariot; (²) and in another, the king is pouring water over the extended hand of an ascetic; the ancient mode of confirming a gift. The subjects, generally, may be described as the gift, by the

(¹) The Burmese women still ornament their long hair, with separate tresses, and strings of beads, silk, etc.: and such coiffures are handed down from mother to daughter. The long plaited hair, mixed with cords of silk, or worsted, tassels, beads, and coins, or metal discs, worn by the women of Ladákh and Tartary, is, also, very like what is represented at Sánchi: and both the costume and the head-attire above described are strikingly like those on a Cornelian ornament from Afghánistán figured, among other "trouvailles" from Topes, in Wilson's "Ariana Antiqua."

(²) Illustrations of the chariots in these sculptures are given in Plates XIV., Fig. 11, and XXXVI., Fig. 12; and representations of other chariots will be seen in Plates VII., Fig. 1; IX., Fig. 2; XV., Fig. 12; XVI.; XX.; and XXXV., Fig. 13. These show, plainly, the construction and mode of draught, and harnessing, of these conveyances; and their points of resemblance to the chariots of other nations.

king to the priests, of his chariot, horses, elephants, wife, and children; and the latter are, in fact, seen on the extreme right of the rear face, seated, in the jungle, near an ascetic's hut; one of the two children holding aloft the symbol described at p. 19.(1)

The "Wessentara Játaka," which appears to be the subject represented on this lintel, is the history of one of the former births, or incarnations, of Sákya, as the prince "Sudatta," or "the generous giver." He is described as giving away, to Bráhmans, or to Indra in the disguise of a mendicant, his royal white elephant; his horses and chariot; his two children; and his wife; successively: but is said to have recovered them again, succeeded to his father's kingdom, and, eventually, become Buddha.

Over each volute there were once seated lions; but, in 1850, these had fallen.

The supports of the second lintel have the following carvings:—

The right cubical prop has, in front, a wheel, on a pillar, with worshippers; and, in rear, a female figure, seated on a lotus; and shaded by a chatta; while two elephants anoint her with liquid poured out of goglets.(2) The left cubical prop has a precisely similar figure, in front; and, in rear, a Sthúpa, shaded by three tís, or umbrellas; attended by "Kinnara"; and worshipped by men and women in Indian costume.

The three small props have, respectively, in front, a mace-bearer, a cháori-bearer, and a sacred chatta-shaded tree, with a chatta, or tí, on either side of it;(3)

(1) For other representations of Ascetics, male and female, see my Plates XII., Fig. 1; XIII., Figs. 1, 2; and XXXVI., Fig. 12. They are evidently, as I pointed out in my original report, the priestly class of the form of religion represented in the sculptures; as will be, more fully, shown later (see remarks on Srámanas and Bráhmanas, at pages 43 to 46).

(2) Other similar figures, both seated and standing, occur at Sánchi: and there is one among the Bharhut sculptures; which Sir A. Cunningham considered to be rather Bráhmanical than Buddhist. ("Stupa of Bharhut," 117; and Plate XXXVI., Fig. 1.) A similar figure is seen on some of the coins of the Bactrian Azilizes. (See Chapter X.) These female figures are the only representations, among the Sánchi sculptures, of anything that looks like an *image*. They are, however, in no instances, the objects of worship; and, indeed, it seems indisputable, that no images of any kind were used by the Buddhists, until at least several centuries after the date of these sculptures. We must, therefore, suppose that these figures are a fanciful representation of Máyadevi, or Mahámáya, the earthly mother of Sákya; who, as such, was not worshipped, in the early days of Buddhism. In process of time, however, the earthly mother was raised to the rank of a celestial goddess; and when so deified, she was evidently invested with many of the characteristics of the great nature goddess, and "Mother of the Gods," who is found in most ancient systems of mythology. And hence it is that we find, side by side with evident plagiarisms from the Gospel narrative, resemblance not only to the Bráhmanical Srí, Lakshmi, and Durgá or Devi; but to the Egyptian Ken, and Isis; the Assyrian Astarte and Mylitta; and the Greek Cybele and Demeter. "Máya" was the common name of the Saktis, or female energies of Brahma, Vishnu, and Siva; and Maya, or Maia, was also, the name of the mother of Sákya Buddha; of the Greek and Egyptian Hermes; and of the Roman Mercury.

(3) This shows that the tí, chatta, or umbrella, that is a horizontal disc, which, after images were introduced, merged into the halo, was, in itself, an object of worship, equally with the tree, Sthúpa, wheel, and disc-and-crescent symbol. It is seen, with an altar in front of it, as an object of worship, in one of the sculptures of the Eastern Gateway: and an instance of its use as a Bráhmanical sacred emblem, also, will be seen on reference to Plate XL., Fig. 6. Pennons, garlands, streamers, and small umbrellas, were, and still

which is shown, in Fig. 14 of Plate XXXVI., and, in rear, double honeysuckle flowers, like those in Plate V., already mentioned. In the spaces between the props, are caparisoned elephants, carrying maháwats, and standard-bearers.

The voluted ends of the centre lintel, are supported by small figures of female dancers, under trees.

The cubical portions of the second lintel have, in front, winged lions, and in rear mounted goats.

On its front face, are seven sacred trees, with altars; (¹) each crowned by a chatta, and guarded by Kinnara; and each attended by worshippers, in Indian costume. These, doubtless, represent the "Bodhis" of the seven "Mánushya," or deified mortal Buddhas, or "Bhagavatas," Vipaswi, Sikhin, Viswabhu, Krakuchanda, Kanaka, Kásyapa, and Sákya (see p. 27). The rear face (Plate IV.) has, on its projecting ends, peacocks; and, in the centre, a subject which, in a Bráhmanical temple, would, at once, be called the "Sabha," or Court, of Indra; in which, peacocks, the párijáta tree, Apsarasas or celestial musicians, and dancing girls, giants, and other supernatural beings,—all of which seem to be included in this sculpture—were prominent features. Some of the giants, it will be seen, are dancing, some singing, and playing on lyres and drums; while others are drinking; and one is feeding a young giant. All have pointed ears, like the "faun" of classic art.

The various myths connected with the Vedic deity Indra, were, as is well known, largely incorporated with the Buddhism of Sákya; and Indra is frequently represented as accompanying, and even worshipping Buddha; (²) so that we may view this subject in either a Buddhistical or a Bráhmanical light.

Other representations of gigantic figures, and heads, will be noticed later; but they merely serve to show that the idea of gigantic beings was familiar to the

are, common offerings to shrines, and sacred trees, among both Bráhmans and Buddhists; and the practice of distinguishing holy trees by flags and pennons, is not only common in India, to the present day, but is alluded to by Buddhist writers as having been followed by Sákya himself; who, while still a Bodhisatwa, made offerings to a pennon-surmounted tree, which was called "the king of all the forest, and of original happiness." ("Foe-Koue-Ki," Chapter XXXI., Note 3.)

(¹) Throughout the sculptures, wherever more than one object of worship is shown, whether tree, Sthúpa, or emblem, there is, always, a group of either three, five or seven. All three numbers were of special significance, among both Buddhists and Bráhmans; as well as in earlier Mithraic forms of religion: and to the Buddhists, in particular, the numbers three, five, and seven, were sacred as the representatives of the "three precious ones," Buddha, Dharmma, Sangha; the five celestial or Dhyáni Buddhas; and the seven Mánushya, or mortal Buddhas.

(²) The Indra of the Buddhist system, which retained so much of the earlier pantheistic faith of the Bráhmans, resided on Mount Sumeru; where his central palace was surrounded by the celestial mansions of thirty-two minor deities; whence the name of the heaven, "Trayastrinsha," the abode of the thirty-three. These thirty-two attendants of the central Indra, have been compared to, and are, there can be little doubt, derived from the thirty-two "Amshaspands," who, in the Zoroastrian myths, are the special attendants on the supreme Ahuramazda: and one of the names of Indra, among the Mongol Buddhists, was Khormousda; which, allowing for differences of pronunciation, is very like the Persian name for the supreme God. (See "Foe-Koue-Ki," Chapter IX., Note 2; and Chapter XVII., Note 17.)

sculptors. (See "Stupa of Bharhut," 94, 104, 105, and Plates XXXIII., Fig. 3; and XLVII., Fig. 7.)

The sculptures between the centre and the top lintel, are as follows. Under the projecting ends, tree-shaded dancing figures, as below; and over the volutes seated lions. The right cubical prop has, in front, a wheel, on an altar, with guardian Kinnara, and worshippers; and that on the left, a standing female figure; anointed by elephants, which are supported on lotus stems and flowers.

The rear of each cubical prop has flowers and buds, in vases. The small props have several representations of a double honeysuckle flower; a chatta-shaded wheel, raised on a short pillar, with capital formed of three lions, and a votive standard, or pennon, on each side of it; and male figures, in Indian dress, holding either a flower or a mace. In the intervening spaces are horsemen.

The third, or top lintel, is sculptured as follows.

On the cubical props, both front and rear, are kneeling winged deer. The front face of the lintel has five Sthúpas and two trees; each shaded by a chatta; guarded by Kinnara; and with worshippers in Indian dress, on either side (see Note 1, p. 37). The rear face shows numerous elephants, standing in, or near water; and attending on or worshipping a banyan tree; the "Nyagrodha," or Ficus indica; to which they seem to be about to offer the lilies growing in the water. In other sculptures, Sthúpas, similarly attended, are represented.(1)

The Nyagrodha, or Banyan, was doubly sacred among the Buddhists: not only was it said to have sheltered Sákya in one of his previous births, or Játakas, as the Chhadánta, or six-tusked, elephant: but it was the "bodhi," or sacred tree, of Kásyapa; the sixth of the seven mortal Buddhas, and the immediate predecessor of Sákya Muni.

Over the volutes of this lintel are seated, winged lions; and it was crowned by a representation of the triad; consisting of a central wheel, of thirty-two spokes, or rays, supported by four elephants; between two of the symbols (see Plates IV., and XXXIX., Fig. 1) which I have called "the disc-and-crescent symbol"; and to which, owing to its importance, I have devoted a separate chapter (Chapter X.).

Originally, there was a chaori-bearer on each side of the central wheel; but only one remained in position, in 1850.

The branched supports of the two disc-and-crescent symbols, resemble some of the fire-altars seen on Sassanian coins; and each is raised on a kind of altar; one of three, and the other of four steps.

Only a portion of the central wheel remains; but it suffices to show that there were, originally, *thirty-two rays*, or spokes, radiating from the central disc, or nave

(1) One of the Bharhut sculptures (see "Stupa of Bharhut," 45, 115; and Plates XV., Fig. 1; and XXX., Fig. 2), represents a very similar scene. Fa Hian, in his description of the Sthúpa, or tower, of Lan-mo (? Rámagráma, on the Gogra river), says. . . . "In this sterile and solitary place, there are no men to sweep and to water; but you may there see, continually, herds of elephants, which take water in their trunks, to water the ground; and which, collecting all sorts of flowers and perfumes, perform the service of the tower." (See English version of the "Foe-Koue-Ki," by Laidlay; Chapter XXIII., and Note 2; and p. 91, Beal's "Fa Hian.")

(see, as to this, Note 2, p. 37). The wheel itself springs from a triform support; resembling, in shape, the triple "Chaitya" symbol, elsewhere compared to the triform Mithraic flame.

On the plinth below the four elephants, is the following Páli inscription,

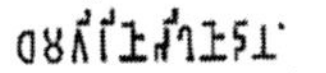

that is, dhama girino bhikhuno dánan: which Sir A. Cunningham read as "gift of Dharmagiri, the mendicant monk." ("The Bhilsa Topes," 262.) It may, however, perhaps, be read, as recording the gift of the sculptured wheel, by (or possibly to) the Bhikshus, or religious fraternity, of the place itself.(1)

Representations of the wheel, or "dhama chaka," are very numerous at Sánchi; and, save perhaps in one instance, which may be intended for a praying-wheel, are all, obviously, objects of worship.

There can be little doubt that the wheel or rayed disc, was, at first, adopted, both by the Buddhists, and by their predecessors, the Bráhmans, as an already long-familiar sacred symbol, in the older sun and fire worship, which Sákya's sect first recognized, and, afterwards discarded and suppressed; and it was doubtless, after this suppression, or attempted suppression, of ancient rites, that the many mystical and metaphorical meanings attached to the wheel, in Buddhist books, were invented and promulgated; perhaps in order to veil the real nature and origin of the symbol.

The universality, in the ancient world, of sun-worship, and of the adoption of so obvious a symbol as a simple, or rayed disc to represent the supreme Sun-god, requires no proof; but the general transition, from the simple disc, to the many-spoked wheel, has been less frequently noticed.

The earliest modification of the plain disc appears to have been the addition of a central point, or smaller disc; as still seen in our astronomical sign for the sun; and, subsequently, to indicate the apparent revolving motion of the luminary, other concentric discs, or rings, were added; which, eventually, suggested the nave, and tires of the solar chariot-wheel. Instances of such concentric discs are common to the symbolism of Assyria, Egypt, Troy, India, Central America, and Scandinavia, and other parts of Europe: and some of them remind one of the triple nave, and six peripheries of the single chariot-wheel of the Indian Súrya.

Next, we find the idea of revolving motion more clearly expressed, by the addition of rays, or spokes; sometimes within the disc, sometimes outside it, and sometimes radiating from the centre and projecting beyond the outer circumference: and specimens of such varieties of the rayed disc, or wheel, with from three to twelve spokes or rays, occur in the symbolism of almost every known system of ancient mythology.

(1) See my Eleventh Chapter, as to this name, and other names ending in "giri," or "hill." Sir A. Cunningham, himself, recognized Dhamagiri as a local as well as a personal name; and suggested that it might have designated the spur of the Sánchi ridge, towards Kána Khera; the main hill being Chetiya-giri.

It would be very interesting to trace the many varieties, and their manifold meanings, in detail; but to do so would involve an elaborate dissertation, and many illustrations; and there is the less necessity for amplification of the subject, here, as there are no wheels of the more archaic types, at Sánchi; all those in the sculptures having sixteen or more spokes, or rays. Such as are represented will be described as they occur: and all that need be said here is, that they serve as important links in the chain of proof, that the Buddhism of Sákya arose out of, and partially adopted, an older, Mithraic, form of worship.

Sir A. Cunningham's valuable researches at Bharhut, have supplied the Páli name for these interesting symbols; one of sixteen rays, being inscribed, in Páli, as "Bhagavata dhama chakam," that is, the wheel of the law of Bhagavata. ("Stupa of Bharhut," 110, 134; and Plate LIV., No. 39.)

The foregoing remarks will suffice to show the widespread use, and the real significance, of the wheel symbol; which has so often been regarded as exclusively Buddhist; and as regards wheels, generally, irrespectively of any particular number of rays or spokes, I may conclude with the following notes.

"A revolving wheel of light" was "turned, as an act of worship, in the temples of the Greeks; who derived the custom from the Egyptians" (see an article on "The Wheel, as a Symbol in Religion," in "Scribner's Monthly," Vol. II., p. 739). The Egyptians, as is well known, drew much of their symbolism from Assyria; where the wheel, or rayed disc seems to have been first used to represent the fiery orb of the sun: perhaps with some traditional allusion to the flame "which turned every way," described in Genesis. (Compare, also, the fiery wheels within wheels, described by the prophet Ezekiel: i. 15 to 21; and x. 2, 6, 9, 12 to 19.)

The ancient Celts represented the supreme God by figures of "the revolving sun; generally under the image of a wheel."

One of the names of the sun, in the "Edda," is, "the fair and shining wheel"; and both the sun-god of the Saxons, and the Scandinavian Seater, had, in common with the Súrya of India, a fiery wheel as their symbol.

I have, elsewhere, shown that the wheel, or "dharma-chakra," and the disc-and-crescent symbol, of which it is a portion, preceded the human-shaped image, as the representative of Buddha; and that these two symbols were seen, as his representatives, by Fa Hian, early in the fifth century of the Christian era.

The earliest known Buddhist books appear to have been written at or soon after this period; and it is in them that we find the metaphorical and mystical interpretations of wheels, which afterwards became so numerous and so popular.

These fanciful meanings of wheels may be enumerated as follows:—

1. The metempsychosis, or passage of the soul, through the various stages of material existence; "which, like a circle, is without beginning or end."
2. Spiritual progress; in which there were three "yana," or modes of advancement.
3. Preaching; which was called "turning the wheel of the law."
4. The different branches of the "law," or "doctrine" (bodhi).

5. Prayer; whence came the idea of praying-wheels.
6. Universal rule, both spiritual and temporal; whence the title "Chakra-vartti," as applied both to Buddha, and to temporal monarchs.

The history of Indian Buddhism shows that whatever reforms of old superstitions and abuses were effected, by Sákya and his earlier followers, were but short-lived. Buddhism, as time went on, relapsed more and more into the old corruptions; and became in time quite as pantheistic as the Bráhmanism which it began by combating.

CHAPTER V.

THE EASTERN GATEWAY OF NO. I STHUPA; AND ITS SCULPTURES.

THE Eastern Gateway resembles the Northern; but is rather smaller: its total height, exclusive of crowning symbols, being only 27 feet 2¼ inches. Its condition, in 1850, was much less perfect than that of the Northern Gateway: and the central symbol, which was, probably, a wheel, (1) and many other details, had entirely disappeared.

The capitals of the gate-pillars are formed by four elephants; which are superior, both in design and execution, to those of the Northern Gateway (see Plate XVII.): and the voluted ends of the lintels are more elegant. The one remaining dancing figure, has her hair short, and unplaited; and decorated with a tuft or plume (see Figs. 5, 6, Plate XIV.).

The left or outer face of the left pillar is covered with floral and scroll work; with, here and there, a few unimportant figures introduced.

The first, or lowest compartment of the front face ("The Bhilsa Topes," III. 205), which is much worn, represents a man of distinction, with two attendants, in a chariot; and followed by elephants and horsemen; leaving a city or palace: whence spectators are watching the procession, as it winds, round the walls, towards an altar; near which are two worshippers. All the figures are in Indian costume.

The second compartment ("The Bhilsa Topes," II. 204), is shown in my Plate XII., Fig. 1; and calls for more detailed description.

It represents a river, or a sheet of (fresh) water; with a small canoe crossing it; and carrying three men, in the ascetic, or priestly costume: two propelling and steering the boat; and the central figure, with hands resting on the gunwale, facing towards four ascetics, who are standing, in reverential attitudes, at the water's edge, below. Close to these figures, is a tree, with an altar in front of it, and garlands pendent from it: and five other trees are growing in the water. One of these (with apes feeding in it) resembles the tree elsewhere called the "bodhi" of Vipaswi; but I cannot suggest any meaning for the others, other than the supposition that the six trees are intended to represent the six predecessors of Sákya.

The other objects in the water, namely, a long flat slab or altar; an alligator (makara); seven geese (hansa); and several open and closed lotus flowers and buds;

(1) I say probably, because I could not find the smallest fragment of a wheel: while there were numerous fragments of such animals as elephants, lions, and deer; all sacred in Buddhism; and any one of which would have been appropriate as a crowning symbol.

are, very probably, used here, symbolically: and, at any rate, both the makara and the hansa are, as will be shown later, highly symbolical; not only in both Buddhism and Bráhmanism; but in other, far older religious systems; while "lilies in a tank" were used, metaphorically, by Sákya himself, as representing human beings, in different stages of religious enlightenment. (See "Buddhism, Mythical and Historical"; in the Westminster Review for October 1856.) Buddha himself is compared, in Buddhist writings, to "a boat and oar, in the vast ocean of life and death" ("Foe-Koue-Ki," Chapter XXIV., Note 11); and other, more or less plausible reasons could be given for regarding the figures in the boat as Sákya Buddha and his two principal followers; which is the view taken by Sir A. Cunningham ("The Bhilsa Topes," 27): but there seem to me to be the following difficulties in the way of this interpretation:—

Firstly. There is reason to believe that no representations of Buddha, in human shape, were resorted to until several centuries later than the date of these sculptures.

Secondly. Had the intention been to represent Sákya Buddha and his two chief supporters; they would probably have been shown, not in a common thong-bound canoe, but in a sacred barge, such as that seen in Fig. 2 of Plate XXI.

Thirdly. There is nothing, in either dress or accessories, to distinguish the central figure in the canoe, from the other men in the sculpture; not even an over-shadowing umbrella.

Fourthly. The central figure is bearded; and, evidently, wore a high conical head-dress: peculiarities utterly unknown, so far as I am aware, to any representations or descriptions of Sákya, in Buddhist art or literature.

I am inclined, on the whole, to view this subject as representing merely the departure, on some expedition or mission, of an ascetic, or priest, of rank, amid the reverential farewells of his followers.(1)

I shall, throughout this book, call the class of persons represented in this and other subjects, ascetics or priests; in preference to using any of the numerous Páli or Sanskrit terms applied to members of the priesthood in Buddhist and Bráhmanical books and inscriptions; such as Bráhmana, Bhikshu, Jhayaka, Parivrajaka, Srámana, Srámanera, Thera, &c.

Fergusson, at one time, treated them as a distinct tribe, the "Dasyus"; but, on my representations, he abandoned this view, and adopted mine, in his second edition of "Tree and Serpent Worship": and there is now, I believe, no question as

(1) I noticed that, in every case, the wearers of the ascetic dress who are distinguished by the high Persian-looking cap, have shaven heads and long beards, two characteristics of the ancient as well as the modern Persians! The Buddhist priests of the present day, are beardless, and have closely shaven heads; and as a rule, are bare-headed: and they are, I believe, invariably so represented in the comparatively recent sculptures of Amarávati. The custom may be partly due to the circumstance that Siddhártha is said, when about to become an ascetic, to have cut off all his hair. (See Bigandet's "Legend of the Burmese Buddha," 52, 60, 63.)

Sir A. Cunningham considers that the wearers of head-dresses in this sculpture belong to a

to their being the priests of the form of religion, whatever its nature, represented in the sculptures.

They are seen in intimate association with the wearers of the ordinary Indian costume; and are connected, like them, with the worship of fire; and with the sacred Sthúpa, and tree: and there is nothing which can show them to be exclusively a Buddhist class, in the ordinary sense of the word Buddhist: while the several terms for priests, above quoted, are at least as applicable to a Bráhman as to a Buddhist sacerdotal order.

The earliest known mention of an Indian priestly order is, I believe, by Herodotus; who wrote about B.C. 420: and in the next century, Kleitarchos mentioned the "Pramnai," and Megasthenes the "Garmanai," as the ascetic priests of the Indians.

Both these terms have been regarded as Greek transliterations of the Buddhist word Srámana: but both are, at least, as much like Bráhmana as Srámana; and there is no mention, in either of the early Greek authors above quoted, of any rites, or objects of worship, which can justify a confident conclusion as to the nature of the religion in force. In later Greek works, we find the "Brahmanai," and the "Garmanai" mentioned, as the two grades of Gumnosophistai; and the "Pramnai" alluded to as an altogether *distinct* class. It seems, therefore, to say the least, doubtful, whether it is safe to argue, from the scanty and discrepant statements of pre-Christian Greek authors, that the Buddhism of Sákya, and its separate priesthood, and peculiar institutions, existed in their time.(1)

higher order of the priesthood than those who are bare-headed; and instances the existing custom in Tibet; where the Lámas have the head covered; and the inferior clergy are bare-headed. ("The Bhilsa Topes," 27, 205.)

(1) The terms applied to the ascetic priests of India, by the Greek writers, "Gumnosophistai," or "Gumnetai," that is, naked, or rather, lightly-clad philosophers, are strikingly applicable to the class of persons now under notice: but neither the Sánchi sculptures, nor the Greek descriptions in any way correspond with the carefully robed, and closely shaven priests of the Buddhists, described by later classical writers, and by the Buddhists themselves; and still to be seen in Buddhist countries! I would point out too, that the principal garment of a Buddhist priest, the "sanghâti," which, by some European writers, is identified with the *kilt* worn by the ascetics of the Sánchi sculptures, is, by others, called a "mantle or cowl." (See "Foe-Koue-Ki," Chapter XXII., Note 12; and Spence Hardy's "Eastern Monachism," 95.)

The principal arguments, for identifying the Pramnai and Garmanai, with the Buddhist Srámanas, only, are, as I understand them, that they are mentioned as the *opponents* of the Bráhmanai; and that the female Garmanai mentioned by Megasthenes, can only be the nuns peculiar to the Buddhism of Sákya. In reply to the first argument, it may, reasonably, be urged that it is by no means clear what assertions are really those of such early writers as Megasthenes and Kleitarchos, and what are to be attributed to the much later writers—such as Strabo and Arrian—through whom, alone, their works are known! Moreover, though the Pramnai and Garmanai appear, in some places, to be opposed to the Bráhmanai; they are, in others, classed, *with* them, without any distinction: so that there is, at least, a doubt on the subject! Again, the existence of a female class in the priesthood, though unquestionably a feature of the Buddhism of Sákya, was in no sense *peculiar* thereto. It was, according to Buddhist writers themselves, an already popular institution, in India, before Sákya's time; and was adopted by him, on the advice of his disciple Ananda, from motives of policy. (See "Foe-Koue-Ki," Chapter XVI., Note 23.) The custom was, doubtless, of ancient, foreign origin; and we know that there were female, as well as male priests, among the ancient Egyptians, Syrians and Greeks; as well as in ancient Rome.

When, however, we turn to classical authors of a much later period, we find unmistakable evidence of the existence of the two hostile sects of Bráhmans and Buddhists.

Clemens Alexandrinus, who wrote between 190 and 220 A.D., speaks of "Butta," or Buddha; and of pyramids—that is Sthúpas, or Chaityas—containing bone-relics; and he distinctly mentions two classes of Indian priests; that is, the "Semnoi" or Srámana; whom, in one place, he calls "Bactrian priests"; and who, he says, admitted female members, or "Semnai": and the Bemnoi, or Bráhmanas, whom he describes as worshippers of Herakles and Pan—the followers, that is, of the old pantheism, which preserved so many traces of its Græco-Persian origin.

Porphyrius (270 to 303 A.D.) classes, as "Gumnosophai," both the "Brachmanai" and the "Samanæi" or "Samanæani"; calling the former a distinct tribe; and the latter, a mixture of all classes; who shaved their heads; wore stoles or tunics; abandoned domestic ties; and lived in colleges or communities: a very correct description of the followers of Sákya Muni, or Gautama Buddha!

If we turn to the Páli inscriptions of the Indian monarch "Devánampiya Piyadasi," we find further reason for concluding that, at their date (3rd century B.C.), when the religion of India was what has been called "Buddhism without Buddha," both Bráhmana and Srámana were titles of *one and the same priestly class*: the terms used, in the Páli, being "bámana sámana," and "sámana bámana"; without any conjunctive or disjunctive, such as would have been used, had the terms meant distinct classes. Both the terms, moreover, meant, alike, in Sanskrit, "purity," and "sanctity."

Professor Wilson, in remarking on this parallel use of the two terms, said, "Although Srámana is usually applied to Buddhist teachers; yet, in its original import, it designates any ascetic or religious character." ("Jour. Roy. As. Soc.," XII., Part 1; p. 177.)

Sákya himself, who was both a Bráhmana by descent, and the chief, or Mahá Srámana of his own sect, is represented, in Buddhist works, as enjoining equal respect to Bráhmanas and Srámanas; and as using, in his discourses, the epithet Bráhmana, as "a term of honour for the Buddhist Arahats, or saints" (see Rhys Davids' "Buddhism," 84): while we learn, also on Buddhist authority, that even as late as the fifth century A.D., the term Srámana continued to be applied to both Buddhist and non-Buddhist priests ("Foe-Koue-Ki," Chapter II., Note 6).

Again, it is ***Buddhist*** writers who tell us that, in the early ages of the world, there was a class of men, set apart to check the growing wickedness of mankind; who were called "Bráhmana," that is "suppressors," or "eradicators"; "Jhayaka," from their custom of dwelling in leaf huts, in the wilderness; and "Parivrajaka," or hermits. ("Jour. Roy. As. Soc.," VI. 362, 363.)

Sir A. Cunningham's views as to these Sánchi ascetics, and those represented at Bharhut, will be found in "The Bhilsa Topes," Preface, xi. to xiv., and pp. 60 to 70; and, "Stupa of Bharhut," p. 30.

The third compartment of this face ("The Bhilsa Topes," I. 203, 204; and my

Plate XII., Fig. 2), shows a three-stemmed, chatta-shaded pípal tree; issuing from a three-arched upper-storeyed shrine; under which, on an altar, is the "disc-and-crescent" symbol; which is thus proved to be of equal sanctity with the tree itself. Kinnara, and four male worshippers, in Indian costume, attend on the tree and symbol; and one of the men has his hair arranged in a top-knot. On either side of the central tree or shrine, are four other trees; one of which resembles the "bodhi" of Vipaswi, elsewhere mentioned.

The aswattha, pípal, or Ficus religiosa, is called, in Buddhist works, the sacred tree of Sákya; and a very similar subject to this, among the Bharhut sculptures, bears the Páli inscription "Bhagavato Sáka Munino bodhi;" that is, the sacred tree of the Bhagavata Sákya Muni. ("Stupa of Bharhut," 45, 114, 115, 134; and Plates XIII., Fig. 1; XXX., Fig. 3; and LIV., No. 28.)

A Páli inscription, over this compartment, records the gift of the pillar by Achhávada Sethi: but makes no mention of the subject.

The fourth, or top compartment shows twenty standing figures, in Indian costume; all praying; ten in, and ten underneath, a balcony or alcove.

The right, or inner face, has four compartments; the lowest occupied by a male janitor, like those at the Northern gateway.

The second compartment ("Bhilsa Topes," III. 210, 211; and my Plate XIII., Fig. 1) shows seven ascetics or priests—without their upper scarves—who appear to be either completing a Sthúpa in a square enclosure, or to be about to build some other structure near it. The action of the figures is very spirited; and the execution good; and their several occupations serve to show not only that the priests designed and erected their own sacred structures, but, also, that wood, brickwork, and metal, were all used in their construction. The Sthúpa stands among five trees; the species of which, save the plantain, I am unable to determine: and it is unlike any of the other Sthúpas represented in the sculptures.

It is of a bee-hive, tumulus, shape; and, apparently, built in successive courses of brickwork; and it has, on its "drum," or cylindrical portion, three symbols; a shell, and some undistinguishable object, on either side of two spheroidal symbols, placed one over the other; which Sir. A. Cunningham considers as analogous to the two eyes represented on Nepálese and Tibetan Chaityas; and as indicating the dedication of the Sthúpa to the supreme, or "Ádi Buddha" (see "The Bhilsa Topes," 8, 9, 209, 210; and Plate III., Figs. 5, 6, 7). This celestial Buddha had various names, as the embodiment of the divine light; such as Chaksha, "the eye"; "light;" "flame-formed;" "the chief lamp of all the regions of space"; "the universally radiant sun;" etc. These titles were applied, also, to the deified *mortal* Buddhas, of whom Sákya was the last: and they are of interest, as supporting the theory of Mithraic origin. A single eye was, as is well known, a very ancient symbol of the deity: but, save in the instances cited by Sir A. Cunningham—in which the symbols are side by side, not one over the other—I am unaware of any use of the double symbol; and I am unable to suggest any connection between them.

The third compartment ("The Bhilsa Topes," II. 207 to 210; and my Plate XIII.,

Fig. 2) is of special interest; as it not only shows, as fire-worshippers, the ascetic, or priestly class; but proves that buildings, as well as caves, were dedicated to "fire"; and that the worship of fire was, equally with that of trees, Sthúpas, wheels, and other emblems, part of the general religion of the country, at the date of the sculptures.

The building here represented—which resembles the fire-temple shown in the frontispiece to Volume II. of Maurice's "Indian Antiquities"—has a domed roof, with a Buddhist railing, on which is perched a peacock. Flames are issuing from two arched openings in the roof; and under the building are a flat altar, and a small fire-altar, overshadowed by a five-headed nága, or serpent. About the building, there are six, or perhaps seven trees; among which are, apparently, a mango; a tála, or tár (Borassus flabelliformis); plantains; and the bodhis of Vipaswi, and Viswabhu.

Eight men, in the ascetic or priestly costume, are worshipping the building and the fire; and the nága appears to be joining in the worship; as, in another sculpture (see p. 52), it does in the worship of a tree. It is possible, however, that it may have been introduced merely to mark the sanctity of the place.(1)

The kilt of the left-hand figure is plain; not plaited like the others: and is open on the right side, exposing the leg; a distinction which doubtless has a meaning.(2)

In the lower part of the compartment, water is represented; and in or near it, an elephant, oxen, sheep, and deer, all symbolic animals in Buddhism. An ascetic is bathing; and three boys are filling their water vessels. To the right of these is a turbaned ascetic, seated, in the attitude called "ukru-patka-bandh," on a mat; and, apparently, addressing, or preaching to, another ascetic, who stands before him in a reverential attitude. Behind this figure, is his leaf-thatched hut; inside which hangs his upper garment or scarf ("uttara sangháti"); and in front of him, and, apparently, guarded by the elephant, are a small fire-altar, fire-tongs, a ladle, and a bundle of either sticks or matting.

Below this group are six (or perhaps seven) small plants, each of seven leaves or sprays; which, from their frequent introduction in the sculptures, have, probably, some symbolic meaning. The seated ascetic is, doubtless, intended for the chief guardian priest of the "ávasatha," or fire temple; whose duty it was to trim, and keep alight, the sacred fire; and who, from his position, was an object of reverence to the subordinate priesthood, and the laity.

The fourth compartment ("Bhilsa Topes," I. 205-207) represents the gateway, and part of the walls of a city, or large building; with two female spectators, and a man holding a kind of wreath, looking out of it. Inside the walls, near a five-pinnacled building, a man and woman are driving, towards the gateway, a couple of

(1) The serpent nowhere appears as an object of worship, at Sánchi; and the same may be said of Bharhut, and I believe, Amarávati. It was, however, a common symbol, both in Buddhism and Bráhmanism; and was, in many older systems, not only a symbol of the sun; but used as the representative of the "genius loci," or guardian deity, of a particular place; the protector of altars and shrines, etc.

(2) Two of the ascetics in Plate XIII., Fig. 1, have, it will be seen, the same peculiar kind of kilt.

bulls or cows. To the left, outside the walls, are two huts; in front of which is a group of a man, seated, with five women, who are engaged in pounding and winnowing grain, and making it into cakes. One of them, as she uses a rolling-pin, is being fondled by the man. Just below this domestic group, is a sacred tí, or chatta, with garlands, near an altar; and with a worshipper on each side. In front of the gateway is water; near which stand three women with water jars; and two men; one with a staff, and a wreath-shaped object, like that seen in the hand of the man on the walls; and the other paying reverence to him. On the left, below the tí and altar, are four buffaloes, three bulls or cows of the humped, or Bráhmini breed, two goats, and two sheep; some in, and some out of the water.

I can suggest no explanation of this curious subject; which Sir. A. Cunningham calls a "kitchen scene." Some of the animals represented, are symbolic, in Buddhism; and the sacred tí has no apparent connection with a purely domestic interpretation: while, possibly, the principal male figure near the water may be intended for a fisherman, with his staff and net; and may, in such case, allude to the former birth of Sákya, as a fisherman.

The figures in this sculpture, though wearing the usual Indian dress, are without necklaces or girdles; and appear to be intended for persons of inferior rank. The hair of the women is done up in a plain knot, or queue; and they have their dhotis or petticoats tightly tucked between the legs, as if to facilitate movement in their menial work.

The left, or inner face of the right pillar has three compartments; the lowest containing the usual janitor figure.

The second compartment (" The Bhilsa Topes," II. 202, 203; and my Plate XVI.) appears to represent incidents in the history of Sákya; combined with tree-worship.

The centre of the compartment shows the storeyed gateway, walls, and buildings of a city, or palace; whence issues a royal procession; winding towards some sacred trees; and watched by numerous spectators.

The procession is headed by seven musicians, mostly of foreign appearance, and a curly-haired boy, perhaps a dwarf.(1) Then comes the king, or prince, in a two-horsed chariot, with his chatta, and chaori-bearers, attended by a mounted elephant, and three archers, one of whom carries a spouted vessel, which appears in almost every procession represented in the sculptures. The rear of the procession, still inside the gateway, consists of two mounted elephants, one carrying a standard; and two horsemen; two loose horses bringing up the extreme rear. The head of the procession is passing round a long low altar, in front of a row of three trees; a tála, or tár; a bodhi of Vipaswi; and a mango; which are worshipped by six men: and near them are three other trees: one, with pendent garlands, and a railed enclosure, which resembles that elsewhere called the "bodhi" of Viswabhu; one like that between two other trees in Fig. 1, Plate IX., and in the centre compartment of Plate V.; and the third, the "bodhi" of Vipaswi. Between the last two trees, is

(1) The frequent appearance of dwarfs, in processions, shows that in India, as in some other countries, European as well as Eastern, dwarfs were part of the royal retinue.

one of the peculiar plants, seen in Plates XII., Fig. 1, and XIV., Fig. 2. At the top of the compartment, is a woman, asleep on a bed, placed on an open terrace; with a peacock perched on the building near her; and an elephant approaching her in the air: evidently a representation of the dream of Máya, the mother of the prince Siddhártha, the future Sákya Buddha, who is said to have dreamt that a chhadanta elephant entered her womb, as a portent of the future celebrity of her expected son. The representation of this legend of the Buddhist "conception," in a sculpture which is certainly as old as the first century of the Christian era, is specially interesting, as proving that the story, whatever its origin, was known in India several centuries before the daté of the Buddhist books which were supposed to have contained the earliest allusions to it.(¹) The costumes, throughout, are Indian; but with some foreign-looking characteristics, among the royal attendants. Some of the women, too, have a peculiar head-gear; wearing tufts or plumes, and a horn-shaped ornament.(²)

There can, I think, be no doubt that this compartment represents the birth, or rather the "conception," of the future Buddha, as the prince Siddhártha; and his

(¹) I cannot afford space to quote the many varying versions of this doubtless ancient myth, which are found in the Lalita Vistara, and other Buddhist writings of India, Ceylon, Burmah, Tibet, China and Japan: but reference may be made to the following, among many other, sources of information, for fuller details:—Foucaux's translation of the "Lalita Vistara," 61, 83; Turnour's "Introduction to the Mahávanso," 22, 134; "Foe-Koue-Ki," Chapter X., Note 4, and XXII., Note 4; Spence Hardy's "Manual of Buddhism," 142; Bigandet's "Legend of the Burmese Buddha," 16; "Trans. Roy. As. Soc.," XX., 287; "The Bhilsa Topes," 202, 203; and "Stupa of Bharhut," 83, 84, 138, and Plates XXVIII. Fig. 2, and LV., No. 89.

The Jainas have a similar legend; and make the elephant one of the "Sola sapne," or sixteen dream portents, which herald the birth of each of their Tirthankaras. Whether, or not, Siddhártha, or Sákya, and his earthly mother Máya, the wife of the petty Sûryavansi Rája Suddhodhana, were ever real historical personages, there is no doubt that both were invested with the characteristics and attributes of old-established deities of mythology, as well as with features imitated from Biblical history. The mortal mother of Buddha, who, at first, was not worshipped, soon became the goddess Máya Devi, or Mahámáya; the counterpart of the great mother-goddess of the Bráhmanical mythology; the Sakti, alike of Brahma, Vishnu, and Siva; and the Indian representative of the "great mother," or "earth mother" of older systems: the Cybele and Demeter of the Greeks (by whom image worship in India has been said to have been introduced): the Isis of Egypt; and mother of the Egyptian Thoth or Hermes: and the still older Astarte or Ishtar of Assyria; the prototype of all. (See Layard's "Nineveh and its Remains," II. 456, 457.)

(²) These remind one of the Abyssinian "horns" described by Bruce; and of the horned head-gear of several ancient nations, to which such frequent allusion is made in Biblical metaphor. The origin of this head-dress was, doubtless, the horned, or rayed, divinities of mythology: the same term, in several ancient languages, designating a "horn," and a "ray of light": ex. gr. the Sanskrit "karna," the Greek "karneios," and the Assyrian "karnaia."

In India, at any rate among the Buddhists, the horn seems to have been sometimes formed by the top-knot of the hair, twisted up with folds of the turban; and the Sánchi sculptures show it as worn by men as well as women. A manufactured imitation of this, called the chuḍamaha, or churamani, is still worn by Hindu women; and is of special value, because it was the distinguishing ornament of Sita, the faithful wife of the god Rámachandra. Among the Indian Buddhists, also, the ornament had a divine sanction and origin. The prince Siddhártha, before he became an ascetic, twisted his top-knot and turban together, and cut them off: and the severed headgear was, at once, carried, by the Devas, to the Trayastrinshas heaven; and became the sacred relic of Sakya, called the chuḍamaha, or "great head-dress" (see description of Plate XVIII.)

departure from his palace, with his royal retinue of "elephants, chariots, horse, and foot"; (1) either on his way to visit, and make offerings to, the sacred trees, below; among the worshippers of which he seems to be again represented as the principal figure: or, perhaps, on one of the excursions during which he witnessed the "four predictive signs," which led him to adopt an ascetic life.

In the third, or top compartment ("Bhilsa Topes," I. 202), are thirteen men, in Indian costume, worshipping a sacred tree.

The front face of this pillar is much defaced. It is divided into five compartments; each representing the same subject: namely, a pillared porch or chamber, in which the king and his attendants are watching a "nách" or dance; the dancing women in which wear plumed head-dresses. The king holds, in one hand, a vase or goblet, perhaps the alms-bowl of an ascetic; and in the other, a "vajra," or thunderbolt: thus combining the regal and priestly offices; a custom which, as well as that of maintaining what may be called religious dancing girls, was common among many ancient oriental nations.

The small compartments on the rear faces have, respectively, a Sthúpa, and a tree; with Kinnara, and worshippers in Indian dress.

It will be noticed that the standard carried on one of the elephants which form the capitals, has, like many other standards, and many of the shields, represented in the sculptures, a device like that of the English Union Jack.(2) On this standard is a badly cut Páli inscription; which will be noticed in Chapter XI.

The supports of the several lintels correspond, in style, with those of the Northern Gateway: and the sculptured subjects are as follow. Front face of the bottom lintel, a tree growing out of a pavilion, or shrine, under which is a disc-and-crescent symbol, on an altar. Kinnara guard the tree; and on either side of it are numerous figures. To its left is a procession of musicians, and men carrying flowers, vases, standards, and long poles, surmounted by discs and other symbols.(3)

(1) That is, the "chaturanga," or four arms of an army, or military escort, or retinue. According to Tod, "chaturanga" is the original of the Persian "shatranj," or chess; a game said to be of Persian origin: and to have been, originally, played with living "pieces," as an expedient for revealing, dramatically, the death of a favourite prince. The story is told in the Sháhnámeh; and it appears to be the basis of the Buddhist accounts of the mode adopted for communicating to Rája Ajátasatru, the death of Sákya. (See J. Prinsep's quotations from Ksoma de Köros, in the "Jour. As. Soc. Beng." VI. 687.)

(2) The heraldic meaning of the Union Jack is, of course, simply the conjunction of the crosses of St. George, St. Andrew, and St. Patrick: but the device of two such intersecting crosses is, in itself, a very ancient one; and was used in Assyria, Syria, Bactria, India, Japan, and other countries. It was the basis, too, of the "labarum" or sacred monogram of the Christian Emperor Constantine, to whom, according to early Christian traditions, it was miraculously revealed.

(3) Long poles, with streamers hanging from them, and supporting discs, birds, and other emblems, are common adjuncts to Buddhist shrines, at the present day; as may be seen in Burmah: and they are analogous to the votive pillars often seen near Sthúpas and temples. Such emblematic poles are common, too, on Bactrian and Indian coins. It is worthy of remark that the Sanskrit word "linga" means, literally, a sign, a pole, or a staff; as also does the Greek word "phallos": so that it is not unlikely that many supposed allusions to Indian and Greek phallic worship, may be based upon passages in ancient authors, which really refer to sun-pillars; or to emblematic poles, carried in religious processions; such as those shown in Plate XXXV., Figs. 42, 45. (See next note, and, also, Note 1, p. 16.)

To right of the tree are worshippers; female musicians;(¹) and a kneeling caparisoned elephant, over which a woman waves a cháori. On the elephant's hind leg stands a man, in undress like that in the similar subject shown in Plate XII., Fig. 1; to whom a woman is speaking; while a child holds the end of his girdle. On the extreme right, is a man approaching in a chariot, attended by a second chariot, and an armed escort. No ascetics are represented; and all the costumes are Indian. This subject, besides its obvious worship of the tree and the disc-and-crescent symbol, would appear to have some partial connection with the Wessentara Jataka, described at p. 36: or perhaps to a dedication of an elephant, to the deity.

On the cubical portions, are winged lions; and on the projecting ends, peacocks.

The rear face of the bottom lintel ("Bhilsa Topes," III. 213), shows the worship of a Sthúpa, by numerous elephants; which surround and pay reverence to it, in the same way as they do the tree on the top lintel of the North gateway. It has kneeling mounted rams, on its cubical portions. Over its left volute was still standing, in 1850, a mounted elephant. The cubical props of the second lintel have, in front, a wheel on an altar, with attendant Kinnara, and worshippers; and the seated female, anointed by elephants, described at p. 36; and, in rear, vases of flowers. The three small props have, respectively, in front, a chatta-shaded tree, a wheel on a pillar, and a pillar crowned by three lions. In rear they resemble those at the North gate, already described.

All the intervening figures had disappeared at the time of my visit. The second, or centre lintel has the following sculptures:—In front ("Bhilsa Topes," II. 211), on the projecting ends, elephants among trees; and, in centre, a sacred tree, surrounded by numerous figures, in Indian costume, some of them with umbrellas held over them. On the left of the tree, are the buildings and walls of a city, with numerous spectators; and on the right a procession, in which are a number of praying figures; a representation of the "Sripáda," or sacred foot-prints, shaded by a chatta; and a horse, similarly shaded. (²)

(¹) The constant union of the two sexes, in the worship of trees, and Sthúpas, at Sánchi, reminds one of the theories advocated in O'Brien's "Round Towers of Ireland," where both the tree and the tower are called phallic, as well as solar symbols. There are, also, at Sánchi, numerous subjects of an amatory character; and representations of the temple dancing-women; who have been compared to the "Kodeshoth," or temple-women, dedicated to the Syrian goddess Ishtar; and who are the earthly representatives of the celestial Apsarasas and Gandharvas, of Buddhist and Bráhmanical mythology. (See as to the Kodeshoth, Conder's "Syrian Stone Lore," pp. 35, 47.) All this tends to prove that, at the time the Sánchi sculptures were executed, the religion in vogue had a strong sensual element in it; quite at variance with the usually recognized characteristics of Sákya's Buddhism. As regards actual linga or phallic worship, however, there is not the remotest trace of it at Sánchi; and though its existence, in many parts of the world, at various times, is unquestionable, it does not seem to have been followed, in India, until some time after the great Saiva movement in the time of Sankara Acháriya. No mention is made of it by such observant travellers as Fa Hian and Hwan Thsang, in the fifth and seventh centuries A.D.: and we find no allusion to it in Muhammadan works of even three or four centuries later!

(²) Though it is probable that the chatta-shaded horse, in this sculpture, as well as the elephant in that of the lower lintel, may be regarded as merely *presented* to the deity, or the priests of the local shrine; there seems no reason why we should not look upon them as intended for sacrifice. I have already (p. 33, and

The whole of the rear face ("Bhilsa Topes," II. 211, 212) is occupied by a representation of a sacred tree, worshipped by numerous animals; among which are the lion, deer, sheep, buffalo, ox, ram, camel, eagle, and, lastly, the five-hooded snake; which I have already mentioned as sharing in the worship of fire (see p. 47).

The cubical portions have kneeling Bactrian camels.

It is possible that the animals and supernatural beings, which are represented as sharing with human beings, in tree worship, and the worship of the Sthúpa, and fire, may be merely intended to show the universal reverence of all creation for the deity represented by those several types: but some of the animals are symbolical of different grades of mankind;(¹) and the Nága or serpent not only represents an important tribe; but is, also, a type of the whole Buddhist church.

A mounted elephant was standing over one of the volutes of this lintel, in 1850.

The cubical props which support the top lintel have, in front, a sacred tree, with Kinnara and worshippers; and a seated female anointed by elephants: and, in rear, terraced Sthúpas, with worshippers. The small props resemble those below.

The front of the top lintel has precisely the same subject as the corresponding lintel at the Northern gateway (see p. 38): and its rear has seven trees, of different kinds; each with two guardian Kinnara, and attendant worshippers.

Its cubical portions have, in front, kneeling, mounted bulls; and, in rear, standing, horned lions, also mounted.

One of the two crowning disc-and-crescent symbols, like those of the Northern gateway, and a mounted elephant over one of the volutes, were still in their places in 1850: but all other details of the entablature, save those specified, had fallen; and many had disappeared altogether.

Note 1) adverted to the "Aswamedha," or sacrifice of a horse to the Sun; and its probable adoption by the Buddhists, as a royal rite; and there is no ground for regarding tenderness for animal life, as more of a Buddhist than a Bráhman tenet; or for doubting that, in early times, among Bráhmans and Buddhists alike, customs were very different from what they became later. The horse was sacred among the Indo-Scythians, from whom Sákya Buddha sprang; and yet they sacrificed it to the Sun-god; and the Indians who had a special veneration for the elephant, may, at one time, both Bráhmans and Buddhists, have made it, as well as the horse, a sacrificial victim.

(¹) Buddhist writers use the metaphors of three yoked cars, and three animals swimming across a stream, to represent the spiritual progress (yana) of the Sráwakas, Pratyekas, and Bodhisatwas, respectively. The Sráwakas, occupied with their own salvation, and regardless of others, are likened to a car drawn by a sheep, an animal which, in flight, never looks back for the rest of the flock; or to a hare, which floats on the surface of a stream, with no power of penetrating deep. The Pratyekas, who do not, in seeking their own emancipation, neglect that of others, are compared to a car drawn by a deer, an animal which, in flight, looks back to the following herd; or to a horse, which, in swimming, sinks deep, but does not reach the bottom of the stream. While the Bodhisatwas, who benefit others regardless of self, and repress error and passion, are likened to a car drawn by an ox, an animal which bears its burden patiently; or to an elephant, which crosses a stream, by walking through the bed of it. All these animals were, according to Buddhist legends, at one time or another, animated by the soul of Buddha: and all (save the hare) occur frequently in the Sánchi sculptures, in connection with the adoration of trees, Sthúpas, or the wheel-symbol. These ingenious metaphors, however, as well as that of the "lilies in a tank," previously noticed, are, probably, all of later date than the epoch of the Sánchi sculptures.

CHAPTER VI.

THE SOUTHERN GATEWAY OF NO. I STHUPA; AND ITS SCULPTURES.

THIS gateway, the oldest of the four, was prostrate long before Captain Fell saw it in 1819; and its sculptures were, with a few exceptions, so broken up, and defaced that I made but few drawings of them.

It resembled the gateways already described, in style and construction; but the gate-pillars, as seen in Plates XVIII. and XIX., Fig. 1, are different in their upper portions; and the abacus is circular.

The capitals are formed by four lions; indifferently carved, and evidently copied from those of the fine isolated pillar, which once stood close to this entrance; and which shows strong traces of Greek influence, if not actual workmanship.(1) Plate XIX., Figs. 1 and 2, show the gateway capital, and the older one from which it was evidently copied.

These gateway pillars are single blocks, 1 foot 9 inches square; and, when complete, were, capitals inclusive, 16½ feet high. The right pillar had, on its left, or inner face, four compartments; but the bottom one, containing the usual door-keeper, is broken off; as is the bottom compartment of the front face.

The second compartment shows three mounted elephants, one carrying a man, and a female standard-bearer, and the other carrying women only (one with a child) besides their maháwats. They are emerging from a gateway, attended by a single horseman; and appear to be driving before them some grotesque giants and dwarfs; one of the latter carrying two bottle-shaped covered jars.

The third compartment has a two-horsed chariot, carrying three men, in Indian costume. In the background is a mounted elephant, with a standard-bearer; and in front of the chariot are five men; one with a sword, and others carrying a spouted vessel, covered vase or caskèt, and other undistinguishable objects.

I can give no plausible explanation of either of these subjects: but possibly,

(1) The use of the well-known "honeysuckle ornament" is one of many indications of Greek influence in Indian art: and the best executed, as well as the earliest Buddhist sculptures are those discovered in the remote north-western parts of India (formerly Gándhára), where Greek and Græco-Bactrian influence was the strongest. The Greeks appear to have derived their honeysuckle symbol from Assyria; among the sculptures of which we find floral symbols closely resembling those at Sánchi, flanked sometimes by mystic animals, and sometimes by birds; being, in fact, as pointed out by Layard, component parts of the "Ashirah" or sacred tree. (See "Nineveh and its Remains," II. 472; and my description of Plate XXXIII., Fig. 2.)

they may have some connection with one represented in the Bharhut sculptures; where a personage of distinction, accompanied by three elephants, carrying women, is called Rája Ajátasatru, the worshipper of Bhagavata ("Stupa of Bharhut," 89, 90, 136, and Plates XVI., Fig. 3; and LIV., No. 63).

The fourth, or top compartment has a representation of the worship of the sacred wheel-symbol, by men and women, in Indian dress, and eight deer. The wheel has thirty-two spokes; each of which ends, on the outer circumference, or tire, in a small disc-and-crescent symbol; and it is guarded by Kinnara, on either side.

The front face of this pillar is in perfect preservation; having been imbedded in the ground from the time of its fall, until turned over and cleaned, on my second visit to Sánchi in 1851. Its three sculptured compartments are shown in Plate XVIII. The first, or lowest compartment shows an open, six-pillared colonnade, with a circular, or oval upper chamber, and a domical roof, ornamented with cross-bands and numerous small discs. Its railed balustrade has a chatta at each corner; and the whole superstructure is supported by beams, which are shown in perspective.(1)

In front of the colonnade below, is a well-executed representation of what appears to be relic-worship. Part of the ceremonial consists of music and dancing; the attitude and gesture of the dancing-woman being exactly like that of the modern "náchní." The principal male figure, who has six attendants, wears a peculiar kind of dhoti and has "Nága"-shaped armlets; and a horned head-ornament: and there are peculiarities of costume, too, among the female figures. Six seated men, are, also, worshipping the displayed relic; some of their features having a Tartar, or Burmese character; as if they were visitors from a distant country.(2) When I first saw this curious sculpture, I thought the object on the altar was a relic-casket; but, since seeing Sir A. Cunningham's work on the Bharhut antiquities, I have come to the conclusion that it represents the chudamaha, or churamani, "hair relic," already alluded to in Note 2, p. 49. Among the Bharhut sculptures, there is one which seems to be identical in subject, though far inferior in treatment; and which is inscribed in Páli, "bhagavato chudamaho"; that is, the head-dress relic of Bhagavata (see "Stupa of Bharhut," 107, 109, 119, 136; and Plates XVI., Fig. 1, and LIV., No. 64). The Sánchi subject has, also, an inscription, on the pent roofing of the colonnade; but it contains no such word as chudamaho, or churamani. It reads as follows:— Vedisa kehidanta káre hirá pakan makanta (or mankata), which Sir A. Cunningham supposed to allude to an inhabitant of Vedisa. ("The Bhilsa Topes," 264.)

(1) See, as to this, and other, indications that the structures at Sánchi are stone copies of what used to be constructed of wood, p. 21, Note 3.

(2) Though foreign-looking in features, these seated worshippers wear the Indian costume. In his first edition of "Tree and Serpent Worship," Mr. J. Fergusson mistook the head of the praying figure nearest the altar, for a severed human head: but, as I convinced him, it is merely the head of a seated figure, thrown backwards while he gazes at the relic on the altar.

The centre compartment (Bhilsa Topes," II. 213) represents a king, or other person of rank, with six female attendants, all in Indian costume. Two of the women hold him in a partial embrace; and the trio seem to be engaged in a kind of devotional dance. A third woman holds an umbrella over the group; and a fourth carries a covered water or wine jar, and a drinking cup: while the remaining two are seated, on a cushion and stool, respectively; one turned towards, and seemingly worshipping a five-flowered plant, or tree; and the other holding a dish or platter. A wreath, or garland, and some drapery hang on pegs in rear of the figures. (See Note 1, p. 51; and Plates VI., Fig. 1, and XXII., Fig. 1, for other amatory and convivial scenes.)

The third or top compartment has a double-storeyed building, of the same style as that in the bottom compartment; but with a plain roof, and three entrances to the upper chamber. This is built round a seven-branched pípala tree, the "bodhi" of Sákya Muni; which is adorned with pennons, and shaded by a double Tí, or chatta.

Under this building (which resembles that shown in Plate XII., Fig. 2) is a large square altar, on which is a triple "disc-and-crescent symbol." On my first visit to Sánchi, I had noticed the resemblance between the single symbol, and the figures in the celebrated triad of Jagannáth; and the discovery of this triform representation was an incontestable proof of what, before, was merely supposition; namely, that the Bráhmanical triad was derived from that of the Buddhists. (See, for fuller remarks, Chapter X.)

The junction of the "bodhi" of Sákya Muni and the disc-and-crescent symbol, as objects of worship, as seen in this Plate, and in my Plate XII., Fig. 2 (and, also, in Plates XIII., Fig. 1, and XXX., Fig. 3 of the "Stupa of Bharhut") is of special interest; as showing that, at the date of these sculptures, the Buddhists of Sákya's sect recognized both tree and symbol, as well as the Sthúpa, the wheel, and fire, as his representatives.

Finally, this interesting sculpture, with its triple arched and chambered shrine, shows the prevalence, in India, as far back at least as the early years of the Christian era, of the triple form of sacred building; specimens of which are found in the religious structures of widely separated ancient races: such, for instance, as the three-celled shrines of Assyria, Egypt, Greece and Rome, from which we derive the three-aisled Christian basilica; the three-chambered and three-spired temples of the Indian Jainas; and, I may add, as a later illustration, the three-domed mosques of the idol-hating Muhammadans; with which we are so familiar in India.

The right, or outer face, has floral and scroll work, as at other gateways. Broken fragments of the compartments of the left pillar, represent processions, draught-bullocks, and the worship of trees; before one of which, are a man and woman clasping hands.

The entablature, which is much broken up, resembled that of the gateways already described. One of its cubical props is shown in Plate XXI., Fig. 1; in which I would particularize the frontlets of the elephants, formed of the curved, and sword-shaped blades noticed at page 19; the snake armlets of the maháwats (which occur only at this gateway); the casket carried by one of them, which exactly resembles the relic-caskets discovered in No. 3 Sthúpa; and one of the standards, with its four "fields," emblazoned with the sun, moon, and small discs, doubtless representing planets. On one face of the lowest lintel ("Bhilsa Topes," III. 215 to 217; and my Plate XX.) is a spirited representation of an attack, from two sides, on a walled city: both the attackers and the defenders—with the exception of a few who seem to represent foreign mercenaries—being attired in the Indian costume. The principal figure, with the left attacking party, is on horseback; and that on the right is a chatta-shaded personage in a chariot; both being accompanied by numerous followers, standard-bearers, armed men, elephants, and bearers of relic-caskets. With the exception of the leading men, in both parties, who are actively engaged with the defenders, the action and gestures of the members of both processions are perfectly peaceful.

This subject evidently represents a contest for, and perhaps triumphal procession of, the relics of a saint, or of some celebrated monarch: and there are several incidents in Buddhist history of which it may be an illustration.(1)

A fragment of the second lintel ("Bhilsa Topes," II. 214, 215, 266), represents, in centre, a double-terraced Sthúpa, shaded by a chatta, and guarded by Kinnara.

On the Sthúpa is a two-lined Páli inscription, to the effect that the donor of the lintel was Balamitra, a pupil of Aryakshudra; the same person as the presenter of one of the pillars of the Western Gateway.(2) On the left of the Sthúpa, are a

(1) According to Buddhist writers, eight Indian cities contended for and ultimately divided, and erected Sthúpas over, the relics of Sákya (see "Foe-Koue-Ki," Chapter XXIV., Notes 8, 12): and this Sánchi sculpture, if rightly interpreted above, shows that the story was current in India several centuries before the earliest Buddhist books were written. The history of Sákya Muni, whether in its earlier traditional form, or as finally elaborated in Buddhist books, is a medley of historical facts, traditional stories, and myths, derived from a variety of sources; together with incidents and imagery borrowed from Sacred Writ: all of which tends to prove that the Buddhism of Sákya was formed into a complete system *after*, and not five or six centuries before, the Christian era!

One coincidence may, appropriately, be noticed here. Plutarch informs us, regarding the celebrated Græco-Bactrian King Menander, that "the cities in common had the charge of his funeral rites; but, afterwards, contended for his ashes. They at last divided his remains equally among them; and agreed that monuments to him should be erected by each." (See "Trans. Roy. As. Soc." I. 130.) Menander flourished between 165 and 130 B.C.; and ruled from the mouths of the Indus—where he captured Potala, the nidus, alike, of the Buddhist Sákas or Sákyas, and the Bráhmanical Súryavansis—to the Doaba, or delta of the Ganges and Jamna.

Traditions regarding him were, doubtless, current, all over this extensive territory, for several centuries after his era: and it seems more probable that the above story regarding his funeral rites should have been adopted by the Buddhists—who adopted so much besides—than that a classical writer should apply to a Græco-Bactrian monarch, an old Indian tradition; which is the only conclusion possible, if we date Sákya Muni in the sixth century B.C.; and is, in fact, the view taken by most European writers who have, hitherto, noticed the above parallel between the history of Menander, and the history of Sákya. (See "Trans. Roy. As. Soc." I. 130, 330; Wilson's "Ariana Antiqua," 283; Tod in "Trans. Roy. As. Soc." I. 317, 330; "Foe-Koue-Ki," Chapter XXII., Note 9; and "The Bhilsa Topes," 126, 127.)

(2) This translation, like most of those contained in this book, is taken from Cunningham's "Bhilsa Topes." See Note 1, page 34, for another proof that the same persons shared in the construction of the Northern, Eastern, and Western Gateways; which shows that though the Southern Gate was first erected, all four were constructed during the lifetime of the same individuals (see Chapter XIII.).

number of men and women, in Indian costume; but standing on the folds of nágas, or snakes, whose hoods canopy their heads. Some of them worship, and make offerings to, the Sthúpa; and some seem to be paying respect to the central figure of the group. On the right of the Sthúpa, a procession approaches, consisting of a royal, or saintly personage in a chariot; shaded by a chatta, and preceded and followed by musicians, horsemen, and standard-bearers on elephants. The chariot is shown, in Fig. 12, Plate XIV. (See pages 60 to 62, as to the "Nágas" represented in the sculptures.) One of the faces of the top lintel ("Bhilsa Topes," I. 214) has alternate Sthúpas and trees; with Kinnara, and worshippers, on either side of each. The central Sthúpa has a three-lined Páli inscription, which contains the name of the Andhra King Sátakarni; and fixes the date of the gateway as between 19 and 37 A.D. (See Chapter XI.)

The cubical portions of this lintel have kneeling mounted bulls; one of the riders carrying a lotus flower, and another, a relic-casket. And on one of its projecting ends is a led horse, issuing from a double-lintel gateway, and attended by a cháori bearer, and a man carrying the spouted vessel, already described.

The summit of this gateway was, it may be assumed, crowned by a central wheel, and two disc-and-crescent symbols; but I did not see any of their fragments; and cannot, therefore, speak positively on the point.

CHAPTER VII.

THE WESTERN GATEWAY OF NO. 1 STHUPA; AND ITS SCULPTURES.

THE right gateway pillar, only, was standing, in 1850; the rest of the gaetway having fallen, a few years previously.

The pillars are 2 feet 4½ inches square; and 16 feet 2 inches high; including the capitals; which are formed by four well-executed grotesque dwarfs (see Plate XXV.), supporting the superstructure, by their up-raised hands, like the Greek Atlantes.

The left pillar was lying with its left or outer, scroll-work, face downwards; and I did not move it. The only distinguishable part of its front face, is the top compartment ("Bhilsa Topes," I. 223, 224), which is shown in my Plate XXII., Fig. 1: and represents four convivial, and rather amatory, couples, seated on beds and matting, in a water-side terraced garden; the two portions of which are connected by a railed flight of steps; on which stand a male and female attendant. The former is, apparently, trying to check the merriment of his female companion. This woman, and also one of the seated women, has the horned head-dress described in Note 2, p. 49. All the figures wear the Indian costume. Five trees are represented; among which are the plantain, the bodhi of Vipaswi, and the jewelled Kalpa darma, or Párijáta, of Indra's paradise. There is, also, at the water's edge, a small five-petalled plant.

The trees and plant possibly have, here, as elsewhere, a symbolical meaning; but there is nothing else in the sculpture to give it any allegorical significance: and we may, I think, take it as representing, merely, a social scene of a convivial and amatory character, in one of the royal gardens. At all events, like other subjects, already noticed, it serves to show that the people represented at Sánchi, whatever their form of religion, were certainly not followers of the strict Buddhism of Sákya; which forbade sensual enjoyment in any shape, and certainly would not have permitted its representation on a sacred building (see Note 1, p. 51).

The right, or inner, face has four compartments: the first or lowest (partly broken) being the usual janitor figure.

The second compartment ("Bhilsa Topes," III. 226, 227; and my Plate XXI., Fig. 2) represents a piece of water, with a barge floating on it; whose prow is formed by a winged gryphon, and stern by a fish's tail. It contains a pavilion, overshadowing a vacant throne; over which a male attendant holds a chatta; while another man has a cháori. A third man is steering, or propelling the vessel, with a large paddle. In the water are fresh-water flowers and buds, and a large shell; and there are five men floating about, holding on by spars and inflated skins; while a sixth appears to be asking the occupant of the stern of the vessel, for help out of the water. All the figures are fully dressed, in Indian costume, with garlands hanging from their head-gear; and those in the water, save perhaps the last mentioned, appear to be quite at their ease, as they float about, with their artificial supports.

It is probable, therefore, that this sculpture may represent, simply, the royal state barge; and the king and some of his court, disporting themselves in an artificial piece of water. State barges, almost identical with that here represented, are used by Indian nobles, to the present day; and aquatic sports are, also, a common pastime.

At the same time, it is impossible to overlook the probability of a symbolical meaning, in such a subject as this.

Captain J. D. Cunningham, in his description of Sánchi, said—"The vessel .... is almost a counterpart of the ark, or sacred boat of Egyptian processions; and which has served to illustrate the Ark of the Jewish Covenant": and many of the sacred Egyptian barges shown in Bunsen's "Egypt's Place in Universal History," and other works on Egypt, not only resemble this Sánchi barge in shape; but, also, contain vacant thrones, and shrines!

Tod ("Rájasthán," I. 572-3) also alludes to the introduction of a boat or ship, in the rites of the Egyptian Isis—which were adopted by the Greeks—and compares them with the analogous Indian festivals of "Gaurí" and the "Dol-játra."

Buddha himself, as already remarked (p. 43), is compared to a boat, on the vast ocean of life and death; and the Brahmanical "Budha," Vishnu, is represented as floating, in the dragon-shaped support, or ark, formed by the mystic Nága, on the waters of the universe, as its preserver: while the shape of the barge here shown is that of the sacred "Makara"—the Makieii of the Chinese writers—the fish avatára or "Játaka" of the Buddhists; who represent that Sákya Buddha was once incarnate in that form; just as the Bráhman mythology makes the "Matsya" or fish, the first of the avatárs of Vishnu, whose latest incarnation was "Budha"! [1]

It is, of course, more interesting to trace, in these curious old sculptures, some of the mystical and symbolical allusions in which, as is well known, both Bráhmans and Buddhists so largely indulged; and the object of which often was, to conceal

[1] See supra, pages 20, 21, and Chapter XIV., as to the "fish" incarnations of Vishnu and Sákya Buddha, and as to the "Makara," Dragon, or Fish-lion, another form of which was the Nága of the waters, as elsewhere shown. The use of this symbol, by both Bráhmans and Buddhists, and their common use, too, of the sacred barge, or ark, in this and other shapes, are proofs of the connection between both forms of religion, and the far older myths of Egypt and Assyria; which, again, as recent discoveries have shown, are traceable to ancient traditions regarding the Creation and the Deluge, which reached, successively, the Persians and Greeks; and thus became, eventually, disseminated in India. Both the fish and the ark or ship, were so widely used in ancient mythology, that a volume might be written on that subject alone; but I can do no more than allude to it, here.

the true meaning and origin of a symbol or legend: but wherever a simple or matter of fact explanation of a subject is clearly admissible, it should, by preference, be adopted. At any rate, my object, alike in my original report on Sánchi, and throughout this book, has been, to suggest such explanations as occur to me, on viewing the subjects in different lights: leaving to more competent antiquarian scholars, the correction or confirmation of my views, as the case may be.

The third compartment ("Bhilsa Topes," II. 225), which is shown in my Plate XXIII., Fig. 1, represents tree worship; or, perhaps more correctly, a festival, in connection therewith; the actors in which are a Nága chief, or king, and eleven female attendants. All are in ordinary Indian costume; but all shaded by snake-hood canopies: the women by single hoods; and the central male figure, by a five-hooded snake, on whose folds he is seated. He holds a lotus sceptre in his right hand; and his two immediate attendants hold, respectively, a cháori and a wine or water goglet.

On his right are three seated women, eating and drinking; and on his left a group of six women; five musicians, and the sixth dancing. The group surrounds a flat altar, in front of a chatta-shaded, and garlanded tree; which may be intended either for a Sála (the bodhi of "Viswabhu," and the tree under which Sákya was born), or a "sirisha" (Acacia sirisa), the bodhi of Krakuchanda. The tree has two guardian male Kinnara; and two female genii, mounted, respectively, on a winged lion, and a winged gryphon, like that forming the barge in the preceding subject.

There are several representations of "Nágas," both in human and in animal form, not only at Sánchi, but at Bharhut; (1) and a sculpture at the latter place supplies an explanation of this compartment. One of its subjects is a Nága rája, worshipping a sacred "sirisa" tree, and altar; and attended by male and female snake-hooded followers: the males with five, and the females with single-hooded canopies, as in my Plate, but on a much less prominent scale. The kneeling figure is on land; but all the others are half-submerged in water, which, as will be seen, is the special element of the Nága or serpent race.

A Páli inscription describes the scene as follows: "Erapato Nága rája bhagavato vandate"; which Sir A. Cunningham translates "Erapátra, the Nága rája, worships (the unseen figure of) Buddha."(2)

This Erapato—the Elápatra of the Bráhmanical Puránas—is described, in Buddhist works, as coming, in his serpent form, to visit Sákya Buddha, under the sacred sirisa trees; and as being converted by him, and endued, afresh, with the forfeited power of assuming human shape. At Bharhut, the entire story is represented: and we may, I think, assume that the same subject is intended in this Sánchi sculpture.

(1) See "Stupa of Bharhut," 11, 25 to 27, and 82; and Plates XIV., XVIII., XXI., XXVIII., and XLII.: and my Plates XIII., Fig. 2; and XXIII., Fig. 1; and descriptions of other subjects.

(2) The title "Bhagavata," which Sir A. Cunningham here renders as Buddha, will be discussed in Chapter XI. Though adopted by the Buddhists, it is in no sense peculiar to Buddhism; but is a common Bráhmanical epithet for the deity: and a compound form of one of the most ancient of divine titles.

Nágas, both among Buddhists and Bráhmans, are of two classes; the mythological and the historical. The former, who, in Buddhist mythology, rank next to the Devas, and Devatás, among the eight classes of superior beings, are, in the Bráhmanical Purânas, "the powerful, many-headed serpent progeny" of Kadru, one of the daughters of the "Prajápati" Daksha; and are described as inhabiting Nágaloka, or Nágadwípa, "the world of waters," beneath "Trikuta," the triangular, or triple-pointed, mountain which supports the sacred Mount Meru: their chief city being called "Bhogávati," or the City of Enjoyment.

The word "Nága," itself, means, in Sanskrit, an elephant, as well as a serpent, or dragon; and is derived from "Naga," which is both a "mountain" and "a tree": so that the mythological Nága is not only the special genius of the element of water; but is intimately associated with the tree, the elephant, and the sacred mount, (of which the Sthúpa is a type); as well as with the serpent, fish, or dragon form; all these being Buddhist symbols, though not of Buddhist origin! (See "Vishnu Purána," 145, 179, 369; "Foe-Koue-Ki," Chapter XVII., Notes 17, 28; Spence Hardy's "Manual of Buddhism," 11, 14; and Cunningham's "Stupa of Bharhut," 23 to 26, and 136.)

The *historical* Nágas, or "Serpent races," are the "Takshakas" of the Bráhmanical Purânas; a race of sun and fire-worshippers, who invaded upper India in the sixth century B.C.: evidently the Pauránik representatives both of the Persians—who conquered parts of India, and introduced their religion, in that century—and of the Indo-Scythians, or Sákas, who rose to power about the commencement of the Christian era, in the Sindh valley; and to whose race "Sákya" belonged.

The Purânas include, among their so-called prophetic dynasties, two series of Nága princes: the Sisunágas, the predecessors of the Mauryas of Pátaliputra, or Pálibothra; and the "nine Nágas" of Padmávati, Kántipura, and Mathura; who are classed as contemporary with "the Guptas of Magadha," whose era commenced in 319 A.D. (see "Vishnu Purána," 479; and Fergusson's "History of Indian and East. Arch.," 10, 14): and we learn, from other sources, that a "Nága" dynasty, named Karkota, ruled, as late as the seventh century A.D. in Kashmir; a country full of traces of Nága superstitions ("Stupa of Bharhut," 23, 24, and Note 2).

In all this jumble of genealogies, the dynastic names are traceable to those of the mythological Nágas enumerated in the Bráhmanical books.(1)

(1) The Indian Rájputs, who still preserve so many Persian and Scythian characteristics and customs, count among their six greater tribes, not only the Súryavansi, Chandravansi, and Agnivansi; that is, the progeny and worshippers of the sun, moon, and fire; but, also, the Nágavansi, or "serpent race." The ancient Persians traced their solar origin under the fable of a mighty serpent ancestor; and the Scythians, who were a branch of the Takshakas, or Nágas, claimed descent from an ancestress who was half woman and half snake; a very common figure, in both Bráhmanical and Buddhist art, as the Nágní, (See Tod's "Rájasthán," I. 35, 36, 53, 56, 57, 103 to 107, 558 and 594.) We have, therefore, both a Persian and a Scythian origin, for the Bráhman and Buddhist fables of Nága-descended races. It is, further, worthy of notice, that the Biblical name of the first mother of the human race, Eve, is, in its old aspirated Hebrew form, Evia, translated by Clemens Alexandrinus, as "a female serpent"; a double signification which is,

Much of the confusion which characterises the interpretations of ancient myths of the serpent is, doubtless, due to the fact that it is used as the symbol both of the good and the evil principle in nature: as representing, that is to say, not only the Sun-god, and the everlasting, all-productive, heat or fire, which he gives forth; but also, water, in its varied forms of sea and river, lake and cloud, rain, mist, and dew, all emanations of, and yet antagonistic to the supreme, solar deity.(¹) There is a like element of confusion, in regard to the Nágas of the Buddhist and Bráhman pseudo-historical books. The Buddhists, for instance, were, originally, foes to the Nága race; whom they conquered and converted, in Northern India; as did the Bráhmanical hero Parasuráma in the South: while they called themselves, and were called by others, "followers of the serpent": that is, votaries of the religion whose symbol was the Nága; which, as elsewhere remarked, was not only a serpent, but an elephant, a mount or Sthúpa, and a tree!

The fourth, or top compartment ("Bhilsa Topes," I. 224, 225) is shown in Plate XXIII., Fig. 2; and appears to illustrate two incidents in the former history of Sákya. A royal or saintly personage in the upper left-hand corner—whose mitre-shaped head-dress has the honeysuckle ornament in it—is bargaining with, or making a gift to, an ascetic; probably, some allusion to the Wessentara Játaka, mentioned at page 36. In the right upper corner are a male and female ascetic, seated near their leaf-thatched huts, between which are a flaming brazier, or altar, a water-vessel, and a ladle. Monkeys on and near the huts, and five deer, show that a wild, or secluded locality is intended. The lower part of the compartment shows a river or piece of water; perhaps the "monkey tank," elsewhere alluded to: in which are flowers and shells, a turtle, and two buffaloes. On the bank, in centre, is a boy, in ascetic dress, carrying a water-jar, and worshipped by a man in Indian costume; and another, or possibly, the same boy appears half immersed in the water, and trying to draw out an arrow with which he has just been shot by one of two kilted archers. Near the water, is a tree, apparently the "bodhi" of Vipaswi; and, scattered about, are twelve of the small multi-foil plants, already described, with five, six, seven, eight, and nine petals. The lower portion of this subject seems to represent an incident in one of the previous births, or "Játakas," of Sákya Sinha; in which he was incarnate as Sáma, the son of the blind hermit Dhukula, and famous

doubtless, the primary origin of the old myth. Mother Eve became, in process of time, mother Earth; the great goddess, the universal mother, always associated, in some way or other, with the serpent form; and her name was invoked alike in the mysteries of Isis, the orgies of Dionysos or Bacchus, and the rites of the Druids of Britain, which Pliny compared to those of the Persians. (See "Notes and Queries," Part XLV., No. 193, p. 41; and "Bhilsa Topes," Preface, p. vi.)

(¹) The custom of representing at once the joint action and the antagonism, of heat and moisture, light and darkness, good and evil, life and death, under the symbol of a solar god in conflict with a snake, dragon, or sea-monster, was universal in ancient mythology: but there were many still more fanciful modes of representing the same general idea. In the earliest Bráhmanical myths, for instance, those contained in the Vedas, the all-supreme Indra, the Lord of the celestial elephant, and tree of life, the god of the sun and the sky, and the regent of rain, has, as his foes, the watery clouds which obscure his radiancy; and which he ultimately subdues and disperses. These clouds are, in Sanskrit, named "Ahi," and "Vritra," both of which words are, also, names of the Nága, or serpent!

(like the Bráhmanical "Sarman") for his care of his parents. One day, when he went to fetch water for them, "surrounded, as usual, by deer," the Rája of Benares, Páliyaka, who was hunting, shot him, with an arrow, just as he was about to lift up his water-vessel. Owing to his virtues, however, he was cured; and his parents were restored to sight. (Spence Hardy's "Eastern Monachism," 275.)

On the abacus of this pillar is a much-worn Páli inscription, recording its donation by a votary.

The left, or inner face of the right pillar has three compartments: the lowest shows a door-keeper; which, as it differs from the others, is given in Plate XV., Fig. 13. The second compartment ("Bhilsa Topes," II. 223) has a chatta-shaded, Kinnara-guarded tree, and altar, with eighteen male worshippers, in Indian dress, seated about it. In the third compartment ("Bhilsa Topes," I. 222; and my Plate XXIV.) is a chatta-shaded, garlanded tree, and altar; with three male, and nine female worshippers, in Indian dress: two of the men are, apparently, performing the ceremony of circumambulation, and gesticulating as they go. In the left upper corner, is a double-roofed, five-pinnacled shrine; and on the other side, approaching the tree, are a horse, ram, hog, buffalo, elephant, and lion, and a gigantic bodiless head. The tree and its worshippers are inside an enclosure, entered by a "torana," or gateway; outside which, near water, are a mango tree, two plantain trees, and the tree elsewhere called the bodhi of Vipaswi; making five in all; also three small five-petalled plants. In the foreground, three men, in Indian dress, are either worshipping, or dedicating, a small altar.

The front face has four compartments: the lowest containing three rampant lions; above which is an inscription recording the gift of the pillar.

The second compartment ("Bhilsa Topes," III. 222) is an unimportant representation of tree-worship.

The third, also, represents tree-worship ("Bhilsa Topes," II. 222), by twelve men, in Indian costume. On either side of the tree are Kinnara, and a figure riding an animal, half lion and half fish. The ground about the tree is rocky; and flames are issuing from its fissures; denoting, probably, a sacred volcanic jet, or thermal spring; and indicative, therefore, of fire-worship.

The fourth, or top compartment ("Bhilsa Topes," I. pp. 218 to 222; and my Plate XXII., Fig. 2), shows the two banks of a river, in which are five fish, two alligators, and a tortoise.(1) On its far bank, are two five-leaved plants; and three trees, growing among rocks; two sleeping deer; and a number of apes; one of which holds, by the left leg, a large male ape; which is springing across the stream, into a "sirisa" tree, in which are two other small apes.

Under this tree, another large ape, and a man in full Indian costume are seated, on a raised platform or "machán," conversing together; and close to them are two men, in the same costume as the soldiers seen below, who appear to be either

(1) The Kachchapa, or tortoise, is the symbol of Kásyapa; the "former Buddha," who immediately preceded Sákya.

carrying, or attemptinp to bend, a bow.[1] Below these figures, a royal personage on horseback, attended by an umbrella bearer, and an escort of armed men, and musicians, is watching an archer; who is aiming a "bhalli," or semi-circular bladed arrow, at a fissure in the distant rocks across the river; whence a waterfall is issuing. The archer wears an Indian turban, and a short-sleeved tunic; the same broad girdle as the other figures, below; and peculiar cross-belts, apparently for supporting his quiver. The three turbaned soldiers and four bare-headed musicians have jackets, broad girdles, and dhotis which display the right leg. Between them and the river, is another tree.

The seated couple under the tree may represent either the visit to Buddha of the "King of the Apes"; the Pauránik Sugriva; that is, some Indo-Scythian; as Scythia was called "the land of apes": or it may be meant for the Prince Siddhártha, under the Sirisa tree on the banks of the river Nilian, in Magadha; which was called "the river of apes;" but the rest of the sculpture seems, clearly, to illustrate an incident in the life of Siddhártha, while prince; who, when competing, like the Greek Ulysses, for the hand of his future wife, is said to have used a mighty bow, which it took *two men* to carry; and, therewith, to have made three wonderful shots, his second arrow piercing seven targets, and striking the earth at a great distance off, "*causing* a *spring of water* to gush forth."

Another Buddhist legend, the "Asádrisa Játaka," relates that Sákya, in a former birth, as the Prince Asádrisa, son of Brahmadatta, King of Váranasi, abandoned his kingdom, and took service, as an archer, with the King of Sámáya; in whose presence he shot an arrow far into the heavens; and caused it, in its return to earth, to cut off a mango, from a tree under which the king was sitting. (Spence Hardy, "Manual of Buddhism," 114.) After other exploits with the same weapon, he became an ascetic, and was translated to heaven.[2]

The entablature corresponded with that of the other gateways; but its fragments were, for the most part, so broken, and difficult to get at, that I only made three drawings of them.

Portions of a central wheel, on four supporting lions, and the two flanking disc-and-crescent symbols, like those of the Northern gateway, were lying among the débris; and, also, the broken female dancers which supported the ends of the lowest lintel. (See Figs. 4 and 7, of Plate XIV.)

The bottom lintel ("Bhilsa Topes," III. p. 229), has, in its centre compartment, a Nyagrodha, or Banyan tree—the bodhi of Kásyapa-muni—attended, and worshipped by elephants; and, on each of its projecting ends, a Sthúpa, with human worshippers.

(1) This action accords best with the legend told of Siddhártha's exploits as an archer: but it must be admitted that the sculpture looks very much as if it were intended to represent the two men, as holding up drapery, perhaps their joined cloaks or mantles, to catch some falling object; such, for instance, as the severed fruit alluded to in the Asádrisa legend.

(2) Sir A. Cunningham is of opinion that a fragment of one of the Bharhut sculptures, which, however, has lost its explanatory Páli inscription, refers to the Asádrisa Játáka legend. (See his "Stupa of Bharhut," pp. 70, 71; and Plate XXVII., Fig. 13.)

On its cubical portions, are kneeling elephants.

The rear of this lintel ("Bhilsa Topes," III. pp. 229, 230), has, in its centre, a storeyed pavilion, with an altar below it, and a spreading tree above it, and, apparently, growing out of it, like those shown in Plates XII., Fig. 2, and XVII.(1) To the left, are worshippers, musicians, and a standard-bearer; and to the right, a group of giants, some dancing, and some fighting; and a party of horsemen, chariots, and mounted elephants, whose riders and drivers are evidently alarmed by the giants; and are trying to restrain their frightened animals. Some of the arms, etc., in this sculpture are shown in Plate XXXV., Figs. 35, 36, 37.

On the cubical portions, are winged, mounted, lions.

The second, or centre lintel ("Bhilsa Topes," II. 229; and my Plate XXVI.), has, on one side, a chatta-shaded wheel, of thirty-two spokes, on a low altar; with hovering kinnara, bearing long garlands. On either side of the wheel stand eight male worshippers, in Indian costume, and eight deer. My Plate shows the right half of this lintel; which is broken in two.

Between the two principal figures, who wear no necklaces, but have long scarves; is a small three-petalled plant; and behind the group, are four trees; one of which somewhat resembles that elsewhere called the "bodhi" of Vipaswi Bhagavata. Another may be a "Jambu": but the three smaller trees are too conventional to be even conjecturally identified.

On the other side of this lintel, is a long procession entering the gates of a city, or palace; whence it is watched by numerous spectators. It appears to represent the same, or a continuation of the same subject as that on the top lintel (Plate XXVII.).

Some of the shields are of peculiar pattern; and are shown in Plate XXXV.

On the cubical portions, are seated winged lions; and kneeling caparisoned horses; (whose heads are shown in Plate XV., Figs. 14, 15).

The third, or top lintel ("Bhilsa Topes," I. 227 to 229; and my Plate XXVII.), has, on one side, what appears to be part of the subject first described. A long procession, escorting a relic-casket, is entering a city, or palace; whence it is watched by numerous (chiefly female) spectators. With a few exceptions, noted below, all the costumes are Indian. The procession is headed by three horsemen, and a led horse, which are already inside the gateway; and consists of horsemen; a second led horse; soldiers; musicians and other attendants on foot, some evidently foreigners; (2) and several elephants; one of whose mahâwats, carries a relic-casket. Just outside the gateway, is a tree, with an altar; apparently the Sála, or "bodhi" of Viswabhu; behind which the procession is passing.

(1) Pavilions, or chapels, round the stems of sacred trees, are frequently mentioned by Buddhist writers; and are common, in India and Burmah, to the present day.

(2) The man immediately behind the leading elephant, and the two horsemen just above him, evidently belong to the same race as the Sthúpa-worshippers in Plate X. As regards the conical caps represented in these two Plates, Sir A. Cunningham says that they are "now only known in Baruáwar, on the upper course of the Rávi" ("Bhilsa Topes," 228).

The shields are of peculiar shape; and are emblazoned both with the "Union Jack" device, and a crescent with three discs; and some of the spearmen who carry them, are rattling their weapons, as if in triumph. The tail of the principal equestrian's horse is, it will be seen, cut in a peculiar manner; and on its crupper is a small tortoise, or "Kachchapa." (1)

The rosettes, plants, and other small objects, seen in the sculpture, may be symbolical; but it is more probable that they were introduced for ornamental purposes, and to fill up unsightly blanks.

The general subject appears to be a triumphant return, with some captured relics —perhaps those of Kásyapa—after an inter-tribal contest, such as that shown in Plate XX.: and the led horses are probably intended either for dedication, or, possibly, sacrifice.

On the other side of this lintel ("Bhilsa Topes," I. 229), are alternate Sthúpas, and trees, with altars; each shaded by a chatta, and attended by kinnara, and two male worshippers in Indian dress. The Sthúpas have rows of projecting pegs; which support long scrolls, of the kind before alluded to (pages 18, 19, and Note 1, p. 19). One of these Sthúpas is shown in Fig. 4 of Plate XXVIII.

On the projecting ends of the lintel are men with standards, and with offerings on salvers; and on its cubical portions, are winged lions.

The smaller objects of the entablature had all disappeared, at the time of my visit: but I found fragments of the wheel, and two disc-and-crescent symbols, which once crowned the summit of the gateway.

(1) The tortoise, as already mentioned, is the emblem of Kásyapa, the Bhagavata, or so-called "former Buddha," who immediately preceeded Sákya. It was, I may add, also an emblem of Mercury, according to Montfaucon. ("Ant. Explained," Vol. I., Book II., Ch. viii. p. 77.)

CHAPTER VIII.

STHUPAS NOS. 2 AND 3; AND THEIR DETAILS: AND THE REMAINS OF STHUPAS 4 TO 8.

No. 2 Sthúpa (E, Plate I.) stands, as already stated, alone, on the lower plateau of the hill.

Captain Fell found it entire, in 1819: but, three years later, the explorers who breached the principal Sthúpa partially destroyed this one also. In Plate XXIX., Fig. 3, I show its state when I saw it in 1850: and Figs. 1, 2, are its restored plan, and section, with the enclosure railing in elevation.

It is less ancient than No. 1 Sthúpa; as one may see by its comparative height; good preservation, where uninjured; decorated enclosure; and lastly, the character of its inscriptions: and Sir A. Cunningham estimated the difference of age as about two centuries.

Like the large Sthúpa, and enclosure, it is put together without any cement: but it had no interior shaft, or mound of brick-work; nor had it ever an outer coating of plaster. Other points of difference are:

1. Its domical portion (39 feet in diameter, and 22½ feet high) springs from, and is structurally connected with, the basement, C; which is perpendicular in section.

2. Its four enclosure entrances (see Fig. 5, Plate XXX.), are of the simple shape which, originally, characterized those of No. 1 Sthúpa; and there are no "torana" or tiered gateways: but the angle pillars at the entrances, are differently carved to the main enclosure uprights; and are, also, in several instances, much more artistically executed.(¹)

3. There are no images of Buddha opposite the entrances.

4. The ascent to the basement terrace (D, E) is opposite the *eastern* entrance; which, therefore, was the principal entrance: whereas in Nos. 1 and 3 Sthúpas, the principal entrance was on the south(²)

(¹) Sir A. Cunningham noticed a like distinction at Bharhut.

(²) The orientation of sacred buildings, that is, placing their entrances to the east, so that the sacellum, or shrine, faced the rising sun, was almost universal among ancient, sun-worshipping races: and the custom has been preserved in modern ecclesiastical architecture. The south, and south-east, however, were, also, important "quarters," in the construction and disposition of sacred buildings; and of the "stone circles," which preceded them as places of worship. Most, but not all, of the Afghán Topes faced east (see "Ariana Antiqua," 57).

Nos. 1 and 2 Sthúpas are called, locally, "Sás bahu ke bitha"; or the wife's, and mother-in-law's stacks: and there is a tradition that the smaller one was constructed of stones stolen from the larger.

The style, and ornamentation of the enclosure, are as in Plate XXX., Figs. 1, 2, 3: and each of the uprights—of which there are eighteen in each quadrant, or seventy-two in all—is ornamented by sculptured medallions, and demi-medallions, or bosses; save the angle pillars, which have sculptured compartments. These last, as already said, are of superior execution; and there are a few fairly carved floral medallions: but the majority are of very poor workmanship; and, moreover, in such low relief; and, when I saw them, so encrusted with moss, and dirt, that many of the subjects were difficult to make out.

The representations of human figures in the bosses, or demi-bosses, are few, and unimportant; but animals, both natural and supernatural, are numerous. Among the former, are deer: elephants, both mounted and dismounted; one of the former emerging from a tiled gateway (which is shown in Fig. 15 of Plate XXXVI.); and another standing over a prostrate woman: lions; one with a bull in its mouth; one killing a deer; and one rearing over an elephant: peacocks, and other, unrecognizable, birds; one of which is killing a snake: (1) and a tortoise; the symbol of the Bhagavata Kásyapa; and, I may add, the form assumed by the Bráhmanical Vishnu, in his second avatára. Among the supernatural beings represented, are alligators (makara), with fish-tails: centaurs, male and female; one of the former ridden by a woman: (2) elephants, with fish-tails: gryphons: human-headed, nondescript animals: lions; some fish-tailed, as seen in Fig. 3, Plate XXX.; and some, with a human face, like the Narasinha avatára of Vishnu, and the man-lions of Assyria, and Egypt: the five-hooded "Nága" (see Fig. 3, Plate XXX.): and the Nágni; that is, a female figure canopied by the Nága hood.

Among the symbols represented are, the disc, with twelve flame-shaped rays, arranged like the petals of a flower (Fig. 3, Plate XXXI.): disc-and-crescent symbols; both single and quadruple (the latter shown in Fig. 6, Plate XXXI.; and found, also,

(1) In India, both Bráhmans and Buddhists adopted the primeval myth, which represented the creative power of the all-supreme sun, acting upon, or, as it was supposed, conquering, the aqueous element, under the form of a serpent, vanquished by a bird. In the Bráhmanical mythology, the mystical "man-eagle" Garuḍa, called "the foe of snakes," is the vahan or vehicle, and the messenger of Vishnu; as was the eagle of the Greek Zeus; and the Bráhmans claimed Buddha as one of Vishnu's emanations, or avatáras. The Buddhists, on the other hand; who were, originally, opponents of the Nágas or serpents; not only adopted, into their system, the Bráhmanical man-bird, Garuḍa; but made it one of Buddha's former incarnations, or "Játakas."

(2) See Fig. 6 of my Plate XXX. The use of the centaur, by both Bráhmans and Buddhists, is one of many indications of the direct influence exercised upon the religious art of both, by the Greeks; and therefore, indirectly, by the myths of Egypt and Assyria, of which the Greek centaur was an embodiment. There is, so far as I know, no mention of the centaur in Buddhist literature, but, in the Bráhmanical Puránas, the "nara," or centaur, is one of the supernatural beings created by Brahma, at the commencement of the present "Kalpa," or age, of the universe: the term being, also, the basis of the name "Náráyana," one of the chief titles of Vishnu. (See "Vishnu Purána," pp. 27, 28, 42.)

in more ornate form at Andher): the symbol marked (C) in Figs. 15, 16, of Plate XXXIX. (see pp. 19, 20,): and the wheel; in some instances alone on an altar with over-shadowing chatta; and in others, combined with the disc-and-crescent symbol.

The more important sculptures, in the compartments of the entrance pillars, are as follows.

On a pillar at the northern entrance, is a wheel of sixteen spokes, resting upon a disc-and-crescent symbol; the whole supported on a flat slab, or altar. Round the outer edge of the wheel, are, alternately, the pointed ends of the spokes, and the semi-circular blades, or arrow-heads already described.(¹) This wheel is decorated with streamers; but there are neither chatta, kinnara, nor worshippers. It is shown in Plate XXXI., Fig. 4. On another pillar, is a precisely similar wheel, crowning a short pillar, whose capital is formed by an elephant and two lions (Fig. 5, Plate XXXI.). On one of the pillars of the eastern entrance, is the subject alluded to at page 39. A plain wheel, apparently of twenty-four spokes, on a small altar, with four steps; on each side of which are a kneeling woman, and a standing man, in Indian costume. The men hold lotus flowers in one hand, and, with the other, are touching, or perhaps turning, the wheel; which may, therefore, be one of the wheels, "whose efficacy is not to be described," mentioned by Fa Hian, as used by the Buddhist priests of Kie-chha; and which M. Rémusat called revolving praying-wheels ("Foe-Koue-Ki," Chapter V., Note 6).

It may, however, be remarked, that the action of the two male worshippers does not, necessarily, imply that they are "turning the wheel;" which, in a Buddhist sense, means both praying and preaching. Maurice, in describing a representation of a sacrifice to the Sun, at Babain, says ("Ind. Ant." II. 307, 309), "the fingers of the worshippers touch the ends of the rays."

Over this sculpture is a much worn Páli inscription, which, so far as I can make it out, appears to record the "dánam," or gift of the pillar, by a resident of Pokhara; an ancient name of Ajmir.

Another pillar, at the eastern entrance, has two men in a pair-horsed chariot; attended by a standard-bearer, mounted on an elephant: and has also, a well-executed figure of a woman, holding a lotus flower, standing in a gateway.

One of the southern entrance pillars, has a chatta-shaded Sthúpa, in a railed

(¹) This kind of blade, the "bhalli," which, as elsewhere pointed out (p. 19), resembles the crescent portion of the disc-and-crescent symbol, is seen in the sacred axes shown in Egyptian monuments; on Indo-Scythic coins; and, I may add, on the sculptured Pictish monuments of Scotland. As the "bhalli," it formed the head of the arrows used, according to the Bráhmanical Puránas, in the conflicts between the gods and the demons, which answer to the Greek legend of the wars between the gods and the Titans. (See "Harivansa Purána," ii. 496, Note 24.) It will be seen that whereas the other arrows represented at Sánchi have all got the ordinary pointed or barbed heads, that used by the archer in Fig. 2, Plate XXII., who represents Sákya as Siddhártha, or Asádrisa, is of this semi-circular shape. The sacred character of this kind of blade, whether as axe or arrow-head, is, at any rate clear from its appearance in conjunction with the wheel symbol.

enclosure; and another has a pillar, with capital formed by three lions supporting a wheel.

At the western entrance is the subject partially represented in Plate XXXI., Fig. 2; a sixteen-spoked wheel, supported by a short pillar, the capital of which has three elephants. On either side are a man and woman, in Indian dress, worshipping the wheel-pillar; and below, are rampant Indian bulls. The Páli inscription on the pillar is read by Sir A. Cunningham, as recording the gift of the sculptured pillar by Vádyuvahaniká, a female lute-player ("The Bhilsa Topes," 282, 283, and Plate XXI., No. 24).

I found no traces of any crowning tí, or chatta; but there were some portions of small pillars and cross-bars; which once formed a square enclosure at the summit of the Sthúpa.

As in the case of No. 1 Sthúpa, the enclosure of No. 2 has numerous Páli inscriptions; which will be treated of in Chapter XI.

After Sir A. Cunningham joined me, at Sánchi, in January, 1851, we excavated this Sthúpa: and found, in a paved chamber, just to the west of its centre, at the spot indicated in Fig. 3 of my Plate XXIX., a square sandstone chest, containing a number of inscribed funereal caskets; which will be described in Chapter XII.

No. 3 Sthupa.

No. 3 Sthúpa (F, Plate I.), which I found almost completely ruined, is nearly due north-east of the principal Sthúpa (D); and about 240 feet distant, from centre to centre. Judging from the remains still traceable, it was, originally, about forty feet in diameter; with a basement terrace six feet wide. And it had a crowning enclosure and tí; fragments of which were still lying about, at the time of my visit. It had, also, a railed enclosure, the raised flooring of which still exists, in several places; though almost all trace of its pillars and rails has disappeared. The entrance was to the south; and had a torana, or tiered gateway, like those of No. 1 Sthúpa; but on a much smaller scale; the pillars, capitals inclusive, being only nine feet two inches high. It was, evidently, copied from the larger gateway. The two gateway pillars and the bottom lintel were still in position, in 1850. The capitals, like those of the large western gateway, are formed by four dwarfs: and the whole surface of both pillars and entablature, is covered by sculptured compartments; the subjects being, principally, Sthúpa, tree, and wheel worship, by people in Indian costume; with attendant kinnara.

One of the compartments of the entablature, shows several groups of Nága-shaded personages, apparently, on a river-bank. In the centre is a pavilion, with hovering kinnara, sheltering a seated Nága-shaded man, who is attended by several women. On the roof of the pavilion, are six spectators; and on either side of it, rocks, amid which are other figures: while on the extreme right, and left, are Nága-canopied men, with one arm encircling the neck of a woman.

The volutes of this (bottom) lintel, are formed of snakes; and on the cubical portions, over the pillars, are men slaying monsters, half elephant and half snake.

The entire subject, may, perhaps, represent "Nága loka," or the abode of the Nága king: or, possibly, a visit by "Nágas," to a Buddhist sacred shrine, guarded by its attendant kinnara.

Sir A. Cunningham traced the remains of a walled enclosure about this Sthúpa, about ninety feet square—built due north and south ("Bhilsa Topes," 296, 297): and this, together with the presence of a sculptured gateway, would have sufficed to prove its importance; even without any other indications. Such indications, were, however, forthcoming: for on digging into the débris of the Sthúpa, we discovered handsome relic caskets, inside stone chests, bearing the names of Sáriputra and Mahámogalána, the two chief disciples of Sákya Muni. (See Chapter XII.)

Close to No. 3 Sthúpa, and within the same square enclosing wall, once stood another (G, Plate I.). But this is a mere mound of débris; and contained no deposits, or relic chambers: and the same remark applies to the remaining Sthúpas 5 to 8, marked H, I, J, K, in the plan; which require no description.

It will be seen that the total number of undoubted Sthúpas, on the main plateau (A) was seven: that is, a large and central one (D); a second (F) similar one; smaller, but of special importance: and five others (G to K) of minor importance, but in peculiar relative positions. And we may, perhaps, be justified in finding, in these circumstances, a further illustration of the allusions to solar and fire worship, of which the Sánchi sculptures and inscriptions contain so many indications.

The presence of funereal relics of Buddhist saints in one of these surrounding Sthúpas (F), does not, necessarily militate against such a theory; since there is much reason to believe that the followers of Sákya, deposited relics in buildings which they appropriated from older forms of worship. (See Chapter XII.)

CHAPTER IX.

ISOLATED PILLARS: CHAITYA, AND OTHER TEMPLES: VIHARAS, OR MONASTERIAL BUILDINGS: AND OTHER MISCELLANEOUS REMAINS, NOT ELSEWHERE DESCRIBED.

WE learn from the Buddhist Maháwanso (pp. 97, 169) that it was customary, before building a Sthúpa, to erect, on the proposed site, a pillar, recording the pious intention. Originally, doubtless, such pillars were merely wooden poles: but, whatever their material, they were, it is said, usually removed when the building was constructed.

It was, also, a common practice, among both Bráhmans and Buddhists, to erect one or more isolated pillars—sometimes with, and sometimes without crowning figures, or symbols representing the deity—near the entrances to their excavated, or structural, temples: and we find many existing specimens of these, in India and Ceylon; just as, in front of the more ancient fanes of Egypt stood symbolic obelisks.

Very often, such "láths," or "sthambhas," bore inscriptions, either votive or memorial: and they seem to have been erected at various dates; some, perhaps, coevally with the Sthúpas or caves near which they stand, and some, subsequently, by successive votaries.

At Sánchi, near the principal, or No. 1, Sthúpa, there were, at least, five of these detached pillars; four of which are shown in my Plates.

One stood about thirty feet to north of the Northern Gateway, at M, Plate I.; and the lower portion of its shaft, five feet three inches high, and two feet six inches in diameter, is still *in situ*, in a small square enclosure. The rest of the shaft has disappeared: but the capital, and crowning figure are lying on the ground, some thirty odd feet off (*e*, Plate I.); and the lower measurement of the former shows that the top diameter of the shaft was two feet three inches. This diminution, of three inches, would, judging from that in other specimens, give a total height for the shaft, of eleven feet eight inches only; and a total height, figure inclusive, of less than twenty-five feet; an inelegant proportion, which, however, may be explained by dearth of larger blocks; and which is, moreover, in accordance with that of some of the pillars represented in the sculptures.(1) The capital and crowning figure are shown in Plate XXXII., Figs. 1, 2; and the restored pillar in Fig. 1, Plate XXXIII.

(1) Sir A. Cunningham considered that the total dimensions of this pillar were about the same as those of the lion pillar near the South Entrance (see "Bhilsa Topes," p. 196, and Plate X.).

Close to the eastern entrance of No. 1 Sthúpa (at N, Plate I.), is the still entire pillar shown in Fig. 2, Plate XXXIII.; the total height of which is fifteen feet two inches.

The birds on the upper capital, are the hansa, or henza, i.e. the duck, or goose; which is sacred in Bráhmanical mythology, to the present day; and is the special symbol of the modern Burmese Buddhists; and they represent, moreover, the same bird as that seen among the sacred symbols of the Assyrians, and still reverenced by the interesting sect of the Yezidis. (See Layard's "Monuments of Nineveh," Plate 95, a., Figs. 11 and 17.) The flowers which alternate with the birds, are identical with the "honeysuckle" of Greece, Phœnicia, and Assyria (see Layard's "Nineveh and its Remains," Vol. II. p. 472, and note); while the crowning winged lion itself has a very Assyrian character! Close to the south, or principal, entrance to No. 1 Sthúpa, are the remains of a fine "sinha sthambha," or lion-pillar, which, when entire, had a total height of 39 feet 9½ inches. The shaft is broken into three pieces; of which about 10 feet is still standing. Its base diameter is 2 feet 11¾ inches, and the top diameter 2 feet 2¼ inches; and the whole shaft, when entire, was therefore, almost exactly ten diameters high. The fragments of its bell-shaped, or "cable-order," capital are lying about; and the fine group of four lions which crowned the summit is, with the exception of parts of the heads, still in very good preservation.

These lions, as already remarked (p. 53), show signs of Greek influence, if not workmanship; and they stand on an abacus, decorated like that just described, but of very superior execution. The lion capital is shown in Fig. 2, Plate XIX.; and the restored pillar, in Fig. 4, Plate XXXIII.

The shaft was highly polished; and on one of its portions there is a well-cut, but much obliterated Páli inscription; as to which, see Chapter XI.

Close to No. 5 Sthúpa (H in plan), a little to north-east of the principal Sthúpa, are two small pillars (P and Q). One (P) is cylindrical; and is in three pieces: the total height, when perfect, being fifteen feet. On its erect portion, is a much worn inscription, in the Gupta character, of the fifth century A.D. The other (Q), nine feet four inches high, is of more modern style: and is shown in Plate XXXIII., Fig. 3.

I could find no traces of the capitals of these pillars; but they were, doubtless of the same style as those of the "cable order," already described; (¹) and the latter,

(¹) I have called this style of capital the "cable order," because its design seems to have been suggested by the coil and pendent loops of a rope, carelessly thrown over a stone slab. It is very common at Sánchi, as may be seen from my plates; more particularly Plates IV.; V.; XXXI., Figs. 2, 5; XXXII.; and XXXIII., Figs. 1, 2, 4, 7: and similar capitals are found in many other parts of India, as well as at Sánchi and the vicinity. One large specimen, the shaft of which has entirely disappeared, still lies at the top of the Lohángi rock, near Bhilsa; and is connected, as were so many of the "láths" themselves, with Pándava legends. Another once crowned a láth, at Firozpur, near Sánchi; and is surmounted by a quadruple group of Nágas and Nágnis, which is called, locally, a "chaumukhti Mahádeo." The well-known iron pillar near the Kutb at Delhi; and the isolated pillars, or láths, at Airan, Kuháon, Mattiah, and other places, have the same style of capital; as, also, has the lion-pillar in front of the Kárli cave; which, from its

perhaps, supported the figure which I found lying at the point marked *f*, in the plan. This is a male figure, wearing a dhoti, girdle, and scarf; and holding a water vase and mace. Behind him, are the folds of a Nága, whose hood overshadows his head. His head-dress is a kind of mitre; like that worn by one of the janitors of a detached temple, which will be noticed shortly.

This figure, and the pillar which supported it, may, I think, be attributed to the Jainas; whose favourite Tirthankara, Páraswanátha, was shaded by, and symbolized by, the Nága.

Chaitya, and other Temples.

Of the six detached buildings whose remains are on the south, south-east, east, and north-east of the principal Sthúpa, marked R to W, in the plan, the most important is the Chaitya-hall, or temple (R); the plan of which is shown in Fig. 1, Plate XXXVII. It consisted, when complete, of an entrance hall of twelve pillars and two pilasters, of the style shown in Figs. 5 and 6 of Plate XXXIII., crowned by a plain architrave; on which, I think, once rested the wooden rafters of a flat roof, or, perhaps, the wooden ribs of a vaulted roof.(¹) This led into an inner hall, twenty-seven feet long, and nineteen feet four inches wide; with a semi-circular end, once enclosed by an uncemented stone wall, four feet thick: and roofed over like the entrance hall. At *g*, in the centre of this sacellum or apse, were the débris of a "chaitya," or relic Sthúpa, from which I unearthed a broken steatite vase, which had once contained relics. (See Chapter XII.)

The plan of this building exactly corresponds with that of the older "Chaitya caves" of Southern India; and there can be no doubt that it was a structural imitation of a cave-temple. The Kárli cave, and the Viswakarma cave at Ellora, both have vaulted roofs; the former with wooden, and the latter with stone ribs: the pillars of the Viswakarma cave being similar to those in this hall.

There was, as seen in the plan, a small entrance porch; one pillar only of which remained, in 1850. The pillars of this porch are small, and entirely different in style from the tall elegant pillars of the main hall: they are, in fact, of a kind usually found in the entrances of Bráhmanical and Jaina temples; and, probably, this insignificant porch was added by the Jainas.

Just to east of this Chaitya-hall, and close to the ruins of Sthúpa No. 6 (I), is a small, rectangular, flat-roofed temple (S, Plate I.), facing north; which is shown in Figs. 2, 3, of Plate XXXVII. It contained the lower portion of a seated Buddha, on a lotus throne, supported by two lions; and bearing a Kutila inscription, commencing with the well-known Buddhist formula, "Ye dharmma hetu prabhava." On the plinth, below the throne, is another, much mutilated inscription, in the same

inscription, was, evidently, like the cave itself, dedicated to the sun, and fire. (See Prinsep, in "Jour. As. Soc. Beng." VI.) The same kind of capital characterizes the buildings represented in the sculptures of Yusufzai; and the gateway pillars at the entrances of the Bharhut Sthúpa: and the list might easily be added to. It resembles, too, the lower part of some of the elegant pillar capitals at Persepolis.

(¹) I found, amid the débris, some fragments of iron clamps; such as would have been used in timber-work; but, of course, all traces of the roof itself had, long since, entirely disappeared.

comparatively modern character. The pillars of the entrance porch are as shown in Fig. 7, Plate XXXIII.

Close to this temple, outside, were two other, much mutilated seated figures, with lions below them; one bearing an illegible inscription.

Due north-east of the principal Sthúpa, at T, is a rectangular flat-roofed temple, shown, in plan and section, in Plate XXXVII., Figs. 4, 5. It has no porch; and its pillars and pilasters are of varied style; some resembling those of the hall just described. Most of them are quite plain, but those marked *a*, *b*, and *c*, are as shown in Figs. 3, 4, of Plate XXXII. At the north end of this temple is a seated Buddha, about seven feet high, halo inclusive; the only peculiarity in which is the absence of the usual scalp tuft, or top-knot.

In the corner to right of the entrance, leaning against the wall, I found a much worn relievo figure of a Nágni, which had, evidently, once been either one of the two flanking supporters of the central Buddha, or one of two door-keepers of the temple. The companion (male) figure was lying just outside the building.

On the pillar marked *d* is the Nágari inscription, which Captain Fell erroneously read as bearing the date of Sanvat 18.(¹)

The remaining three buildings are on the upper plateau (C) of the hill. The largest (U, Plate I.), due east of the principal Sthúpa, is a ruined vihára, or monastery. Such residences, for the priests of a temple, were common, in India, long before the time of Sákya Muni; though, after his date, they became a specially Buddhist class of buildings. The ranges of cells appear to have had uniform, flat roofs, and were grouped round one or more open quadrangles; the extreme dimensions of the enclosure being about 115 ft. by 85.

The style of the pillars and pilasters of the cells and their verandahs is shown in Fig. 6 of Plate XXXVIII.

I have alluded, elsewhere, to the probable identity of Sánchi, with the "Chetiya-giri" of the Buddhist histories; and, if we accept the identification, this would be the site of the "magnificent vihára" erected by Asoka's wife, "Chetiya Devi," for the accommodation of their son Mahindo, or Mahendra.

The existing ruins, however, present no trace of magnificence, either in size, or style, and are certainly far more modern that the date assigned (from Buddhist data) to Asoka's reign. We must, therefore, suppose, either that an older and finer vihára has entirely disappeared, or that Chetiya Devi (and, consequently, Asoka himself) existed some centuries later than has been hitherto supposed; a view which there are many other grounds for maintaining.

A little to the south-east of this vihára is the ruined building, marked V, in Plate I.; the plan and sections of which are shown in Plate XXXVIII., Figs. 1, 2, 3. I have called this a vihára-temple; as, when complete, it consisted of a central temple, with "sikhara," or tower, lightened by an upper chamber,(²) and supported partly by its

(¹) Captain Fell's mistake as to this date led to other mistakes on his, and Colonel Sykes's parts, which, however, it is unnecessary to particularize.

(²) These inner chambers, or cells, in the solid-looking Sikharas of structural temples, were, doubtless,

own sustaining walls, and partly by the side and rear walls of the two flanking ranges of cells; thus leaving a vaulted passage all round the temple, as shown in the plan.(1)

The floor of the central temple is several feet higher than that of the flanking cells: and on a raised daïs, at its eastern end (that is, facing west), is the colossal seated Buddha, shown in Plate XXXIV.; which once had a rich canopy or niche over it, as is evident from still existing fragments.

On its lotus throne is a mutilated "Ye dharmma" inscription, in the "Kutila" character; which, as elsewhere shown, fixes its date as from the eighth to the tenth century of the Christian era.

In a corner of the southern verandah of the vihára portion, I found another figure of Buddha, very much like the above, but with a belt, instead of a robe, falling over the left shoulder.

Near the building were lying several Hindu-looking, sculptured figures, but none that could be identified with any member of the Bráhmanical Pantheon.

A further indication of the comparatively recent date of this "vihára-temple," and its figure of Buddha, is afforded by the presence of modern-looking letters, on stones in its side cells, which letters are upside down, and were, therefore, evidently carved some time before the building was erected.(2)

The remaining building (W, Plate I.), which also faces west, is a small, flat-roofed range of three cells, with a common verandah, or entrance chamber, forming a small vihára. The central cell is lower than the others, and has a vault, four feet deep, below it. The plan and section are given in Plate XXXVIII., Figs. 4, 5.

At Z, close to the multi-form model Sthúpa, mentioned at page 14, were some more Bráhmanical-looking sculptures, like those near V; but none of any importance.

The only object still to be noticed is the large stone bowl or basin, which lies near the pathway connecting Nos. 1 and 2 Sthúpas, at L, Plate I.; about 170 yards from the central plateau of the hill.

This is a large block of stone, hollowed out to form a hemispherical bowl, 4½ feet in diameter, and 2½ feet deep; which was evidently intended to be either sunk in the ground, or let into an artificial bed.

I am not aware that stone vessels of this kind were ever used in purely Buddhist worship; but, in a Bráhmanical locality, they would be, at once, recognized as "homa" pits, or receptacles used in sacrifices by fire (see "Jour. As. Soc. Beng." for August, 1847, p. 754). The so-called "Druidical rock-basins," found in Great Britain, are supposed to have been used in expiatory sacrifices (see Nicholson's "Encyclopædia": "Antiquities"); and the "cup-hollows" which have been dis-

partially, an expedient for lightening the weight of the superincumbent mass; but they are, manifestly, analogous to the relic-chambers of the Sthúpas, which were the originals of the Sikhara; and, very possibly, they may, once, have enclosed deposits of some kind.

(1) Such narrow and dark passages round the "Garbha Griha," or inner shrine, is part of the construction of most large Indian temples; and its origin is the enclosed passage, for "parikráma," round the Sthúpa whence the structural temple was derived.

(2) These letters, as they appear on the walls are, 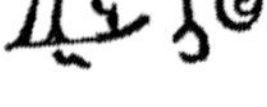 and 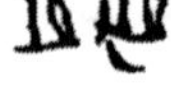

covered in India, and in so many other parts of the world, may, perhaps, have some analogy to this curious object. (See, on this subject, "The Bhilsa Topes," p. 180.)

In this chapter, and, indeed, throughout the book, I have described everything just as I found, and left it, in 1850—1851.

Since my visit, as already said, there have been extensive clearances and restorations at Sánchi; and many detached sculptures, and fragments of figures, pillars, rails, etc., have been collected and re-arranged: a process which, however desirable and advantageous in some respects, is not always, in an antiquarian sense, an unalloyed advantage!

CHAPTER X.

THE DISC-AND-CRESCENT SYMBOL.

THE curious symbol, which I call the disc-and-crescent, is one of the most prominent objects among the Sánchi remains.

I have given it the above descriptive appellation, in preference to any purely Buddhist title: for though, as the "Tri-ratna," it is, unquestionably, a Buddhist symbol, of very varied significance, it is neither exclusively, nor originally, Buddhist; but is of an antiquity much more remote than any phase of what is now called Buddhism.

I propose, in this chapter, firstly, to show how extensively it is used, at Sánchi, and elsewhere in India; and secondly, to trace it in the symbolism of other countries, and of non-Buddhist forms of religion.

In its usual, and complete, form, that is, a plain or ornamented disc; surmounted by a crescent, either a simple semi-circle, or dentated into a trident, or "trisula"; it is met with, as follows, at Sánchi.[1]

1. As the right and left members of the triad; the central emblem being the wheel, or "dharma chakra"; over the gateways of the principal Sthúpa. (Plates IV. and XXXIX., Fig. 1.)

2. On altars; either singly, or in triple form. (Plates XII., Fig. 2; XVIII.; and XXXIX., Figs. 2, 5, and 5, *a*.)

3. On a votive pillar; shaded by three chattas. (Plate V.)

4. In quadruple form; in one of the medallions of No. 2 enclosure. (Fig. 6, Plate XXXI.) It also occurs, in like shape, at Andher.

5. As the central symbol of votive necklaces. (Plates IV.; and XXXIX., Figs. 15, 16, *b*.)

6. Round the outer circumference of wheels, raised on pillars; corresponding, in number, with their rays or spokes.

7. On a vacant throne, in a (? sacred) barge. (Plate XXI., Fig. 2.)

8. Crowning the poles of standards. (Plates VII., Fig. 1; X.; XVI.; XVII.; XX.; XXI., Fig. 1; XXXV., Figs. 42, 43, 44, 47, 48; XXXVI., Fig. 7; and XXXIX., Figs. 3, 4.)

9. On sword scabbards. (Plates XV., Figs. 13; XXI., Fig. 1; and XXXV., Fig. 27.)

10. In the plumed head-stalls of the royal chariot horses. (Plate XVI.)

[1] See pages 18 to 20, 38, 46, 52, 55, 68, 69, and Notes.

Each of the component parts of the symbol is used separately, as well as in conjunction ("sangha") with the other.

Instances of the disc, alone, plain, annulated, foliated, rayed, or in the form of a star, will be seen in Plates IV.; V.; XV., Figs. 14, 15; XXI., Fig. 1; XXVI.; XXVII.; XXXI., Figs. 1 to 5; XXXV., Figs. 30, 33, 43, 45, 48; and XXXIX., Figs. 15, 16, *d*, *g*. And the crescent, in various shapes, occurs, without the disc, as follows:—Round the circumference of wheels (Plate XXXI., Figs. 2, 4, 5): as a blazoning on standards and shields (Plates X.; XXI., Fig. 1; XXVI.; and XXXV., Figs. 33, 43, 48): as the blade of a sacred axe; and of an axe carried by a giant (Plates V.; XXXV., Fig. 37; and XXXIX., Figs. 15, 16, *h*): as the blade of the "bhalli," or sacred arrow (Plates XXII., Fig. 2; and XXXV., Fig. 39): as an ornament in the frontlet of an elephant (Plates XVII.; and XXI., Fig. 1): and, as a simple trident, on a staff, apparently, a giant's weapon (Plate XXXV., Fig. 36).

It appears, also, both single and quadruple, in some votive inscriptions, at Sánchi.(¹)

The symbol was, apparently, equally significant and sacred, whether erect, as above, or inverted; and among the sculptures of both Bharhut and Amarávati, it occurs very frequently in both forms; one specimen, at the latter place, having the two forms conjoined, thus; forming a symbol which occurs among the Assyrian sculptures, and which resembles the thunderbolt of the Greek Zeus, and the "Vajra" of the Vedic Indra. In this form, it also reminds one of some varieties of the Sassanian fire-altar, and, finally (without its central winged disc), it is like the Runic letter, K.

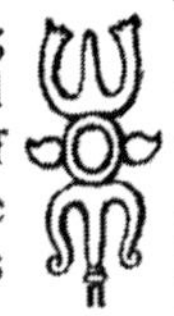

We also find the "disc-and-crescent" symbol, sometimes erect, and sometimes inverted, in other inscriptions, as well as in those at Sánchi; as, for instance, in the cave inscriptions of Junir, Khandgiri, Sainhadri, and Udáyagiri in Cuttack; and also, as will be separately shown, among the devices, or so-called monograms, of Indian coins (see my Plate XXXIX., Fig. 9): and in all, or almost all, of these instances, it has been, hitherto, treated as an exclusively Buddhist symbol. In fact, its presence on an Indian coin, or in a sculpture or inscription, in India, has been generally accepted as a sufficient proof of its Buddhist character.

The first European writer who remarked upon this symbol was, I believe, J. Prinsep; who called it, in its erect form, "the Buddhist monogram," and in its inverted form, "the Buddhist Chaitya": as did, also, Professor Wilson, and Colonel Sykes: and all three viewed it, in both forms, as representing the Buddhist triad, "Buddha, Dharma, and Sangha." Prinsep, however, did not treat the "Chaitya" as an *exclusively* Buddhist symbol: but compared it to the "Mithraic flame, Mount Meru . . . the holy flame, trilingual and pyramidal, of the Sassanian fire-worship."(²)

(¹) Allusions to some of the above uses of the symbol will be found in "The Bhilsa Topes," pages 37, 38, 40, 191, 203, 204, 213, 278, 329, 351, 352 and 354 to 360; and in its Plates XIII.; XIX., No. 183; XXX., Fig. 1; and XXXII., Figs. 1, 3, 8, 9, 10, 15, and 19 to 22.

(²) See "Jour. Roy. As. Soc." VI. 451; "Jour. As. Soc. Beng." IV. 686, and VI., 389; and "Ariana Antiqua," 413, 414. This Persian "triple Mithraic flame," a symbol of the triad, was the direct forerunner

Beal, in his "Catena of Buddhist Scriptures," 147, 149, called it "the sacred symbol of the mani, or three-fold gem, indicating the all-supreme Buddha"; and, also, "the triple object of veneration, Buddha, the Law, and the Church."

Sir A. Cunningham ("Stupa of Bharhut," 8, 110, 111, 114, 118), also called the disc-and-crescent, the "triple gem," or "tri-ratna" symbol; and pointed out that the term "symbol of dharma," which had formerly been applied to it, is, strictly, applicable to the separate disc, or wheel, only; which has that title inscribed over it at Bharhut.(1)

I need not multiply instances of the use of this symbol in Buddhist or quasi-Buddhist sculpture and inscriptions; or of its many verbal descriptions by European scholars: but will now advert to the evidence of its widely extended use, both in and out of India; and the grounds there are for the views I hold as to its nature and origin.

We learn, from the unquestionable evidence of coins, that some form of the disc-and-crescent symbol was, for a long period, in common use in Bactria, India proper, and Ceylon; and we find it on specimens of coinage varying from the purely Buddhist characteristics of the more recent types, through many gradations of Bráhmanical, sun, fire, and elemental worship, to coins whose characteristics are Persian and Greek figures, and legends in Greek, either alone, or conjoined with Ariano-Páli. In other words, we can trace this symbol, or some variety of it, on authenticated coins, from as recent a date as the latter part of the seventh century of the Christian era, up to about two centuries B.C.: and with less and less of clearly *Buddhist* character, as we ascend in the scale of antiquity.

These coins may be divided, for my present purpose, into eight categories:—

1. The most recent, and those which are principally, if not exclusively, Buddhist, have been found, chiefly, in Central and Southern India, and in Ceylon; and I need do no more than refer to them. (See, as to some of these, "Jour. Roy. As. Soc." VI. 487; and "Jour. As. Soc. Beng." IV. 686; and VI. 389, and Plate XX.)

2. Next, in order of antiquity, are coins, bearing this symbol, which belong to the groups known as the "Gupta" coins of Kanoj, Magadha, Málwa, and Saurâshtra; and which range in date from about 670 A.D. up to 319 A.D., the now ascertained date of the commencement of the "Gupta era."

Some coins of this extensive series are almost purely Buddhist; while others combine the disc-and-crescent symbol with figures, animals and devices which pertain to the Bráhmanical Pantheon, and to the worship of the sun, fire and other elements. And on the older specimens we find Indo-Scythic, and debased Greek

both of the Buddhist Chaitya, and of the Bráhmanical "trisula" and "tretagni." The Buddhist interpretations of it will be found elsewhere: and the Bráhmanical Puránas explain such terms as "tretagni," "trilochana," etc., by the legend that, "in the beginning," there existed but one god (Naráyana), one fire (Agni), and one Veda; and that, in the "Treta," or third yuga, all were made triple, by Pururavas, the son of Ila; who was, also, the first producer of the sacred fire itself, by the attrition of sticks of the áswattha or pipal, and the sami tree. ("Vishnu Purána," 396, 397, and Note 6.)

(1) The full Páli inscription is "Bhagavato dhama chakam"; that is, The wheel of the law of Bhagavata. ("Stupa of Bharhut," 110, 111, and Plate XIII., Fig. 3.)

characteristics, which will be adverted to later. See "Trans. Roy. As. Soc." I. Plate XII.; "Jour. As. Soc. Beng." III. 25, and VI. 1053; and Fleet's "Gupta Volume."(¹)

3. The symbol appears on the Sassanian coins of Persia; large numbers of which have been found in Afghánisthán; dating in the third and fourth centuries A.D. On these coins the disc-and-crescent is found in conjunction with stars, wheels, crescents, flame-crowned figures, fire-altars, and Magian priests. ("Jour. As. Soc. Beng." VI., Plates XIV., XV.; and Wilson's "Ariana Antiqua," 382 to 385.)

4. It is common, also, on coins of the "Satraps," or local princes, known as the "Sáhs" of Sauráshtra: whose dates range from about 320 A.D. up to about the middle of the first century B.C.(²)

5. The next group of coins bearing this symbol, are those, found principally between the Indus and Jamna, to which belongs the specimen shown in Fig. 8 of my Plate XXXIX. (See "Ariana Antiqua," Plate XV., Fig. 23; and "The Bhilsa Topes," 354, 355, and Plate XXXI., Fig. 11.) Some of the symbols on this coin are shown, on a larger scale, in my Plate XXXIX., Figs. 9 to 14.

Professor Wilson compared these coins with those of several Indo-Scythic princes; but considered their symbols as "no doubt eminently Buddhist; although

(¹) So far as I am aware, the earliest instance of the occurrence of this symbol on any Indian coin, is on the Græco-Bactrian coinage of Pantaleon; whose date is supposed to have been between 120 and 195 B.C. ("Jour. As. Soc. Beng." V. 389; "Ariana Antiq." 283; and Prinsep's "Historical Results," etc., 65) There seems, at any rate, no trace of its use, either on coins, or in inscriptions or sculpture, at any period antecedent to the era of the Greeks in India; while it abounds on Buddhist coins and monuments of dates *subsequent* to the Christian era: a circumstance of marked importance, in connection with the question of the antiquity of the Buddhism of Sákya; in which it became so popular and significant, as a symbol.

(²) See, as to these Sauráshtra princes, and their coins, "Jour. Roy. As. Soc." VI. 451; "Ariana Antiqua," 384, 385; Thomas's "Sáh Kings of Sauráshtra"; and Fleet's "Gupta Volume." The date of the rise of the Sáh dynasty, about 57-56 B.C., coincides with that of the first appearance of the Indo-Scythians in the neighbourhood of the Indus; and, also, with the alleged commencement of the Bráhmanical era—still used in India—known as the Samvat of Vikramáditya. The real date of the favourite Hindu hero, Vikramáditya of Ujain, has been the subject of much learned discussion, and much difference of opinion. Mr. J. Fergusson and Professor Max Müller, for instance, have both maintained that his true date is more than five centuries *later* than that indicated by the era attributed to him; a theory which has been, quite recently, disputed by Professor Petersen, who claims to have rebutted it. The question can scarcely, however, be considered as decided, either one way or the other; and the Sánchi remains seem to throw fresh light upon it. There certainly appears much reason for supposing that the Vikramáditya of Ujain, to whom the Samvat era is attributed, was one of the "Gupta" princes, whose inscriptions exist at Sánchi, as well as on some of the Indian láths; and on numerous coins. Chandra Gupta II., the monarch mentioned in the Sánchi inscriptions, and who ruled over Ujain, and a large part of India, in the fifth century A.D., was called "Vikramáditya," and he, at any rate, was no mythical personage. (See "Field;" and "The Bhilsa Topes," 141 to 143.) How far the Bráhman and Buddhist writers of the fifth or sixth century A.D., were acquainted with European chronology, can only be conjectured; but it is a well-known fact that Christian chronology itself was readjusted and finally settled, at about the above date: and many European writers have asserted that Bráhmans and Buddhists, alike, purposely falsified their history and chronology, at about the same period, in order to give them a superior apparent antiquity to Christianity. It was about the same time, too, that the Bráhmans invented the now popular god Krishna, the so-called eighth avatár of Vishnu, and immediate predecessor of the ninth avatár, Budha. (See Chapter XIV., for remarks on the date of Krishna.)

why they are so, we are not apprised." ("Arian. Antiq." 413, 414.) It appears to me that not only the disc-and-crescent, but *all* the symbols in Fig. 8, however Buddhist, in character, are derived from pre-Buddhist sources.

These coins are supposed to belong to about the first century A.D.: that is, the same date as the Sánchi sculptured gateways.

The Páli and Ariano-Páli legends of Fig. 8 read, according to Sir A. Cunningham, "(Coin) of the royal Kunanda, brother of Mahárája Amogha": but the dynasty is not, I believe, decided.

6. The disc-and-crescent, in conjunction with symbol *f*, of Figs. 15, 16, Plate XXXIX., and the female figure anointed by elephants, alluded to in Note 2, page 36, occurs, also, on some coins, with old Páli legends, and such Bráhmanical names as "Dhana Deva," "Mula Deva," and "Visákha Deva," which I saw in Sir A. Cunningham's possession, in 1851; and which he attributed, I think, to an Ajodhya, or Oudh dynasty, of a somewhat earlier date than the preceding coins.

7. The disc-and-crescent is a common symbol on the coins of the Indo-Scythic, and other so-called barbaric princes, who immediately succeeded the Græco-Bactrians; and whose dates ranged from about the end of the first century A.D., up to a little before 50 B.C.

It is found, for instance, on coins of Varáoro or Varáhran, Kanerkes or Kanishka, Kadphises, Undopherres or Gondophares, and Azes; in conjunction with what have been called Saiva figures, and such significant symbols as the moon, crescent, trident, axe, club, bull, jet of flame, fire-altar, etc. Some specimens have figures in Indian and in Persian costume; female figures between trees; figures carrying the caduceus, cornucopiæ, palm-branches, and tridents; and figures of the Græco-Persian Helios, or Mithras (the Bráhmanical Súrya, or Mitra): and, finally, on the oldest examples, we find such purely Greek figures as Zeus, Pallas, Hercules, and Victory; with legends in both Ariano-Páli and Greek; pointing to the period when Greek influence was still predominant. (See "Arian. Antiq." 439, 440; and Plates V., Fig. 20; X., Figs. 5 to 21; XIV., Figs. 12, 13; and XXI., Figs. 17, 19; and Prinsep's "Hist. Res." 76, 77.)

Professor Wilson said, regarding this group of coins, ". . . . To the Greeks succeeded the Barbarians, about a century B.C.; viz., Sâkas, Getæ, Parthians, Huns, and Turks; who, at first, retained Greek divinities; and, afterwards, combined fire-worship with Hindú polytheism. Later princes, of different dynasties, tried to introduce a form of the Mithraic faith, combined with partial Buddhism; but both gave place to Hindú types, when Indian princes once more regained ascendency in the Paropamisus."

Figs. 6 and 7 of Plate XXXIX. show two coins, of the above class, which strikingly exemplify the mixed Persian, Greek, Indo-Scythic, Buddhist, and Bráhmanical symbolism above adverted to (compare Figs 8 and 9 of Plate XL.).

8. Other coins of a mixed Indo-Scythic and Greek character, are those of Mauas or Mayes; of which specimens are shown in Figs. 28, 29, of Plate XXXIX. These do not actually show the disc-and-crescent symbol itself; but have varieties

of it in the trident and the caduceus:[1] and the elephant on one, and female figure between trees on the other, are connected both with the Indian Buddha, and the Greek Hermes. The coins which bear the name Mauas or Mayes (Mayasa), in Greek and Ariano-Páli, have been compared with those of Azes (legend Ajasa or Ayasa), who has been supposed to be the "Ayus" of the Bráhmanical Puránas, and the "Ayu," or Asoka, of Buddhist literature; and, also, with coins of the Græco-Bactrian princes, Apollodotus, Straton, and Demetrius: and it has been suggested that the word rendered Mayes may be the name, not of the king himself, but of his tutelary deity. In this point of view, the coins would possess, still more strikingly, a mixed Buddhist and Greek character, Mauas, or Mayes, Páli "Mayasa," representing a matronymic of either Buddha, or Hermes, as the son of Maya.

As an illustration of the use of the "disc-and-crescent," on coins which are entirely unconnected with Buddhism, I may cite its occurrence on coins of Herod the Great of Judæa!

The simplest, and oldest forms of this symbol, ♉, ♉, both of which occur at Sánchi, represented the sun and moon; the two earliest objects of worship, throughout the ancient world.

The sun typified the supreme male, creative spirit, which, in India, was embodied as Íswara, and "Ádi Buddha." The moon represented the female power; passive nature, or matter; in India, Pradhána, and "Dharma": and the conjunction of the two—called, in India, "Sangha"—produced the five elements; and, therefrom, mankind and the material universe at large.

When, and how, this very ancient doctrine reached India, is too wide a question for discussion here; but it is, evidently, the basis of both Bráhmanical and Buddhist cosmogony.

The combined disc and crescent, therefore, represented, not only the two principal objects of ancient worship; but, also, the elements which were created by their joint agency: and eventually, types and symbols were replaced by human-shaped representations of the supreme male and female divinities; or by androgyne figures of the two conjoined: the result being, in most ancient nations, as it so manifestly was in India, widely-spread corruptions.

That symbols preceded images, as objects of worship, in most if not all of the systems of mythology known to scholars, is a well-established opinion: and among the Indian Buddhists, the exclusive use of symbols, seems to have lasted until the early part of the fifth century of the Christian era: as the Chinese traveller Fa Hian, who traversed India, at that period, from the far north to Ceylon, saw no images of Buddha; though he mentions several of his symbolical representations; such as

[1] The analogy between the Greek caduceus, the Egyptian symbol of life, the Buddhist disc-and-crescent, and the Bráhmanical trisula, or trident, will be noticed later. Some authorities have explained the resemblance between Hermes, or Mercury, and the primitive Budha, and their symbols, by the theory that the Greeks derived their Hermes and his emblems from India: but it seems a sounder opinion that India borrowed from the Greeks, who had previously derived Hermes and his peculiar symbol from Egypt.

the wheel; the ox's head; and the emblematic stones, which he calls "towers of deliverance." The ox-head symbol, and its apparent identity with the "disc and crescent," will be noticed under another head: but I will refer, here, somewhat in detail, to the emblematic Sthúpas mentioned by Fa Hian. In his account of the ancient temple of Fo, or Buddha, at Hilo, near Peshávar, he wrote as follows:—"There are towers of deliverance, adorned with all manner of precious things; some open, the others shut; and about five feet high.(1) To supply these, there are constantly, every morning, dealers in flowers and perfumes, before the gate of the chapel; that such as wish to perform their devotions, may buy of every variety." ("Foe-Koue-Ki," Chap. XIII.)

In all probability, the "shut" towers, here alluded to, were what I have, elsewhere, called minature Sthúpas (see Figs. 1 to 9, Plate XV.): and the "open" towers were, there can be no doubt, symbolic objects such as are now under notice (see Figs. 1, 2, and 5*a*, of my Plate XXXIX.). Such symbols had doubtless been clustered round sacred buildings, or placed on easily accessible altars, and decorated as described, long before Fa Hian's time. The sculptures of Sánchi, Bharhut and Amarávati, show that at their respective dates, it was customary to decorate both the disc-and-crescent and Sthúpas, with flowers, wreaths, and streamers: and to the present day, floral offerings and scented unguents, are used alike by the Buddhist worshippers of Sthúpas and Pagodas, and by the Bráhman worshippers of Vishnu, and the Linga of Siva (itself a "miniature Sthúpa"); who still, as of old, purchase their "flowers and perfumes" as they approach the shrine.

Rémusat, in his learned notes to the "Foe-Koue-Ki" (Chap. XIII., Note 6), remarks as follows, on the "Towers of deliverance" of Fa Hian:—

"The word 'tower,' Sanskrit Sthúpa, applies not merely to great religious buildings, but, likewise, to those miniature structures, which are the model of the former, on a reduced scale; . . . simple stones, which by their form, symbolize the five elements, ether, air, fire, water, and earth, and consequently the human body, which is compounded of these, . . . are called Sthúpa, by analogy. The annexed cut(2) may give some idea of the figure assigned to each element. The lowest, or the earth, is rectangular; water, immediately above, occupies a circle; fire a triangle; air a crescent; and ether a smaller acuminated circle.(3) Instead of Chinese names, Sanskrit letters, being abbreviations of the Sanskrit name of each element, are inscribed on the different parts of the Sthúpa."

I did not find these designatory letters on any of the symbols at Sánchi; but there can be no doubt as to the identity of the elementary monogram, figured by M. Rémusat, with Fig. 1 of my Plate XXXIX.; in which, the triangle (fire) is repre-

(1) The representations of the "disc-and-crescent" over the Sánchi gateways are about this size; and, perhaps, this may have been the usual size for such symbols, when intended as adjuncts to worship. The "miniature Sthúpas" are of smaller dimensions.

(2) This cut is reproduced in my Plate XXXIX., Fig. 17.

(3) In the account given, in the Bráhmanical Purànas, of the creation of the elements, by the joint action of spirit and matter, earth, water, fire, air, and ether, are enumerated in the same relative order, as in Rémusat's Note.

sented by the blade-shaped projections, marked *a*; and the acuminated circle (ether) is elaborated into the peculiar symbol marked *b*, on which I have remarked at pages 19, 20.[1]

Sir A. Cunningham ("The Bhilsa Topes," 40, 355, 356) also treated the disc-and-crescent, as symbolizing the five elements; represented by a combination of the radical letters 𑀬, ya, air; 𑀭, ra, fire; 𑀮, la, earth; 𑀯, va, water; and 𑀦, na, ether; "which, when combined, contain the letter 𑀲, s, for Sumeru, and the letter 𑀫, m, for manas, or mind."

Colonel Sykes ("Jour. Roy. As. Soc." VI. 283, 293), on the other hand, compared the "towers of deliverance" mentioned by Fa Hian to the altars seen on Bactrian coins; and suggested that, in both cases, what was intended was the "Buddhist family altar," and not any object connected with sun or fire worship.[2]

We find analogous combinations of the disc and the crescent in the Assyrian symbols shown in my Plate XXXIX., Figs. 10, 11, 12: which are described, by Layard, and other authorities, as representing the Assyrian triad, composed of the sun, moon, and Ishtár or Ashtoreth ("Nineveh and its Remains," II. 449, 464, 465).

Figures 10 and 11, were adopted, almost unaltered, by the Persians; as the emblems of Ahura Mazda; and were, doubtless, as elsewhere supposed, introduced by them into Upper India. Fig. 12, if not the prototype of, is, at all events, strictly analogous to, the well-known winged globe of Egyptian mythology;[3] and its five

(1) Several of the component parts of the elemental symbol here noticed, are among the symbols strung on the necklaces shown in Plates V. and XXXIX.; and are, also, Bráhmanical sectarial marks. (Compare Figs. 15, 16, 30, 31, 32, 36, and 41 to 44, of Plate XXXIX.) It will be seen, too, that the disc, and the simple crescent, or bident, are among the sacred symbols on Assyrian necklaces (see Fig. 1, Plate XL.): and there is a further Assyrian resemblance, in the conical, or acuminated symbol, in Figs. 17, 43, 44, and 45, of Plate XXXIX.; which is identical, in shape, with the so-called "fir cone" carried by the Assyrian deities and priests.

(2) If the Buddhists ever used "family altars," it must have been when Buddhism was still largely mingled with the sun, fire, and elemental worship which it first adopted, then modified, and finally, for a time discarded; and when, therefore, the "fire-altar" of the older worship, was commonly used, in both public and private rites.

It is to be noted, that both Sykes and Rémusat, in their remarks upon Towers of deliverance, advert to the significant fact, that there is no mention of sun, or fire worship among the *unorthodox* cults enumerated in Buddhist works. The latter writer says ("Foe-Koue-Ki," Chap. XVII, Note 21):—"Amongst all passages, in Chinese authors, relative to what the Buddhists term heresies, I have met with none that was particularly applicable to the fire-worshippers of Persia." The heretical sects alluded to were the worshippers of earth, air, water, and ether, respectively, as the "great first cause" of all things; and the non-mention of fire-worship fortifies the conclusion that it was recognized as a part of the orthodox Buddhist religion.

(3) A symbol identical with the Egyptian "winged globe," but reversed, was seen over the doorway of a three-chambered shrine, at "Ocosingo" in Central America, by Stephens: and at Palenque, were found other symbols, which more or less, resemble the disc-and-crescent. ("Central America, and Yucatan," II. 311, 317, 346, 349.)

Some of the earlier representations of the Egyptian sacred scarabæus, also, bear a strong resemblance to the conjoined symbols of the disc and crescent: see, in particular, those on the celebrated Shush stone.

The winged globe, or, more properly, winged disc, was one of the pagan symbols which were adopted by the early Christians; and was etherealized into the beautiful winged heads known to Christian art as "cherubs."

clustered discs, within a larger disc, are exactly reproduced in what is called, in India, the "panch-mukhti," or "panchánan" linga, and its encircling yoni; a representation of which is given in Fig. 15 of my Plate XL.[1]

In the Persian sculptures at Naksh-i-Rustam; which are of the time of Darius Hystaspes (sixth century B.C.), the disc-and-crescent symbol appears on the dress of a figure, which is supposed to represent one of the foreign kings, made captive by Darius (Ker-Porter's "Travels," I., Plate XXIV.).

The symbol is, unquestionably, identical with the "caduceus," the staff, or wand of Mercury (the Greek Hermes, and Egyptian Thoth): and it is, also, the astronomical sign of the *planet* Mercury, the Indian Budha (see Figs. 26, 27, of my Plate XXXIX.).

Maurice, in his "Ancient History of India," described the caduceus as uniting "the solar and lunar emblems with the mystic cross; which not only represents the four cardinal points, but the four elements, and universal matter."

The speculations of the same learned writer as to the serpents sometimes seen entwined round the caduceus, are inapplicable to its *older* form; which had neither serpents nor cross; but was a simple disc-and-crescent, on a staff ☿ (in which precise form, we find it at Sánchi). This afterwards became ☿; and, eventually the disc was discarded, and the symbol merged into the plain trisula, or trident Ψ.

In the Preface to "The Bhilsa Topes," p. viii., Sir A. Cunningham compares this archaic form of the caduceus with the Sánchi symbol.

Hermes was the Greek copy of the Egyptian Thoth, whose representations—like the caduceus itself, and the disc-and-cresent symbol—combined the solar and lunar symbols. Thoth, moreover, in common with most of the male divinities of Egypt, carried the tau, or crux ansata; the so-called "symbol of life," ☥ or ♀; which, itself, is a modification of the "chaitya" form of the symbol now under discussion; with the two arms of the crescent, or trident, represented by straight in lieu of curved lines.[2]

[1] This combination of five discs is, itself, a very ancient symbol; and is met with frequently in both Assyrian and Greek mythological representations; and on the sculptured crosses of Great Britain; as well as in India. Like the winged disc itself, of which it sometimes formed part, it was adopted as a Christian symbol; and eventually came to signify the "five wounds" of the crucified Saviour of the world.

[2] The first of the two forms of the crux ansata above shown, occurs on Indian coins; sometimes as ☥, and sometimes as ☥; which reminds one of some of the Egyptian representations of the sun's disc, with its triple descending ray. The two tridental forms ♆ and ♆, are mere varieties, the one of the other: and, in fact, the planetary sign of Mercury may be said to combine both forms of the disc-and-crescent symbol, the erect and the reversed; like the double symbol shown in p. 104.

The second figure of the crux ansata, ♀, which forms part of the caduceus, is, also, the sign of the planet Venus; and, in its reversed form ♁, is the sign for the earth.

In this last shape, it occurs, as a royal symbol, in many parts of the world; and as the familiar, "ball and cross," is still the emblem of earthly sovereignty. It also, still denotes spiritual supremacy; and is so used, alike on Christian churches and Muhammadan mosques and tombs. But over the latter, the crescent, instead of the cross, surmounts the ball.

There is another curious, if not important, feature to be noticed, in connection with the resemblance between the disc-and-crescent symbol, and the caduceus, or wand of Mercury or Hermes; the "Thoth" of Egypt; the planetary, "Budha" of India; and the "Woden" of Scandinavia.

Among the Páli letters which, as already shown, are conjoined in the Indian symbol, and which, together, form the caduceus, we may, I think, particularize, as the principal, 8, ma; +, ka; and I, ra; which are not only, singly, names of sacred import both in Egyptian and Indian mythology; but, in conjunction, form the word "makara": a term which, while curiously like "Mercury," is the name given, in Sanskrit, to the mystical fish, dragon, or sea monster, which figures so prominently in almost every known system of mythology; and which was adopted, from more ancient myths, by both the Buddhists and the Bráhmans.

So favourite a symbol was it, with the Buddhists, that they described Buddha himself, as having once existed in that form; while, among the Bráhmans, the Makara, Matsya, or Machh, was the first avatára of Vishnu—whose last avatára was Budha—the Zodiacal sign which we call "Capricorn"; and the vahan, and emblem of Varuna, god of the sea; and of Káma, god of love; whose name combines the titles both of the Sun and the Moon, an evident allusion to the primitive myth of the junction, for creative purposes, of the principal male and female deities!

I cannot better illustrate the comprehensive significance of the above three syllables, than by quoting their several meanings, in Sanskrit and in Egyptian.

"Ma," in Sanskrit, is Brahma; Vishnu; Siva; Yama; Lakshmi; mother; the moon; time; light, or lustre; mind: and, also, a magical or mystical formula; that is, the tri-literal Aom. In Egyptian mythology, "Ma" is the moon; a goat; and one of the components in the name of the god "Num"; whose emblems (like those of the Vedic fire-god Agni), are a water-vase, and goat.

"Ka," in Sanskrit, is Brahma; Vishnu; Yama; Kámadeva; Daksha; Prajápati; the sun; fire; light, or splendour; water; time; air, or wind; mind; soul; a prince; the head; the hair; and a peacock, or king of birds. It is, also, applied to *any* principal god, or object of worship.

In Egyptian, "Ka" is part of the divine name; and also signifies a bull; or, if in conjunction with the crescent, or "female sign," a cow.

"Ra," in Sanskrit, is fire; heat; warmth; burning; speed; and, also, desire and love; the god of which is Káma, or Kámadeva.

In Egyptian mythology, "Ra" is the sun; a creator or doer; and, also, a common component in the names of deities.

A further indication that the Sánchi "disc-and-crescent" was, originally, the joint emblem of the sun and moon, is afforded by its exact resemblance to the Zodiacal sign "Taurus" (Fig. 25, Plate XXXIX.): which, as is well known, represents the head and horns of the Bull; one of the most ancient, and widely used, of solar types.

The adoption of the bull and the cow as the material emblems of the principal male and female deities—that is, the sun and the moon—was, doubtless, due, partly to the early-noticed resemblance between their horned heads, and the conjoined soli-lunar symbol; and partly to the fact that, among the pastoral races who were the earliest idolaters, the bull and the cow were the "first" or chief of animals; and therefore, the most appropriate representatives of the supreme Godhead. But, be this as it may, we have, in the mythology of various races, abundant proof of the use of tauri-form symbols and figures, which have always been viewed as Mithraic; and which can be clearly traced, from the simple "disc-and-crescent" form, to the complete animal figure, or the horned, or rayed human figure.(1)

The sign "Taurus," gradually merged into the common ornament, on Classic altars and friezes, called the "bucranium," which has been, erroneously, regarded as symbolizing, merely, the taurobolia, or bull-sacrifices to Cybele: (2) and the same symbol formed the "first," or principal letter, in the earliest Hebrew, Phœnician and Greek alphabets; in which, "Aleph" or "Alpha" signified both "the first" or supreme being, and a bull, or ox! (3)

In India, as in other countries, *symbols* of the deity were worshipped long before images, whether of animal or of human shape; and though the Buddhists never went so far as to worship the bull itself, we have evidence that they *did* worship, as representing Buddha, either the bull's head symbol, or some variety of the "disc-and-crescent," which closely resembled it: and Fa Hian affords us proof that such a symbol was of equal sanctity with the wheel or "chakra," as late as the commencement of the fifth century A.D.

In describing the Buddhist temple of Jeta, near Sravasti ("Foe-Koue-Ki," Chapter XX), he wrote:—"There are two pavilions, and two stone pillars. On the pillar to the left side is executed the figure of a wheel: and on that to the right side is placed that of an ox": and he added that Rája Prasenajit made a sandal-wood image of Buddha, in the shape of "an ox's head"; which received Buddha's approval; and was "the first of all the statues of Foe; and that which men of subsequent times have copied."

Besides the above illustrations of the transition from the simple "disc-and-crescent," to a horned human or animal head, I may refer to others, among the rude rock-carvings of Central America, and the neighbourhood of Mentone! (See pp. 54,

(1) The horns of the crescent, or bident, not only represented the moon's, as distinct from the sun's shape, but also the solar and lunar *rays;* and the names given to the horned deities were, in Assyria, "karnaim," and, in Greece, "karneios" and "karnaia"; both of which answer to the Sanskrit "karna," which means both a horn, and a ray of light; more particularly a sun-beam.

(2) Many illustrations could be cited, of the gradations from the simple "disc-and-crescent" to the horned human head, or the horned ox-skull; and some are particularized elsewhere. A variety of this form occurs on Indo-Sassanian coins; and on coins of the Ujain series; in the latter case, in a three-fold group. (See "Jour. As. Soc. Beng." VI. p. 290, and Plate LXI.)

(3) The oldest form of the Hebrew, and Phœnician Aleph, was ∀, which, reversed, was the old Greek Alpha A; both being varieties of the disc-and-crescent, or bull's head symbol; that is, ♉, ♈. The triangle and the circle were convertible, and equally sacred and significant symbols of the triune deity; and both, alike, represented the most perfect and mystical of numbers, three. Aleph, or Alpha, therefore, denoted all three members of the sacred triad, as well as "the first," or principal member.

362, 363, and Plates, in the "Transactions of the International Congress of Prehistoric Archæology" for 1868).

I have already (p. 55), adverted to the evident connection between the Bráhmanical Jagannáth triad, and the Buddhist triad of "Buddha, Dharma, and Sangha."

Faber wrote, as follows, many years ago, in his "Anct. Myth." (II. 482, 487):—"All sects, in this triad, or rather in the component parts of the figures, worshipped the sun and moon, the basis of all mythology": (¹) and, as illustrating this, he compared the triad itself to the "pránava," or mystic triliteral syllable "Aom," as written in the *Persian* character; and, the individual figures to the lunar god of Heliopolis, and the Carrhenians.(²)

Colonel Sykes ("Jour. Roy. As. Soc." VI. 274), remarked upon the "uncouth figures" of Jagannáth, as "more like chaityas, than beings with human form;" and described the temple itself as being on or near the site of an older Buddhist shrine.

Laidlay, in his translation of the "Foe-Koue-Ki" ("Travels of Fa Hian," Chapter III. Note 13, and XXVII. Note 9), gives a very conclusive summary of the several proofs that the triad, and "Rathjátra" procession of Jagannáth, were borrowed from the Buddhists; and the like views are stated by Sir A. Cunningham, both in his "The Bhilsa Topes," as already quoted, and "Stupa of Bharhut" (111, 112), where he recognizes the "unquestionable identity of the figures in the Bráhmanical triad with the 'tri-ratna,'" or "disc-and-crescent" symbol.

Finally, Conder ("Syrian Stone Lore," 72, 73), has some interesting remarks on the resemblance between the Jagannáth figures, and the Akkadian, Egyptian, and Phœnician "symbols of life;" and his illustrations are noteworthy, as tending to show the transition from the symbol, to a rude human figure.

Whether the Bráhmans of Jagannáth borrowed from the Buddhists, or the latter from the former, is, after all, of minor importance; as the symbolic figures used were, in either case, of a foreign origin. The Buddhists of Ceylon, however, where the *Buddhist* car procession still survives, in the yearly procession of the dalada, or "tooth-relic," allow that, originally, the ceremony was purely Bráhmanical.

The disc-and-crescent symbol is the exact counterpart of the Páli letter or syllable, "ma"; the several meanings of which, in Sanskrit and Egyptian, I have already given (page 87). It is used in Buddhist Páli inscriptions, both as a prefix and an affix, to represent the mystic word Aom, Aum or Om; similarly used by the Bráhmans.(³)

(¹) Faber's illustrations are reproduced in my Plate XXXIX., Figs. 19 to 24. In all pictures or models of the Bráhmanical triad, the central figure, or Jagannáth himself, differs from the other two in being armless: in explanation of which, an absurd legend is told. (See "The Bhilsa Topes," 358-360.)

(²) The Carrhenian symbol (my Fig. 24), besides its analogy with the disc-and-crescent symbol, has Assyrian and Egyptian features. The crescent, the disc or oval, and the star, are Assyrian emblems; and the star within the crescent is the Egyptian, or five-rayed star, elsewhere alluded to. It occurs, also, on many ancient coins and medals; sometimes with the interlacing of its two arrow-heads fully indicated.

(³) This sacred triliteral syllable is universally used, by both Bráhmans and Buddhists, as a prefatory,

Other uses of the symbol are, on memorial "Sati" pillars; where, as already stated, it represents, as it did in the earliest times, the Sun and Moon, which are invoked as witnesses of the self-immolation. Another common symbol, on such monuments, is a human hand; also a common Buddhist symbol, traceable, probably, to ancient Egypt.

In the form ☿, which, as elsewhere pointed out, is the oldest form of the caduceus, it tallies with the Bráhmanical symbol of the sacred scorpion, an emblem not only common in Indian sculpture, but connected with representations of Mercury and Mithras. The same form of the symbol is seen attached to the four arms of a plain cross, among the Buddhist coin emblems collected by Colonel Sykes. ("Jour. Roy. As. Soc." VI. 456, 457.)

Colonel Sykes called it a form of "praying wheel;" but it is, rather, a variety of the Swastika, and probably represents the "pancha dhyána," or five celestial Buddhas; the central cross being the supreme, or Ádi Buddha.

I have, now, to remark upon other combinations of the disc and the crescent; in which the disc is within the crescent, and the latter is in its earlier or bi-dental form.

The most striking of these is the symbol shown in Fig. 18 of Plate XXXIX.; which forms the head-ornament of the Egyptian deities Hathor, Isis, Nub or Num, Osiris, and Thoth, and of the symbolic bull and ram. (See Bonomi and Arundale's "Egypt. Ant. in the Brit. Mus." Plate XVI., Figs. 57, 58; and XXVI., Figs. 102 to 105: Coleman's "Myth. of the Hind." 255, 258: and Bunsen's "Egypt's Place in Univ. Hist." Plates III., V.)

A similar symbol (on a staff) occurs on Babylonian seals; in Greek representations of Artemis, as the Moon (where the central disc appears as the head of the goddess; and among the symbols at Palenque in Central America. (See Layard's "Nineveh, etc.," 2nd Series, 596; Piroli and Zoëga's "Bass. Rel. Ant. di Roma," II. Plate LVIII.; and Stephens's "Cent. Amer. and Yucatan," II. 311.)

Other varieties of this combination of the disc and bident, are shown in the upper portions of Figs. 1, 17, 19 and 24 of my Plate XXXIX., and in the Sectarial Mark, Fig. 37.

The bident, or horn-shaped crescent, thus shown to have been a common symbol in both India and Egypt: was, also, sacred in Assyria. (See Figs. 32, 33, 36, 46 of Plate XXXIX.; and Fig. 1 of Plate XL.)

and final invocation, in prayers and ceremonials, in books, and in inscriptions: and it has numerous meanings; including the ineffable name of the supreme deity.

It is impossible to say, how far, if at all, the mythologists of India were cognizant of the sculpture and epigraphy of the Romans; but it is, at least, a curious circumstance that the Indian triune divinity—both Bráhman and Buddhist, should be represented by the triliteral A.O.M.; which is almost identical with the Roman I.O.M.; the common representative of the supreme Jupiter, Optimus, Maximus.

The dentated, or tridental form of the crescent, which forms the upper portion of the disc-and-crescent symbol, has its own separate significance.

At page 79, I have instanced some of its uses at Sánchi; and I would now point out that, in Greece, the trident was not only the symbol of Poseidon or Neptune—of whose planetary form it is still the sign—but was connected, also, with both Phoibos and Hermes. In Assyria, a flame-shaped trident was the symbol of the god "Vul;" representing lightning.

The Indo-Scythians, as their coins show, adopted the trident from their Greek predecessors; and, at a later period, it became the emblem of the Buddhist "tri-ratna" or triad of "precious ones," and the special emblem of the Bráhmanical Siva. Among the Bráhmans, however, as among the Greeks, it was not the exclusive appanage of one deity: for it is found in representations of Vishnu, and of Súrya (see Figs. 8, 9, Plate XL.): and, as a weapon, it is borne by many other divinities; and is fabled to have been formed from a fragment of the sun's disc.(1)

As pointed out by Sir A. Cunningham ("Stupa of Bharhut," 113, 114), this portion of the disc-and-crescent symbol resembles the minuscular form of the Greek "omega"; the great or double *o*: while, I may add, the small, or single *o*, "omikron," is represented by the disc. This junction of the two letters is, doubtless, in itself, significant; and forms, I may remark, the sacred "trefoil," as well as the "disc-and-crescent."

In some of the Catacomb inscriptions at Rome, the omega is so peculiarly formed, that but for the juxtaposition of the alpha, it would be called a trident.

It is noteworthy that the initial, as well as the medial and final form of the omega, was a sacred symbol, in Egypt, and elsewhere, long before it was adopted as a Greek letter. In the symbolism of ancient Egypt, Ω was a component part of the name of the god Khem: and we find it, also, on either side of a star, on Phœnician seals.

The reversed trident, I may remark, in conclusion, is the Zodiacal sign of the Ram; an animal almost as common, as a solar type, as the bull: and a prominent feature in the mythology of Greece and Egypt, as well as in that of India.

In order to economize space, I have limited myself to some, only, of the many illustrations I have collected of the wide-spread use of this so-called "Buddhist emblem."

I have, doubtless, overlooked many, of importance, which will, at once, occur to

(1) See Chapter XI. In the Bráhmanical mythology, the symbols, weapons, and special attributes and qualities of a divinity, are as sacred as the deity to whom they belong: and are even represented as having, occasionally, become incarnate, as separate objects of worship. The "Alware Kathá," for instance, relates the impersonation of the weapons and ornaments of Vishnu: and the Básaveswara Cheritra" is a history of the human incarnation of Nandi, the sacred Bull of Siva: while the Puránas allude to the separate deification of the attributes and qualities of celestial beings. (See Wilson's "McKenzie Collection," I. 281, 285; and "Vishnu Purána," 158, 267; and Langlois' "Harivansa Purána," I. 18; and note 31.)

more competent students of symbolism: while some of those adduced will, I have no doubt, appear fanciful and strained, if taken alone.

I cannot but think, however, that my illustrations, taken collectively, will support the view that the Buddhism of Sákya is a composite religion; far less ancient, and far less "sui generis," than has been generally supposed; and that though it possesses many features connected with cults of high antiquity, such as the worship of the sun, fire, and the elements in general, its own date is not more remote than about the commencement of the Christian era.

The Swastika Symbol.

The well-known symbol called the "crux gammata"; in Sanskrit Swastika, and Sauvastika; is not represented in the Sánchi sculptures; nor, so far as I am aware, at Bharhut or Amarávati.

It occurs, however, in several of the Páli inscriptions; and once, in association with the "disc-and-crescent" symbol; and I, therefore, notice it, in this chapter (see "The Bhilsa Topes," Plate XIX., Figs. 186, 188, 192, 195).

There is no proof, so far as I am aware, of its use as a *Buddhist* symbol, at any time anterior to the date of the Sánchi gateway, on which, only, it occurs; but like the "disc-and-crescent"—with which it is often associated, both in inscriptions and on coins—it is of very ancient origin; and can be traced back, among various races, to the earliest times; as will be evident from the following (alphabetical) detail of countries or peoples, in and by which it is known to have been used; viz., Ashanti, Assyria, Bactria, Britain, Celts, Central America, Central Asia, China, Cyprus, Egypt, Etruria, France, Germany, Greece, India, Japan, Persia, Roman Empire, Scandinavia, Sicily, Spain, Syria, Tibet, and Troy!

From its resemblance to the simple cross, and to the initial letter of the Greek word "Χριστος," it was adopted by the Christians, as a sacred symbol: and is found, in the Roman Catacombs, marked on the dress of "the Good Shepherd," and other figures: and it continued to be used, on ecclesiastical vestments, in Europe, to a comparatively recent date.(1)

It is the "cross fylfot" of heraldry; and as an armorial bearing, is said to have been introduced, from the East; probably about the time of the Crusades; but according to some authorities, in the sixth century A.D.

(1) An instance of this later use of the symbol occurs on the monument of Bishop Edington, at Winchester (A.D. 1361); where, according to Mr. C. E. Ponting, it signifies "perfect submission to the divine will." The writer adds, "There is no reason why it should not have been a symbol of submission, in the religious faiths of the ancient world." ("Wiltshire Archæol. and Nat. Hist. Magazine" for November 1890; p. 230.) This opinion is borne out, at any rate as regards India, by the Sanskrit meaning of "Swastika"; which, according to Sir A. Cunningham, is derived from su, and asti, that is, "it is well"; or as Professor Wilson expresses it, "so be it"; either implying resignation ("The Bhilsa Topes," 18).

The Indian sect, of the Swástikas, the Tao-tsse of China, whose emblem was the Swastika, are described as a heretical sect, who denied the immortality of the soul: whereas the orthodox Buddhists, and their Bráhman predecessors, like the Egyptians of old, heldthe ancient doctrine of the metempsychosis. Both the Swástikas and the Tao-tsse were, admittedly, anterior to the sect of Sákya; which, doubtless, adopted the symbol, directly, from them.

Its *earliest* signification appears to have been, a representation of the apparent motion of the sun; whence it came, also, to typify celestial fire, as well as its source, the sun: and it was, thus, made the "keraunos," or symbol of lightning; and the so-called battle-axe, or hammer, of the Scandinavian Thor.

The Swastika was found, as one of the commonest symbols, on the vases, balls, and spindle-whorls, of Troy; and was supposed, by the late Dr. Schliemann, to represent the revolving apparatus used for producing the sacred fire. Professor Max Müller communicated a learned note, on the two varieties of the symbol; namely, the "Svastika," with arms pointing to the right; and the "Sauvastika," with arms pointing to the left: both of which, however, whatever their later meanings, he treated as solar emblems. (See Schliemann's "Troy and its Remains," 101 to 105, and 119; and "Ilios," 346 to 354.)

There are, so far as I know, no satisfactory data from which to decide when or from what particular source, the Swástikas of India, or the Chinese Tao-tsse, adopted the Swastika as their sacred symbol. All that I wish to make clear is that it is, in no sense, exclusively Buddhist, any more than it is exclusively Bráhmanical; and that it was extensively used, in widely separated parts of the world, long before it was known in India, at all.

The late Mr. E. Thomas, of the Indian Civil Service, published, in 1880, a valuable treatise on "The Indian Swastika, and its Western Counterparts": but, to my great regret, I have failed to obtain a copy.

CHAPTER XI.

INSCRIPTIONS, UNCONNECTED WITH RELIC DEPOSITS.

OWING to the loss of my original transcripts of the Sánchi inscriptions, and the non-receipt of their translations (see p. 1), I am at a considerable disadvantage, in drawing up this chapter: but I have the authority of Sir A. Cunningham, to make full use of the transcripts and translations published by him (¹) and I gladly acknowledge the great assistance I have derived, not merely as regards inscriptions, but in other respects, from his valuable works, "The Bhilsa Topes," and "Stupa of Bharhut"; as well as from his replies to my occasional references.

The total number of inscriptions at Sánchi, irrespective of those on relic-caskets, appears to be 315; distributed as in the following tabular detail.

Character of the inscriptions, and proximate dates.	On the uprights, cross-bars, and copings of the enclosures; and on the sculptured gateways		On sthambhas or isolated pillars.	On the thrones or pedestals of images.	In other places.	Totals.
	of No. 1 Sthúpa.	of No. 2 Sthúpa.				
I. Old Páli } From the 3rd century B.C., to 1st century A.D.	232	50	1	...	...	283
II. Later Páli } From the 3rd century B.C., to 1st century A.D.	18	2	...	...	...	20
III. Gupta Páli, between 319 and 600 A.D. ...	2	...	1	...	...	3
IV. Kutila, 8th to 10th century A.D.	...	...	...	3	...	3
V. Nágari, of and after 14th century A.D. ...	3	...	...	...	3	6
Totals ...	255	52	2	3	3	315

The 303 Páli inscriptions, of Classes I. and II., have no dates; and with but one or two exceptions, contain no names, or other particulars, whence a date can be inferred; and the forms of the letters used, though, to some extent a guide as to relative age, only enables us to fix the actual dates of the records within rather wide limits of time.

(¹) See "The Bhilsa Topes," Chapters XVI., XIX., pp. 235 to 268, 280 to 284; and Plates XVI. to XIX., and XXI.

The old Páli character, for instance, is, undoubtedly identical with that of the rock and pillar edicts of "Devánampiya Piyadasi"; which are of the third century B.C.: and it was, according to some authorities, used even as early as the sixth century B.C. But it was, also, in use, concurrently with successive variations, all over India, for several centuries *after* the date of the Piyadasi edicts; and we find the character, in its oldest form, not only on the Græco-Bactrian coins of Agathokles and Pantaleon; and the Brahmanical coins of about the first century A.D. mentioned at p. 82; but on the Sánchi sculptured gateways: the *oldest* of which was erected as late as between 19 and 37 A.D.

OLD, AND LATER PALI INSCRIPTIONS.

The most important, and, probably, one of the oldest of the Páli inscriptions, is that on the broken "sthambha," or láth, near the Southern Gateway of No. 1 Stúpa; which is numbered 177 by Sir A. Cunningham.

It is a seven-line, and evidently complete, inscription, in the oldest form of Páli; and very well cut: but is so defaced, in parts, that all that can be made out, by the combined acumen of Mr. J. Prinsep, and Sir A. Cunningham, is, that it records the gift of the means of providing refreshment for the members of the "Sangham" (¹) or religious community. As I have kept a copy of my transcript of this inscription, I subjoin a fac-simile of it; with conjectural readings in Roman character.

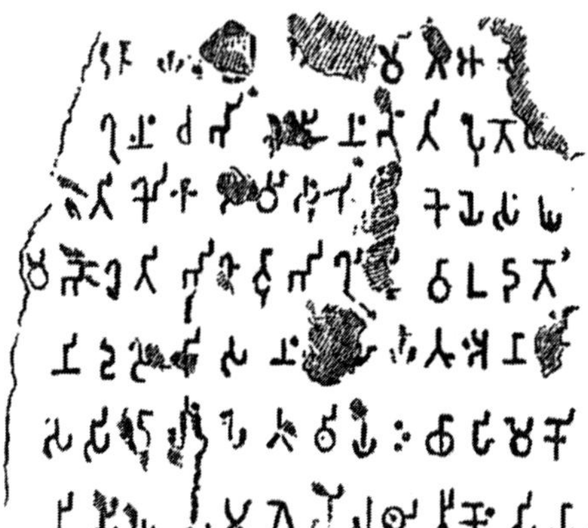

ḍa ra ya ma't á the

khu nan cha bhi í nan ḍá ti pu ta
to

ti khki ka vi san ri ke ye san gha

ma bhe dha ti bhi kha tá bhi khi i vá u dá to
vá

ni du se ri sa nan ha ya tu a ná
dí

sa si vá pe ta vi ya i chhá hi me ki
ko
kai

ti si gha sa ma ge chi la thi tí kan si yá ti
san kon

Its character is the same as that of the majority of the inscriptions in the enclosure of the Sthúpa: but it is much better carved than, though probably of about the same age as, those records. All that can be asserted, with reasonable certainty, however, as to its date, is, that it is older than the Southern Gateway, near which it stands; as its fine lion capital was, evidently, the model for the gateway capitals.

(¹) See "Jour. As. Soc. Beng." VII. 565, *et seq.*; and "The Bhilsa Topes," 181, 182, and 259 to 262 and Plate XIX., No. 177. The hypothetical readings which, originally, led Sir A. Cunningham to regard

Among the short votive inscriptions, on the enclosure, near the Southern Gateway, there is one, also in the oldest Páli character, which reads Subáhitasa Gotiputasa rájalipíkarasa dánam; that is, "Gift of Subáhita, son of Goti, the royal scribe"; of which Sir A. Cunningham says, "This is the most valuable of all the inscriptions on the Sánchi colonnade: as it belongs to the family of Goti; whose eldest son, Gotiputra, was the teacher of the celebrated Mogaliputra. This inscription, therefore, serves to fix the date of the Sánchi enclosure in the early part of Asoka's reign." ("The Bhilsa Topes," 251; and Plate XVII., No. 110.)

Both Gotiputra, and Mogaliputra, were, according to Buddhist works, celebrities of Asoka's time; and both names occur on relic caskets which we excavated at Sánchi, and elsewhere: but the books which connect them with Asoka's time, were not written until, at earliest, the fourth or fifth century A.D.; and, moreover, the Sthúpa in which the relics inscribed as Gotiputra's were found, is 200 years more modern than the enclosure inscriptions of the larger Sthúpa (see "The Bhilsa Topes," p. 281): so there is a difficulty in regarding Subáhita and Gotiputra, as brothers; and, probably, the safer conclusion is, that the term Gotiputra, in both the inscriptions, refers to a sect or tribe, named after some common ancestor.(1)

Next, in apparent order of date, is a three-line inscription, in a more recent form of Páli, which is carved on the representation of a Sthúpa, on the top lintel of the Southern Gateway; and which records the gift, either of the lintel or of the whole gateway. It reads: Rájnye (or perhaps Rájnyo) Siri Sátakanisa
Avesaṇisa Vásiṭhi putasa
Ánandasa dánam

that is, "Gift of Ánanda, son of the neophyte Vásishtha, in the reign of Sri Sátakarni." ("The Bhilsa Topes," 264, 265; and Plate XIX., No. 190.)

In the "Vishnu Purána" (472, Note 4) Srí Sátakarni appears as the third king of the Maghada dynasty called Ándhra, or Ándhrabhritya; one of the "future" or prophesied dynasties which, in the falsified Puránas, misrepresent history.(2)

His reign, according to the varying lists in the Matsyu, Váyu, and Vishnu Puránas, and calculations based on the known date of Chandra Gupta Maurya, commenced between 12 and 20 A.D.; and lasted, according to Sir A. Cunningham, from 19 to 37 A.D.

This inscription, therefore, which records the completion of the oldest of the sculptured gateways, shows that prior to the commencement of the Christian era,

this inscription as recording a grant by Asoka of Magadha, to the members of the Sánti, or Sánchi, community, have, I understand, been abandoned by him, after repeated scrutiny of the original inscription.

(1) This supposition is supported by the fact that the name Gotiputra, which is that given to one of the missionaries, whose relics were found in No. 2 Sthúpa, does not occur among the missionaries to the Hemawanta enumerated in the Maháwanso. (See "The Bhilsa Topes," 122 and 293.)

(2) All the Pauránik dynasties which contain names which have been recognized in Greek or Buddhist authors, on coins, or in inscriptions, are represented as "prophetic"; and in so garbled and confused a manner as to be next to useless for chronological purposes. The confusion has, evidently, been an intentional perversion, by the Bráhman writers, of real history: and it has, frequently, been remarked that *Buddhist* written history is quite as unreliable as that of the Bráhmanical Puránas.

the four entrances to the large Sthúpa were like those of No. 2 Sthúpa: and shows further, that there was nothing about the Sthúpa, prior to that date, to identify it with the Buddhism of Sákya.

I have, next, to notice a long inscription, in later Páli character, which is cut across the capital of the left pillar of the Eastern Gateway; and of which I am able to give a fac-simile of my original transcript, with its apparent Roman character equivalents.

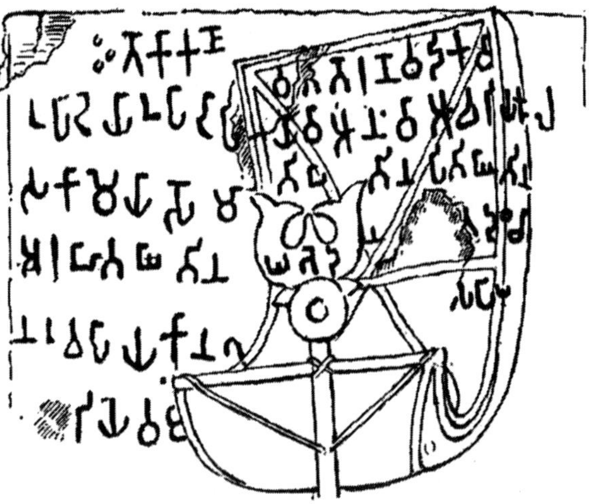

. . . . i to ká ka ṇá
va t to ra ṇa va di ka vá
u pá ḍe yá u pá á pi ya vá á naṅ vá á cha ri ya ku la
ti ba ti na pi ti ghá ti na
sa ká me yá so má (?)
na . . . ta dun chá
a ra há ta ghá ti na gha (?) da
sa pá gha
na ru cha pá ya ká na kka (?)
(?)
. . . . ri yeva ja

This inscription is only partially given in "The Bhilsa Topes" (p. 263, and Plate XIX., Note 183), and is not translated: but the words ito, kákaṇá, upádeyá, toraṇa, ácháriya kula, somá, ghátina, arahàta, and, perhaps, kánakkariya, are legible; and, I think, enough can be made out to show that the inscription records the gift of the pillar, or perhaps the whole gateway (toraṇa) by a member, or members of a religious class.

In my original Report, I suggested that, perhaps, the last word quoted was the name of the place, Kánakhera: but on further scrutiny, aided by a rubbing given me by Sir A. Cunningham, I am inclined to think this doubtful.

Of the remaining 299 Páli inscriptions, the majority (244 at least) are merely short records of the dánam, or gift (ꖉ⊥), by individuals or communities, of portions of the enclosures, or gateways.

Their chronological value is next to "nil"; but they contain certain personal, sacred, and topographical terms, some of which call for notice; and they are interesting, as proving that, at the time they were inscribed, it was customary in India, as it had been among the ancient Egyptians and Hebrews, to receive the aid of the general community, in the building and embellishment of sacred structures.(1)

Many of the personal names combine a sacred name with some secular affix; which is a *Bráhmanical* rather than a Buddhist practice; and is inculcated in the Code of Manu, and in the Puránas (see "Manu," II. 30-32; and "Vishnu Purána," 289, 297, Note 4). We find, for instance, among other affixes to the names of deities, or sacred objects, such terms as Dana, Data, Dina, Mita, Pála, Pálita, Piya, Rakhita, Sana or Sena, Siha, and Vaḍhana, or Vaṛhana: and, in some instances, both the components of a name are sacred terms.

It would be tedious and useless to notice all these composite names in detail; but their importance lies in the fact that, howsoever combined, the names indicate what were the sacred terms in use at the time, and thus serve to show the nature of the worship then in vogue.

I therefore notice, in alphabetical order, some of these terms, which, though used by the Buddhists, are common Bráhmanical terms; and, in some instances, traceable to a very remote source.

1. Áchariya; which even now, is one of the commonest components in names of Bráhmans, means, in Sanskrit, a teacher of the entire Veda.
2. Agi; is the Sanskrit Agni; the Vedic god of fire; and the Indian representative of the Egyptian Num, or Nub, and the Assyrian Nebo.
3. Ahi; which occurs only in conjunction with Mita, or Mitra,(2) is, in Sanskrit, the sun, a snake, a cloud, vapour, water, and "the celestial serpent."
4. Araha; though used by the Buddhists, in common with Bodhisatwa, as the title of their highest priestly order; was a common term among the Bráhmans: and, in fact, the terms Arahata, and Bráhmana, are used, correlatively, by Buddhist writers themselves. Arahat was, also, the distinctive appellation of the Jainas (see "Vishnu Purána," 163, 164, Note 7; and 339, Notes 3, 4).
5. Asa—which occurs, also, as Asva—has the affix Deva, and Giri. It is the Sanskrit "Aswa," a horse: an animal which, as a solar emblem, and

(1) Most of the inscriptions at Bharhut, are of the same character and purport as these. The custom still exists, and has long existed, among the Buddhists of Ceylon and Burmah, in regard to their pagodas, zayáts, images, and sacred bells.

(2) The word Mitra, which, in these inscriptions, Sir A. Cunningham translates as "friend"; though it has that meaning, in Sanskrit, means, also, the sun; and has been read, with such meaning, in many other Indian inscriptions, by well-known European scholars. See, for instance, Dr. Bird's "Historical Researches on the Origin and Principles of the Bauddha and Jaina Religions"; where he gives translations of a number of inscriptions from the Caves of Ajanta, Ellora, Kanári, Kárli, and Násik; and traces the connection between Buddhism and the old sun-worship. (See, on this point, however, "The Bhilsa Topes," p. 5, and note.)

a sacrificial offering, is prominent, not only in Bráhmanical as well as Buddhist literature and sculpture, but in many ancient systems of mythology. The horse was, for instance, specially sacred among the Scythians, or Sáka; from whom was derived "Sákya," the tribal name of Gautama Buddha.

6. Bhagavato, or Bhagavata; though it only occurs once at Sánchi, is common at Bharhut; where it is found in connection with the sacred wheel, or Dharma-chakra; and with the bodhis, or sacred trees, of Sákya Muni, and five of his predecessors. (See "The Bhilsa Topes," 241; and "Stupa of Bharhut," 83, 84, 132, 134, 137, 138 and 139.)

In one of the Bharhut inscriptions (pp. 14, 143; and Plate LVI., No. 19), the term is connected with Mahádeva! Though adopted by the Buddhists, it was by no means an exclusively Buddhist appellation; but was used by the Bráhmans; among whom, in the form Bhagaván, or Bhagwán, it is a common name for Vishnu, to the present day. Professor Wilson derives "Bhagavata" from the dissyllable "Bhaga"; which means power, dominion, glory, splendour, wisdom, etc.; and the possessive affix "va," or "vat" ("Vishnu Purána," 122, and 643, Notes 8, 9, 10). The full meanings of "Bhaga," in Sanskrit, are, an apportioner; dispenser; distributor; lord; patron; an Áditya regarded in the Vedas as bestowing wealth; the brother of the dawn; a name of the sun, moon, and Rudra; good fortune; happiness; beauty; majesty; pleasure; etc.

Other Pauránik explanations, give numerous meanings to each of the three syllables, "bha," "ga," and "va"; and apply the whole tri-syllabled name to the supreme Vásudeva, or Vishnu (ib. 643, Note 9). "Bhaga," moreover, is one of the numerous names of the sun, in the Vedas: but it is not, even there, a purely Indian term. It is derived from the very ancient Aryan root "bhaj"; meaning to apportion, or divide; and was the name of the supreme deity of the ancient Aryans before their separation into the Iranian or Persian, and Indian branches. I have, already, quoted some of its many Indian meanings: and, among the ancient Persians, as we learn from the Zendavesta, and the Achæmenian inscriptions, one of the titles of the supreme deity—Ahuramazda, or Mithra—was "Bhaga Bhagánan" or "God of Gods." (See "Vishnu Purána," as above; Wilson's "Rig Veda Sanhita," 34, Note *c*; and 120, Note *c*; and Cook's "Origin of Religions and Languages," 19, 42, 69.).

7. Bhikhu, and its feminine form Bhikhuni, also spelled Bhichhu and Bhichhuni; are very common terms, in the inscriptions; and denote the mendicant order of the priesthood. They are, however, in no sense, *exclusively Buddhist*. Among the Bráhmans, the Bhikshuka was the fourth order of the religious community (see "Inst. of Manu," VI. 33; and "Vishnu Purána," 295, 296, and Note 6): and it was the sight of one of this class which, finally, led Sákya to abandon his secular life.

Mendicant priests, of both sexes, were, as is well known, an institution among the ancient Greeks and Egyptians. (See Montfaucon's "Antiq. Expld."; Wilkinson's "Mans. and Custs. of the Anc. Egyptians," I. 258, 259; II. 320; and III. 347, 368; and "The Bhilsa Topes," 33.)

8. Budha occurs frequently on both the Sánchi enclosures; and, generally, with an affix indicative of respect, worship, or protection, such as mita, pálita, or rakhita.

Throughout the Sánchi inscriptions; as, also, at Bharhut; and, I believe, in the only rock edict (at Bhabra, near Jaipur) in which it appears, the word is spelt with a single d, Budha (Páli, 𑀩𑀼𑀥); whereas, in Buddhist books, and in (later) inscriptions which are, manifestly, connected with the Buddhism of Sákya, the word used is "Buddha," with the double d.

The former is the Budha of Bráhmanical mythology, identified with the planet Mercury; and, according to the Puránas, the son of Rudra, Mahádeva, Soma, or Chandra, "the moon"; and the ninth, or last, avatára of Vishnu. (See "Vishnu Purána," 59, 238 to 240, and 393.)

Professor Wilson says, regarding this Pauránik Budha:—

"Much erroneous speculation has originated, in confounding this Budha, the son of Soma, and regent of the planet Mercury, 'he who knows,' the intelligent, with Buddha, any deified mortal, or 'he by whom truth is known,' or, as individually applicable, Gautama, or Sákya, son of the Rája Suddhodana; by whom the Buddhists themselves aver their doctrines were first promulgated. The two characters have nothing in common; and the names are identical only when one or other is misspelt."

9. Dhama (Páli 𑀥𑀫), occurs frequently, at Sánchi; with such affixes as data, deva, giri, guta, kathika, naka, pála, rakhita, sena, sihi, siva, and vaḍhána, or vaṛhana.[1]

It may represent either of the Sanskrit words "dhama," which means the moon; Krishna; Yama; Brahma; and the supreme spirit: or "dharma," which has the meanings, an attendant of Súrya, Yama, or Dharmarája (the Indian Pluto); material, concrete, and elemental nature; personified matter; etc.

On the other hand, the word used in Buddhist books, and in inscriptions, *subsequent* to the Christian era, and of purely Buddhist character,[2] is not "dharma," but "dharmma," with the double m; of which the proper translations seem to be, that which is kept, or held fast; an ordinance or usage; a law, statute, or custom; piety; religion; virtue; morality; and, also, a drinker of the soma juice; and a personification of right, justice, law, or virtue.

[1] At Bharhut, "dhama" appears in conjunction with chaka, or chakra, as well as with guta, and rakhita —i.e., gupta, and rakshita.

[2] See, for example, the "Kutila" inscription (of the eighth to tenth century A.D.), on one of the large figures of Buddha, or Tathágata, already described; and the similar inscription, at Bhojpur, noticed in "The Bhilsa Topes," p. 329: in both of which we have the common Buddhist sentence, "Ye dharmma hetu prabhava, hetun teshán tathágato," etc.

The distinction between "dharma" and "dharmma," has not been sufficiently recognized, even in some dictionaries; and, consequently, as with the confusion between "Budha," and "Buddha," much that, strictly, refers to older forms of worship, has been connected, exclusively, with the Buddhism of Sákya.

10. Isa, Isá, and Isi, occur frequently; and with the affixes daka, diti, dási, datá, diná, kasa, lasa, mita, pálita, and rakhita. All three are connected, etymologically, with Íswara, which is not only one of the titles of Ádi, or the supreme *celestial* Buddha, but is the special appellation of the Bráhmanical Vishnu, and Siva. It is, also, synonymous with "Mahat" or embodied intellect. (See "Vishnu Purána," 2, Note 3; 14; 15, Note 22; and 121, Note 17.) As a purely Buddhist term, Isi is a sanctified mortal; from the root "esa," to investigate. ("Maháwanso," 21.)
11. Mita—the Sanskrit Mitra—appears, mostly as an affix, in the following composite forms, Ahi mita; Bala mita; Bála mita; Búla mita; Isi mita; Mita majhaya; Nasaya mitaya; and Sagha mita (see page 98, and Note 2). It is one of the names of the sun-god, in the Persian, Greek, and Bráhmanical systems of mythology.
12. Naga, and Nága are found in such compounds as Aya nága; Nága dána, or Nága dina; Nága hapati; Nága mita; Nága pálita; Nága payasa, or piyasa; Nága rakhita; and Nagilasa: all, more or less, indicative of reverence for the Nága; a term already discussed at pages 61, 62.
13. Rakhita, and its feminine rakhitá, occur very frequently; as an affix to Budha, Dhama, Isi, Nága, Sagha, and Siha (or Sinha), "the lion." The joint terms may, or may not, represent personal names: but the true meaning of the Sanskrit word rakshita is, like pálita, guarded, protected, preserved, or maintained, by.
14. Sámana, the Sanskrit Srámana, occurs once only, at Sánchi; I have, already, discussed it, at length; and shown it to be quite as much Bráhmanical as Buddhist.
15. Tapasa, or tapasi, and its inflexions tápasyána, tapasiyá, etc., represent the Sanskrit tapasya, a hermit, or ascetic; and are applicable more strictly to a Bráhmanical than to a Buddhist class of religionists. The term is common both in the Vedas and Puránas.
16. Upaḍaya, or Upáḍiya; which Sir A. Cunningham translates as "the abbot, or head of a Buddhist monastery," is still a common second name for a Bráhman: and is the Sanskrit Upádháya, one who teaches a part of the Vedas; whereas the Ácháriya taught all.

Among the many personal or tribal names, two are of special interest, as showing that, at the date of the inscriptions, the dynastic names Pánḍava and Gupta were known; and were applied to private individuals.

In two of the inscriptions on the enclosure of No. 2 Sthúpa, rough copies of which I still have, the word Pádu, or Paḍu occurs, as the name of a "kula" or tribe: the full inscriptions (Cunningham's 3 and 8), reading as follows:—Páḍukulikáya gámasa dánam; and Budha pálitasa sethino Paḍukulikiyase dana.

Sir A. Cunningham ("The Bhilsa Topes," 280) says, of these inscriptions:—"The celebrated name of the Pándus is here met with, for the first time, on a genuine ancient monument."

Whether we read the word as the name of a tribe, or the name of a town or village (gáma, or gráma), it proves equally that the "Panch Pánḍava," or "five Pándu brothers," were not the purely mythical personages they have, often, been called: and there are other grounds, too, for giving them, a historical reality; and connecting them, as long ago suggested by Dr. Mill, with the "Guptas" of the fourth and fifth centuries A.D.

Buddhist writers mention a "Panḍu," as King of India, about the commencement of the fourth century of the Christian era: and if this be taken as the Panḍu of the Bráhmanical Puránas, we have an exact parallel with the "Gupta" dynasty of inscriptions and on coins, as seen in the following table.

Names and Titles.	A.D.	Gupta Era.	Remarks and References.
1 Panḍu	302	...	King of India; and a convert to Buddhism; according to Buddhist writers ("Jour. As. Soc. Beng." VI. 861).
2 Bhima, or Gupta	319	1	
3 *Ghatotkacha	340	21	Son of Bhima, by Hidimbá; according to the Puránas: and son of Gupta, according to the later láth inscriptions.
4 *Chandra Gupta I.	360	41	
5 *Samudra Gupta, or Parákrama ...	380	61	
6 *Chandra Gupta II., or Vikramáditya	401	82	According to an inscription at Udáyagiri, near Sánchi.
	408	89	According to Jaina works.
	412	93	According to an inscription on the Sánchi enclosure.
	428	109	According to Chinese writers; who give the name as "Yu-gai," or "moon-protected." (1)
7 *Kumára Gupta, or Mahendra ...	430	111	Son of Chandra Gupta Vikramáditya, according to the láth inscriptions: and son of Asoka, according to Buddhist works.

The names marked with an asterisk, in the above list, are those mentioned in

(1) I have already (page 81, and Note 2) adverted to the possible identity of the "Chandra Gupta Vikramáditya" here mentioned, with the Bráhmanical "Vikramáditya" of Ujain; the alleged founder of the

inscriptions, or on coins, or both: and I may add, as a further indication of a connection between the "Guptas" and the "Pándavas," that the "láths" which bear the names of these "Gupta" princes, are always called "Bhima gaja"; that is, the staff of "Bhima" Pándava.

The word "Gupta," in Sanskrit, means, protected, guarded, preserved; and, also, concealed, secret, and a Vaisya affix: and, in the Sánchi inscriptions, it occurs as follows: Ajita guta, Araha guta, Chada guta, Dhama guta, Nadi guta, Sati guta, Siri guta, and Vaji guta.

Among the very numerous topographical names contained in the Páli inscriptions, the majority appear to be unimportant; and, at any rate, unidentifiable: but some few are of interest, as showing the early use of local names still current in various parts of India, or mentioned in Indian or Cingalese literature.

Among these may be specified the following:—

1. Bhoga vadhana, or Bhoga varhana, which resembles the "bhoga vati," or "city of joy," which was the Nága capital (see page 61).
2. Chakatikaya. The name of a "Mandala," or temple; probably dedicated to the sacred "chakra."
3. Káboja, apparently Kámboja, or Kámbhoya; the habitat of the Kámbojas, who are classed, in the Bráhmanical Puránas, with the Chinas, Sákas, and Yavanas (*i.e.* the Chinese Tartars, Indo-Scythians, and Bactrian Greeks), as Mlechchas, or "fierce barbarians." ("Vishnu Purána," 194, 374, and notes.)
4. Kekateya, or Kekateyapura. The Warangal dynasty of Southern India—said to have been of Pándava origin—bore the names Kákateya, and Ganapati. ("McKenz. Coll." 123, 126.)
5. Kujara, given, by oversight, as Kundura, in "The Bhilsa Topes," 249. This resembles Kajaráha, or Kajurahi (*olim* Jajávati), near Chattarpur, in Bundelkhand; where there are some fine Bráhmanical and Jaina ruins.
6. Kurara or Kurari. This is given, in the Bráhmanical Puránas, as the name of one of the ridges, radiating from the sacred Mount Meru. ("Vishnu Purána," 169.)
7. Madhuvana. Sir A. Cunningham ("The Bhilsa Topes," 253), considers this to represent Mahoba. The Puránas give the name "Madhu," or "Madhuvana," "the grove of Madhu," to the site of the holy city of Mathura. ("Vishnu Purána," 90.)
8. Nava Gáma, or Nava Gráma; "new town"; a place, according to the context,

Sanvat era; whose date was put back, by the Hindú historians, to B.C. 56: that is, to the period of the Sákas, or Indo-Scythians, to whose race Sákya belonged. But it seems to me that we may go beyond this, and see, in this "Chandra Gupta" of the fifth century A.D. (the Yu-gai of the Chinese historians), the historical original of the "Ayu," or "Asoka," of Buddhist writers: whom they, also, put back, in order to connect him with the older Maurya dynasty of Pátaliputra, or Palibothra. It is, at any rate, a very suggestive coincidence, that there is an etymological analogy between "Samudra," the name of Chandra Gupta Vikramáditya's father, and "Vindusára," the name of Asoka's father; and that each had a son named "Mahendra."

connected with Ujain. The name Navagáma or Náogaon (Nowgong) is still used, in Assam and Bundelkhand.

9. Padenekayika, and Pádukulikáya: evidently called after the Pándavas or Pándus. (See previous remarks, at pp. 101-103.)
10. Patithána, or Patithiya: apparently a rendering of Pratistháná. A city, so named, on the Godáveri, was the capital of Sáliváhana, King of Southern India, and founder of the Sáka era (A.D. 78). According to the Vishnu Purána (p. 350), "Pratistháná" (at or near Allahabad), was a city given by the Manu Vaivaswata, to his son Sudyumna.
11. Pokaraya, or Pokhareyaka: that is, Pokhara, or Pushkara; an ancient name of Ajmer; and still the name of a very sacred place of Bráhmanical pilgrimage, near Ajmer.

    The Puránas mention "Pushkaravati" as one of the two principal cities of Gandhára; the abode of Pushkara, the nephew of "Ráma Chandra." ("Vish. Pur." 191, 385, 386, Note 17, and 443, Note 2.)
12. Sanghala, or Sanghila, resembles Singhala, or Sinhila, one of the old names of "Lanka," or Ceylon.
13. Ujena, or Ujeniya; the still existing city of Ujain; the "Avanti" of the Bráhmanical Puránas; and capital of the celebrated Vikramáditya. According to the Buddhists, it was the seat of government of "Asoka," when Viceroy under his father, Vindusára. (See pp. 3 and 75.)
14. Vahila, supposed to represent "Bhilsa" ("The Bhilsa Topes," 243).
15. Vedisa, or Vidisa. This is identified by Sir A. Cunningham, with "Besnagar" the "Wessanagara" of Buddhist works, near Bhilsa ("Stupa of of Bharhut," 132, 137). Professor Wilson ("Vish. Pur." 183, Note 52) calls Bhilsa itself Vidisa.
16. Vejaja, and Vejaja gáma; the village of Vraja, or Vrija, according to Prinsep (see "The Bhilsa Topes," 240). In the Bráhmanical mythology, Vraja, or Vrija, is the district round Mathura; and the scene of Krishna's exploits and sports.

Besides the foregoing names, there are ten ending with "giri," or "hill"; some, at least, of which, must, I think, be held to allude to the place itself (see pp. 3, 4). These are, as follows:—

Asagiri; i.e. Aswagiri, the hill of the sacred horse (see pp. 98, 99).

Devagiri, or the hill of the Devas.

Dhamagiri, or Dharmagiri: the hill of Dharma: as to which, see pp. 100, 101.

Dhanagiri: the hill of Dhana, or perhaps Dharana.

Dhana, both in Páli and Sanskrit, means wealth, treasure, an object of affection, etc.: and forms part of the epithet "Dhanapati," or Lord of wealth, a title applied to both Indra and Kuvera; Vedic deities adopted by the Buddhists.

Dharana means the world; the sun; a Nága king; the king of mountains, Himálaya; and, in its feminine form, the earth; a female breast, etc.

Mahágiri, is the great hill.

Malagiri, or Mulagiri: perhaps the same as the Maragiri of the Bharhut inscriptions (the l and r being permutable). "Mala" may be the Páli rendering of "Malwa"; and "Mula" is one of the Bráhmanical lunar asterisms.

Nadagiri, or Nandagiri: the hill of Nanda, or Nandi.

Nanda, in Sanskrit means joy, pleasure, enjoyment; and Nandi is the sacred bull of Siva.

Most of the varieties of this name occur at Bharhut, also; and Sir A. Cunningham identifies them with Nander. ("Stupa of Bharhut," 138, 143, Nos. 91, 95.)

Pusagiri; the hill of Pusha, or Pushya.

In Bráhmanical works, "Pusha" appears as a celebrated teacher of the Vedas; and Pushya is the name of one of the lunar mansions, and also, of an ancestor of Sákya, in the Ikshwáku line ("Vish. Pur." 226, Note 21; and 387, 463).

Sabhagiri; the hill of Sabha; or perhaps, Sambha or Sambhava.

Sabhá is the Sanskrit for an assembly, court, council, or congregation; and is specially applied to the Court of Indra.

Sambha and Sambhava are, respectively, the thunderbolt of Indra, and a title of Siva.

Yasogiri; the hill of Yaso; which is the Páli rendering of the Sanskrit "Yasas"; meaning glory, splendour, honour, praise, fame, etc. It is a very common component in both Buddhist and Bráhman names, both of persons and places.

The foregoing remarks will, I think, suffice to show that the Páli inscriptions at Sánchi contain no indications of an exclusively *Buddhist* allusion.

Gupta Inscriptions.

There are only three inscriptions in the form of Páli which is usually called the Gupta character (Nos. 197, 198, 199 of Sir A. Cunningham's list). The first and most important of these (on the principal enclosure railing) records the gift, by "the great king, Chandra Gupta," of lands and money, to the Srámanas of the great Vihára; the followers of the Ávasath ceremonial; [1] and contains a date, read by both Prinsep and Cunningham, as "San. 93, bhádra pada 14." (See "Jour. As. Soc. Beng." VI. 455; and "The Bhilsa Topes," 152-154.)

(1) The terms Sámana and Vihára, here applied to the local priesthood, and their place of abode, have been already noticed (see pp. 43, Note 1; 44, Note 1; and 45). They do not occur in any of the older Páli inscriptions: and even in the more recent inscriptions of No. 2 Sthúpa, "Sámana" is only used once. The word "Ávasatha," which is old Persian as well as Sanskrit, means, not only "a peculiar religious ceremony," but a "fire-temple," or "place for sacred fire": and it is thus evident that fire-worship, of which there are several indications in the sculptures, was still a part of Buddhist ritual, in the fifth century of the Christian era: although Buddhist writers represent it as having been suppressed, and its votaries expelled, at the third synod; that is, according to Buddhist chronology, in the time of Asoka, six and a half centuries before the date of this inscription!

The epoch of these later "Gupta" princes—whose coins and inscriptions are numerous—has been satisfactorily ascertained to have commenced in A.D. 319: and this inscription, if dated in their era, is of A.D. 412 (see p. 102). It was carved, therefore, and Chandra Gupta of Magadha was reigning, when the Chinese pilgrim, Fa Hian, was travelling through India: but though Fa Hian visited Kanoj, which belonged to the Gupta territory, and, also, Pátaliputra, the capital of Magadha, he nowhere mentions the name of the reigning monarch.

The second Gupta inscription (also on the principal railing), is very badly cut; but has been satisfactorily read as recording the building of an alms-house, and donations for providing lights for the "shrines of the four Buddhas," by a female devotee, with the very Bráhmanical name of Hariswámini.

This, also, has a date; which, however, is variously rendered, by Prinsep and Cunningham. The former considered it *posterior* to the Chandra Gupta inscription just noticed ("Jour. As. Soc. Beng." VI. 459): and the latter reads it as between 264 and 314 A.D., if of the Sanvat era; or between 399 and 441 A.D., if of the Sáka era.

If it be dated in the "Gupta era," it would be of the seventh century.

As my transcript of this date differs, slightly, from Sir A. Cunningham's ("The Bhilsa Topes," 193, and Plate XXI., No. 198), I give a fac-simile of my own reading.

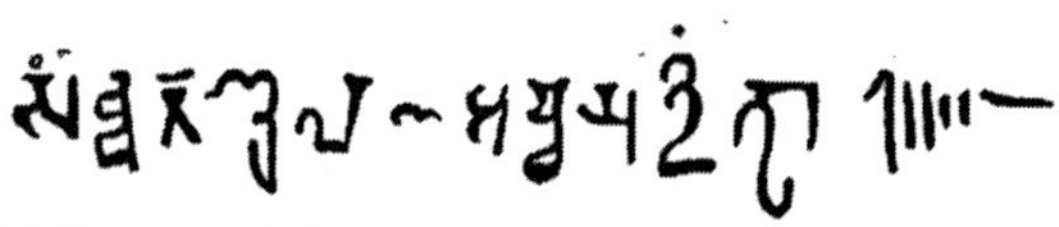

The third Gupta inscription is on the small detached pillar marked P, in Plate I. It reads—di hariswámi gosha sinha Valiputra: and appears, therefore, to be connected, as to date, with the second inscription. ("The Bhilsa Topes," 199.)

Kutila Inscriptions.

There are three inscriptions in the "Kutila" form of Nágari: two on the thrones or plinths of large images of Buddha; and one on the plinth of one of the small Sthúpas shown in Plate XV.

These inscriptions are not given by Sir A. Cunningham; and in the absence of my transcripts, and their translations, I am unable to particularize their details. This, however, is of the less consequence; as the character of the inscriptions is as recent as the eighth, or perhaps even the tenth century A.D.; and they appear to contain merely invocations to Buddha; commencing with the well-known formula, "Ye dharmma hetu prabhava hetun teshán tathágato," etc.; to which I have referred (p. 100, Note 1), as using the more modern term "dharmma," and not the older word "dharma," of the Páli inscriptions.

Inscriptions in ordinary Nágari.

The remaining inscriptions at Sánchi, six in number, are in varieties of the ordinary Nágari character.

The three oldest, carved on the enclosure of No. 1 Sthúpa, are identical: and read as follows:

Rá srí sáva deva praṇamati nitya:

a salutation, apparently, to the Bráhmanical Devas, generally; that is, to the "Viswa Devas."

The third inscription is on a Sati pillar; and is dated Sanvat 1321 (A.D. 1265). It contains the name Srímá; a divine name common to both Buddhists and Bráhmans: being that of the mother of Buddha, Maya, or Maya Devi; and of the Bráhmanical Srí or Lakshmí.

Sríma, or Sirima, appears, at Bharhut, as one of the guardian "devatás" of the enclosure to the Sthúpa (see "Stupa of Bharhut," 20, 22, 136).

A fifth Nágari inscription is on one of the pillars of the small detached temple marked T, in Plate I. It is dated Sanvat 1852; and inscribed, by Daṇḍa Náyaka, to "Srí nága buddhí."

This is the inscription, I conclude, which Captain Fell read as dated Sanvat 18.

The sixth inscription is undated. It is cut on a flat piece of rock, at the foot of the Sánchi hill; and contains, so far as I could make out, the words Sríma, Saktayah, Saktih, and Mitránandasya: which seem to point to a mixed Tantric and Mithraic worship: while the rude carving below it is of a Buddhist character. This is a mere outline sketch; representing two rather well-drawn elephants; each with a maháwat, and a monkey holding on behind. They support, with their trunks, a seat or throne; above which, but seated in the air, is a cross-legged, long-eared figure, with hands in his lap; like the common representations of Buddha: and with either a light robe, or the sacred Bráhmanical thread, over one shoulder.

In concluding this unavoidably imperfect chapter, I can but express my regret that, with the exceptions noticed, the Sánchi inscriptions have proved to be of so little historical value.

CHAPTER XII.

FUNEREAL RELICS; AND THEIR INSCRIPTIONS.

RELICS, or traces of their deposit, were discovered, by Sir A. Cunningham, and myself, in 1851, as follow:—

At Sánchi; in two out of eight Sthúpas; and in the chaitya-hall, marked R, in Plate I.

At Sonári; about six miles to the S.W. in two out of eight Sthúpas.

At Satdhára; about six and a half miles to the W.; in two out of seven Sthúpas.

At Bhojpur, or Pipliya Bijoli; about six and a half miles to the S.E.; in eight out of thirty-seven Sthúpas.

And at Ándher; about eleven miles to the S.E.; in each of three Sthúpas.

Full particulars of these "trouvailles," with translations of their accompanying inscriptions (which I have permission to make use of), will be found in "The Bhilsa Topes," pages 117 to 123, and 285 to 350; and Plates XX. and XXII. to XXX.

The principal Sthúpa at Sánchi yielded no relics: nor could we find any trace of a cell for their deposit: though we sank a shaft, five feet square, through the central brick-work, down to a point below the level of the basement terrace.

In No. 2 Sthúpa (E of Plate I.), however, we found numerous relics, of great interest.

Just to the west of the centre of the structure, and thirteen feet above the ground line, we came upon a chamber or cell, formed of six, uncemented, stone slabs; in which was a square covered sand-stone box; inscribed in Páli, as follows, on the side towards the east. (I have numbered the inscriptions, for reference.)

No. 1. Savina vináyakána aran Kásapa
Gotan upádaya aran cha Váchhá
Suvijayátan Vanáyaka.

Sir A. Cunningham translates this as follows ("The Bhilsa Topes," 286):

"Teacher of all branches of Vináya, the Arahata Kásyapa
Gotra, Upádiya (or Abbot); and the Arahata
Váchhi Suvijayata, teacher of Vináya."

The stone box contained a few fragments of calcined bone; and four small steatite caskets (which I have numbered I. to IV.); each containing calcined bone, and each inscribed, in Páli.

No. I. Casket (see "The Bhilsa Topes," pp. 287, 289, 290, and Plate XX., 1) has three inscriptions; outside and inside the lid, and on the bottom of the casket, respectively; viz.:

No. 2. Sapurisasa Kásapagotasa sava hemavatácharíyasa: that is, "(Relics) of the emancipated Kásyapagotra, the missionary to the whole Hemawanta."

No. 3. Sapurisa Majhimasa. "(Relics) of the emancipated Madhyama."

No. 4. Sapurisasa Háritíputasa. "(Relics) of the emancipated Háritíputra."

Kásyapa, who in No. 1 is called Upádaya, and teacher of Vináya, is mentioned in No. 2 as the Áchariya of the Hemawanta, or Himálaya region (see pp. 98 and 101, as to these two terms): and we found his relics at Sonári, also, with a similar inscription to No. 2; in which his patronymic is given as Kotiputa; that is, "the son of Koti." Relics of Majhima, or Madhyama were, also, found at Sonári; in the same Sthúpa as those of Kásapagota, Gotiputa, Kosikiputa, and Álabagira. He is there called Kodiniputa; i.e., "the son of Kodini," or Kohudinya, one of the eighty principal companions and disciples of Sákya Buddha.

Both Kásyapa and Madhyama—whose relics were thus found together, in two different places—were, according to the Buddhist Mahâwanso, among the five missionaries sent to the Hemawanta region, at the time of the third synod; which is said to have been held at Pátaliputra, in the reign of Asoka; about 300 years after the nirvána or death of Sákya Buddha: that is, according to the usual computation, B.C. 243! (See "The Bhilsa Topes," 118 to 123.)

Other relics of Háritíputra were found at Ándher; inscribed as the gift of Asa Deva, or Aswa Deva.

No. II. Casket, which is more elegant in shape than No. I., has two inscriptions; round the outside of the lid, one inside the other. (See "The Bhilsa Topes," 288 to 290), viz.:

No. 5. Sapurisasa Váchháya Suvijayátasa Gotatevásino; that is, "(Relics) of the emancipated Váchhá Suvaijayá, the pupil of Gota" (or perhaps Goti).

No. 6. Kákanava pabhásasáhana dana: that is, "The gift of Kákanava prabhásana.

Váchhá Suvijáyata was, evidently, an Arhata of equal importance with Kásyapa Gotra; as their names are conjoined on the outer stone box. We found no more of his relics, however: but, at Ándher, we found relics of Váchhiputa, a pupil of Gotiputa ("The Bhilsa Topes," 346); who seems to have been his son.

In the same Sthúpa, were found relics of Kákanava pabhásana, who is there called a son of Goti, and of the race of Kodini, or Kohudinya; and, also, relics of Mogaliputa, the pupil of Gotiputa (ib. 346 to 348).

Sir A. Cunningham is inclined to identify Kákanava pabhásana, with "Káka bhása"; who, according to the books of the Burmese Buddhists, was employed, by Asoka, to discover hidden relics, and superintend their enshrinement in a chaitya or dagopa (ib. 290).

No. III. Casket, which resembles No. II., has the two following inscriptions.

No. 7. (Outside lid.) Sapurisasa Mahavanáyasa Sapurisa Ápagírasa: that is, "(Relics) of the emancipated Mahavanáya and of the emancipated Ápagíra."

No. 8. (Inside lid.) Sapurisasa Koḍiniputasa. "(Relics) of the emancipated Kohuḍinya putra."

Mahávanáya, as a personal name, is unknown: but Sir A. Cunningham is inclined to identify Ápagíra with the Álabagira, whose relics were found—together with those of Majhima, Kásapagota, and Kosikiputa—in one of the Sonári Sthúpas.

Koḍiniputa appears, in one of the Sonári relic inscriptions, as the patronymic of Majhima, or Madhyama. (See "Bhilsa Topes," 271, 288, 290, 293 and 317.)

No. IV. Casket, which resembles No. I., has three inscriptions; outside and inside the lid, and underneath the casket respectively.

No. 9. Sapurisasa Kosikiputasa. "(Relics) of the emancipated Kausikiputra."

No. 10. Sapurisasa Gotiputasa. "(Relics) of the emancipated Gotiputra."

No. 11. Sapurisasa Mogaliputasa. "(Relics) of the emancipated Maudgalaputra.

Kosikiputa's relics were found, also, at Sonári; in the same Sthúpa as those of Gotiputa, Majhima, Kásapagota and Ápagíra. Gotiputa, that is, Gotiputra, "the son of Goti," is not mentioned, at any rate by that appellation, among the missionaries to the Hemawanta enumerated in the Mahâwanso; but the name appears on other relic caskets; not only, as just stated, at Sonári—where he is called the brother of religion amongst the Dhardabhisáras of the Hemawanta—but at Ándher, in three relic inscriptions; which represent him, respectively, as the teacher of Váchhiputa; as Kákanava pabhásana; and as the teacher of Mogaliputa.

Mogaliputa; i.e. Maudgalaputra, or the son of Mudgala; was, according to Buddhist writers, another name for Tishya, the son of the Bráhman Mudgala, and head of the third Buddhist synod, held at Pátaliputra, in the reign of Asoka; the result of which was the despatch of nine missions: some of whose members I have already mentioned. (See "The Bhilsa Topes," 115 to 123.)

His relics were, also, found at Andher; in the same Sthúpa as those of Vácchiputa, pupil of Gotiputa, and Kákanava pabhásana, son of Goti: and he is there, also, called a pupil of Gotiputa.

Mudgala, who, according to these inscriptions, and to Buddhist works, was the father of Mogaliputa, or Tishya, is mentioned, in the Váyu and Vishnu Puránas, among the five disciples of Veda Mitra, or Sákalya, one of the early teachers of the Rig Veda ("Vishnu Purána," 277, Note 8): and as the Vedas, to which such a fabulous antiquity has been assigned, are, at any rate, far older than any known Buddhist work or inscription, we may conclude that the Buddhists adopted the Bráhmanical name as that of one of their own sages. (See "The Bhilsa Topes," 120, 271, 272, 288 to 293, 316, 318, and 346 to 348.)

Relics in No. 3 Sthupa.

In No. 3 Sthúpa (F, in plan), exactly at the level of the basement terrace, we found a rectangular cavity covered by a stone slab six feet by three feet, lying north and south. Under this, embedded in the floor of the cell, were two massive stone chests:

that on the south inscribed, in old Páli characters, Sáriputasa, "of Sáriputra"; and that on the north inscribed Mahámogalánasa, "of the great Maudgalána."

Inside each chest was an elegant steatite casket; under a cover or saucer of black glazed earthenware, eight inches in diameter, and of very delicate manufacture.

The southern casket—near which lay two bits of sandal wood—had the Páli letter ᖷ, the initial of Sáriputa, written in some kind of ink, inside its lid: and contained a small fragment of bone, and seven jewels, evidently once strung as a necklace; viz. a piece of pearl, or mother-of-pearl, in the shape of a shell; two seed pearls; a lapis lazuli rosette or star; a ruby or garnet bead; a crystal bead; and an amethyst bead: probably representing, as suggested by Sir A. Cunningham, the "seven precious things," which it was customary to bury, with the ashes of holy persons.

The northern casket, had, written inside its lid, the Páli letter 8, the initial of Mahámogalána; and contained two small fragments of bone.

I have, elsewhere, pointed out that, in representations of the Buddhist triad, the central figure, or emblem of Buddha, is supported, on either side, by two other figures, or emblems; called, according to the intention of the group, "Dharma" and "Sangha," or "Bodhisatwas": and that various names are given to the latter; Sáriputra and Mogalána, among others. These two are called, emphatically, Buddha's right and left hand disciples, or Bodhisatwas: and as the central figure faces the east, the right hand supporter is on the south,(1) and the left hand supporter is on the north; which are the relative positions in which we found the relics of Sáriputra and Mahámogalána.

According to Buddhist writers, both Sáriputra and the great Mogalána were, like Buddha himself, of Bráhmanical descent: and both were converted from Bráhmanism to Buddhism, by the preaching of Sákya; whose principal, "right and left," disciples they became.

Sáriputra, according to Buddhist authors, was, also, named Upatisso, or Upatishya, after his father the Bráhman Tishya, "the most learned of all the Bráhmans at the court of Rájagriha": and his mother was Sárí, or Sáriká; so named from the resemblance of her eyes to those of the Sáras, or Indian crane.

"Tishya" was, apparently, a common name, among both Buddhists and Bráhmans. It was (see p. 110) given also to Mogaliputra, the son of Mudgala, and alleged contemporary of Asoka.

Fa Hian says that Sáriputra was born and died at Nalo, or Nalada, near Rájagriha; and he also mentions towers, or Sthúpas, in his honour, at Nalada and Mathura. (See "As. Res." XX. 52; Turnour's "Introd. to the Maháwanso," XXVII.; "Foe-Koue-Ki" (Laidlay's), Chap. XVI., Notes 16, 17; and XXVIII., Notes 6, 7, 8; and "The Bhilsa Topes," 297 to 305.)

Mahámogalána, i.e., the great Maudgaláyana, is the patronymic of Kálika, or Kolita; who—like Maudgaliputra—was, also, the son of a Bráhman named Mudgala see page 110); a coincidence which points to the probability that there has been some

(1) Dakshina, in Sanskrit, means both "the right hand," and "the south."

intentional falsification. Fa Hian mentions a tower in honour of Mogalána, at Mathura.

(See "As. Res." XX., 89; "Foe-Koue-Ki" (Laidlay's), Chap. XV., No. 18; and XXVIII., Note 10; "Vishnu Purána," 227, Note 8; and "The Bhilsa Topes," 297, 299, 300, 305, 306.)

Other relics of Sáriputra and Mahámogalána, inscribed with their names, were found in one of the Sthúpas as Satdhára.(¹)

The only other relic discovered at Sánchi, was a broken steatite covered vase, which I dug out of the *débris* of the chaitya at the curved end of the chaitya-hall (R, Plate I.).

The vase is without inscription; and any relics it ever held, had disappeared, save small bits of bone, and two crystal heads.

It had, evidently, been dug up before; and the relic chamber, if any, had been destroyed.

Besides the names already mentioned as occurring at Sánchi, and other adjacent places, on relic caskets; I must add two which we found, without the prefix Sapurisa, on small earthenware caskets in one of the Sthúpas at Bojhpur (see "The Bhilsa Topes," 335, 336); viz. "Patito" (or perhaps Patibho); and "Upahitaka." These are included in the following table; which I have prepared to show, in alphabetical order, all the names given in the relic inscriptions: with the places where they were found; and specifying those which refer to personages, whose relics were deposited.

No.	Uninflected Names as they appear in Pali.	Relics, where discovered.	Particulars given in the Inscriptions, and Remarks.
1	Álabagíra	Sonári ...	Supposed, by Sir A. Cunningham, to refer to the same person.
2	Ápagíra	Sánchi ...	
3	Asadeva (Aswa Deva)	... ...	Giver of the relics of Háritíputa (No. 6).
4	Goti	... ...	Teacher of Váchhásuvijayáta (No. 21), and father of Kákanava pabhásana (No. 7).
5	Gotiputa (Gotiputra)	Ándher ... Sánchi ... Sonári ...	Teacher of Váchhiputa (No. 22).

(¹) The French writer, M. Manupied, in his "Essai sur l'origine des principaux peuples anciens" (1844), put forward some curious speculations, tending to identify the ten principal disciples of Sákya Buddha with the patriarchs, and principal prophets of Biblical history: and compared Mogalána, or Moukian, with Moses!

The same writer discussed the "two grand epochs of Buddhism"; the first extending from the sixth century B.C., to the first century A.D.; and the second from the first century A.D. to the eighth century. In the second phase, which is the Buddhism of Sákya, the personal triad replaced the spiritual triad of the earlier phase: and it does not seem unreasonable to connect the triple group of Sákya and his two supporters, "on his right hand and on his left," with a Biblical source! There is no doubt that before the period when the custom arose, of associating two human attendants or Bodhisatwas with Buddha, the Christian writings were known to the learned in India: and there is, certainly, a marked resemblance, between the group of the deified Sákya Buddha between the two Bodhisatwas Mogalána and Sáriputra, and the description in the Gospels, of the glorified Saviour, at his Transfiguration, attended by his two supporters, Moses and Elias; the leading representatives of the "law" (Dharma), and "the prophets" (Sangha)!

No.	Uninflected Names as they appear in Pali.	Relics, where discovered.	Particulars given in the Inscriptions and Remarks.
6	Háritíputa (Háritíputra)	Ándher. Sánchi.	
7	Kákanava pabhásana (Kákanava Prabhásana).	Ándher ...	Giver of the relics of Váchhásuvijayáta (No. 21).
8	Kásapagota (Kásyapagotra) ...	Sánchi ... Sonári ...	Son of Koti (No. 12).
9	Kodini (Kohudinya)	... ...	Father of Majhima (No. 16).
10	Kodiniputa (Kohudínyaputra) ...	Sánchi. Sonári.	
11	Kosikiputa (Kausikiputra) ...	Sánchi. Sonári.	
12	Koti	... ...	Father of Kásapagota (No. 8).
13	Kotiputa (Kotiputra)	Sonári.	
14	Mahá Mogalána (Mahá Maudgaláyána).	Sánchi. Satdhára.	
15	Mahá Vanáya	Sánchi.	
16	Majhima (Madhyama)	Sánchi. Sonári.	
17	Mogaliputa (Maudgaliputra) ...	Ándher. Sánchi.	
18	Patito (Patitya)	Bhojpur ...	Translated, by Sir A. Cunningham, as "degraded." In my transcript, the word looks like "Patibho."
19	Sáriputa (Sáriputra)	Sánchi. Satdhára.	
20	Upahitaka	Bhojpur ...	Supposed, by Sir A. Cunningham, to have been a member of the local fraternity.
21	Váchháyasuvijayáta (Váchhásuvijayáta)	Sánchi.	
22	Váchhiputa (Váchhiputra) ...	Ándher.	

Several of the above names, Nos. 8, 14, 16, 17 and 19, occur as those of Buddhist celebrities in the Maháwanso and other Buddhist works: and could we be sure that these Sánchi relics were deposited in Nos. 2 and 3 Sthúpas, at the time of their erection, the discovery would be of special interest, as proving that these names were known, in Central India, at least three centuries before the date of the earliest Buddhist works which mention them. Indeed, at first sight, the existence of these relics, with their inscriptions in the old Páli character, seems to support the generally received theory as to the antiquity of the Buddhism of Sákya.(1)

(1) The date assigned, by Sir A. Cunningham, to these relic inscriptions, or, rather, to the missions to

The general arguments against this view will be more conveniently treated of in the next chapter; and I have already (p. 95) shown that the style of character in itself, is no proof of pre-Christian date. As regards the deposit of the relics, at Sánchi, there is, I think, at least a strong probability that they were brought—perhaps as already old relics—from elsewhere, to Sánchi; and were there enshrined in Nos. 2 and 3 Sthúpas, long after the Sthúpas themselves and their enclosures and gateways were constructed. In other words, it seems probable that the Buddhists who brought these relics to Sánchi, appropriated, as their relic shrines, buildings already ancient, and sacred in connection with the older form of worship.

We know that the earlier caves of India, which, it is generally allowed, were excavated by the followers of an old Mithraic religion, were appropriated successively, by the followers of Sákya, and by the Bráhmanical pantheists, who had preceded, and who finally ousted them: and we have an instance of this Buddhist appropriation of pre-existing buildings, in No. 1 Sthúpa, at Sánchi itself; which, at a date certainly long after its erection, was dedicated to the "four Buddhas," that is, to Sákya, and his three acknowledged predecessors, Kásyapa, Kanaka, and Krakuchanda.

Such appropriation of old shrines, and "holy places," was, indeed, a common practice in India—as it was in other countries—and has, often, led to confusion and misconception: and as to the removal of relics, from one place of deposit to another, often after long intervals of time, Buddhist history abounds with instances of it; and it has, frequently, been remarked upon by European writers. (See, among many others, "The Bhilsa Topes," 30, 99, 100, 290 to 292, and 307.)

In support of my view, I may point out that the relic chamber, of No. 2 Sthúpa, is not in the *centre* of the structure; which, we may fairly assume, it would have been had the building been constructed purposely to cover the relics: and secondly, that neither in the sculptures, nor in the inscriptions on the enclosing railings of Nos. 2 and 3 Sthúpas, is there any mention of, or allusion to, any deposit of relics; or any one of the names found in the *relic* inscriptions. It can scarcely be doubted that had the Sthúpas been *erected* as relic shrines, some allusion to the object of the structures, and to at least the leading personages commemorated, would have appeared in either the sculptures, or the inscriptions on the enclosures of the Sthúpas; or in both.

Finally, had Nos. 2 and 3 Sthúpas been originally erected as shrines for the relics of leading disciples of Sákya Buddha, it could only have been because the principal Sthúpa either contained his relics, or was, otherwise, expressly dedicated to him: and of this there is not the slightest indication.

On the contrary, it is clear that there were never any relics whatever in the principal Sthúpa; and there is nothing in either its sculptures or enclosure inscriptions, to show that there ever was, or ever was supposed to be, a relic deposit: while, as I have, elsewhere, pointed out, neither Sánchi nor any of the numerous

which they refer, is about the middle of the third century B.C.; that is, six or seven centuries prior to the earliest authenticated Buddhist books which contain allusions to missions.

names of places already adverted to, can be found mentioned in any of the Buddhist works which enumerate the places which possessed Sthúpas over the "Sarira" or mortal relics of Sákya; or Sthúpas commemorative of incidents in his career.

Exclusive of a few apparent allusions, in the sculptures of the principal Sthúpa, to Játakas, or previous incarnations of Buddha (see pages 35, 36, 49, 51, and 62 to 64), which were, not improbably, based upon Bráhmanical myths; the only direct indication of any connection of the main building with Sákya's worship, is in the reference made in the Gupta inscription of the early part of the fifth century A.D.; and even in that, the Sthúpa is not called the shrine of Sákya alone; but the shrine of the "four Buddhas," of whom he was the last.

How long *before* the date of this inscription the large Sthúpa was held sacred by the followers of Sákya Buddha, can only be conjectured; but it evidently became so sacred, between the date of the sculptured gateways and the date of the Gupta inscription; that is, between A.D. 37, and A.D. 412; and we may, therefore, assume that the deposit of relics in the more recent Sthúpas Nos. 2 and 3, was made as late as nearly the middle of the third century A.D. (see pp. 116, 117).

CHAPTER XIII.

THE AGE, AND PURPORT OF THE SANCHI STHUPAS; THEIR ENCLOSURES; AND GATEWAYS.

THE question of the age of the Sánchi Sthúpas, and their enclosures, is of importance, as connected with the nature of the religion which they indicate: as it can scarcely be doubted that such striking religious monuments must have been completed *soon*, and not long, after the spread of the form of worship represented.

All that can, with any certainty, be concluded, as to Nos. 2 and 3 Sthúpas, is that they are more modern than the principal Sthúpa, No. 1; from which they were evidently copied.

This is shown, in the case of No. 2 Sthúpa—which was quite complete in 1819 A.D.—by the general inferiority of its sculptures, more particularly the figures of men and women: by the ornamental style of the enclosing railing; which is transitional between the simple style of the large enclosure, and the highly ornate specimens at Bharhut and Amarávati: and by the perfect preservation of the uninjured portions of the main structure. . The character of its votive inscriptions, too, is, to some extent, indicative of a relatively modern date, as compared with that of the inscriptions of No. 1 Sthúpa: but this test, as I have elsewhere shown, is not, in any way, conclusive.(1)

In the case of the principal Sthúpa, however, we have something more than conjecture to go upon, both as regards its age and its purport; and what has been said, in previous chapters of this book, seems to me to justify the following conclusions.

Firstly. That there was, originally, a perfectly hemispherical Sthúpa, or Tumulus, probably entirely of brickwork; without basement terrace, superstructure, enclosure, relic-deposit, or anything whatever, apart from its symbolic shape,(2) to

(1) Sir A. Cunningham estimates the difference of age between the *enclosures* of Nos. 1 and 2 Sthúpas (as evidenced by their inscriptions) as 200 years; and considers that the Sthúpa itself was erected between 220 and 200 B.C. ("The Bhilsa Topes," 281, 291) As regards No. 3 Sthúpa, he dates the Sthúpa itself between 550 and 250 B.C.: its railed enclosure about the latter period; that is, the era of Asoka: and its sculptured gateway, in the first century A.D.; the same date as that of the large gateways, from which it was, evidently, copied (ibid. 296, 306, 307).

(2) This hemispherical shape is characteristic of the more ancient Sthúpas, and distinguishes them from the more elevated modern structures. It is said, in Buddhist works, to have been imitated from the air bubbles floating on the surface of water ("Mahâwanso," 175): but its original meaning, as seen from Egyptian and Assyrian examples, was a representation of the rising sun.

connect it with any particular form of religion: and certainly, without anything connected with Sákya's Buddhism.

Secondly. That a basement terrace was subsequently added; obviously for the purpose of circumambulation: a ceremonial which, though adopted by the Buddhists, was known to, and practised by their Bráhmanical predecessors; and was an essential feature in the ancient worship of the sun, and of fire as a type of the sun.

Thirdly. That either at, or after the time when this basement was added, the four-entranced, railed enclosure, was constructed; the form, and the inscriptions of which show that the religion then existing was closely allied to sun, fire, and elemental worship.

Fourthly. That, at a still later period, that is, after the Buddhism of Sákya had been mingled with the older faith, the hemispherical mound was truncated; and the top enclosures and crowning tís, or umbrella, were added. And that, in all probability, the outer stone casing, and plaster, of the Sthúpa, are of the same period.(1)

Fifthly. That the four sculptured gateways, which are clearly more modern than the main enclosure, were erected in the first century of the Christian era; the oldest between 19 and 37 A.D.; and the others very soon after: and that their sculptures and inscriptions prove that relic-worship, and some other features of the Buddhism of Sákya, were then *co-existent* with the older worship of the sun, fire, and elements generally.

Sixthly. That between the date of the sculptured gateways; and the commencement of the fifth century A.D., the building acquired a still more pronounced Buddhist character: by the addition, opposite the four entrances to the enclosure, of the four images of Buddhas; which, with their overshadowing canopies, are mentioned in one of the Gupta inscriptions, as "the shrines of the four Buddhas"; an indication that, even at that date Buddhism continued to be mixed up with the older pre-Sákyan faith; which other Sánchi inscriptions show to have been connected with fire-worship.

As regards the age of the principal Sthúpa, such high authorities as J. Prinsep, Sir A. Cunningham, and Fergusson, among others, favour the view that it was, originally, erected either in the time of Sákya himself, i.e. about 2434 years ago; or in the time of Asoka, as one of many Sthúpas erected by him after his conversion from Bráhmanism to Buddhism; i.e. about 2150 years ago!

There is nothing, in the construction or appearance of the building, to warrant its attribution to so remote a period as either of these dates; and, on the other hand, there are several reasons for believing it to be much more modern.

Had it been *originally* connected with Sákya Buddha, and his royal apostle Asoka, the connection would, surely, have been mentioned, or alluded to, in the local sculptures or inscriptions, and in the Buddhist works which profess to give the

(1) Sir A. Cunningham ("The Bhilsa Topes," 271), is also of opinion that the original Sthúpa was of brickwork; and thinks it may be as old as 500 B.C. Its stone casing was, he supposes, added as early as the time of Asoka (third century B.C.).

history both of Sákya himself, and of Asoka; but there is no such allusion; nor, as elsewhere observed, is Sánchi anywhere mentioned as one of the places where Sthúpas in honour of Buddha were erected. Even the Chinese travellers Fa Hian and Hwan Thsang, in the fifth and seventh centuries A.D., make no mention of any such structure; and though neither of them actually visited Sánchi, they must have heard of it, if it possessed a Sthúpa dedicated to Sákya, and believed to have been erected by the great Asoka.(¹)

Another theory, as to the age of the hemispherical mound, which was the original form of the largest Sánchi Sthúpa, is that this type of building was introduced by the Sacæ, Sáka, or Scythians, who succeeded the Græco-Bactrians, shortly before the Christian era; and to whose race Sákya belonged.

Professor Wilson said, regarding Topes, "Their prevalence, in all likelihood, originated with the establishment of the Indo-Scythic rule" ("Ariana Antiqua," 90, 91).

H. Prinsep, in his "Historical Results from Recent Discoveries in Afghánisthán," 120-122, said: "They seem to be of Scythian origin; and are, in all respects, analogous to the mounds and tumuli left, by invaders of the Scythian and Gothic races, in all parts of the world over-run or traversed by them."

This view, which is certainly much more in harmony than the preceding one, with the apparent age of these buildings, strongly supports the theory as to the date of Sákya's reform, advocated in this book; for it establishes a close synchronism between the epoch of the Scythian mound-builders, and the epoch of the (Scythian) Sáka Muni, or Sákya Buddha, the admitted originator of the relic-Sthúpa!

Be this as it may, however, there seems reason to believe that Sthúpas of some kind existed in India, before that type of building was adopted by the followers of Sákya, as the "dagopa," or *relic*-shrine. How long, before his time, such buildings existed in any part of India, can only be conjectured: but their existence is, at any rate, admitted by Buddhist writers themselves; who state that Sákya recognized and adopted them, and inculcated their continued worship.

Their use, in Central India, would, necessarily, have commenced some time later than in the north-western regions, where they were first introduced; and we have a limit for their antiquity in the fact that no buildings of the kind appear to have been seen by the all-observant Greek invaders of the fourth century B.C., who would certainly, have mentioned such curious structures, had any existed.

This kind of building, therefore, cannot have been introduced into the countries on the extreme north-west of India until some time after the Greek era: and if we allow a reasonable interval for its gradual spread, southwards, over India Proper, it seems safe to conclude that the *earliest* Sthúpas at Sánchi, whatever their nature and object, were not erected before 100 B.C.

The principal, or No. 1 Sthúpa, had its enclosure added between that period, and the completion of the structure by the four sculptured gateways; and these last were, it is now known, erected early in the first century A.D.

(¹) Hwan Thsang mentions at least fifty Sthúpas, which, he says, were attributed to Asoka; but Sánchi is not one of the places he names.

As to the meaning of Sthúpas, there has been almost as great variety of opinion, as there is respecting their antiquity. Some authorities have treated them exclusively as relic shrines; others as chief's tombs, afterwards dedicated to the deity worshipped by the deceased. Some, again, have regarded them, solely, as sacred structures, or temples, symbolizing the deity, and his emblem Mount Meru. Masson divided them into regal cenotaphs, and saints' or priests' tombs: Fergusson, again, also divided Sthúpas into two classes, viz., the sacred, and commemorative; and the relic Sthúpa: and, finally, Sir A. Cunningham, who has entered more fully into the subject, than any previous authority, classifies them as follows, in the light afforded by these Sánchi specimens.

1st. Religious edifices; dedicated either to the Celestial or Adi Buddha; or to one of his emanations, the "Mánushi" or mortal Buddhas: to which class he attributes the large Sánchi Sthúpa.

2nd. Funereal Sthúpas; erected over the relics of mortal Buddhas, or their disciples, and other ecclesiastics.

3rd. Memorial or commemorative Sthúpas; such as Mánikyála.

It is unnecessary to quote all the above varying views in detail: but full particulars of each will be found, as follows:—Wilson's and Masson's "Ariana Antiqua," 45, 90, 91; H. Prinsep's "Hist. Results," etc., 120, 123; J. Prinsep, "Jour. As. Soc. Beng." III. 570-572; J. Cunningham, Ibid. for August, 1847, 473; Fergusson's "Hist. of Ind. and East. Arch." 50, 62; and Sir A. Cunningham, "The Bhilsa Topes," 7 to 9, 12 to 14.

Some of the above-mentioned opinions are, it will be seen, too sweeping in their terms; applying one general definition to structures of several different classes; a confusion doubtless due to the often noticed resemblance between the emblematic Sthúpas, and the relic and funereal Sthúpas, which it was customary to group near them.

This resemblance, however, was not peculiar to Buddhism; but is noticeable in the ancient remains of Persia and Egypt, as well as in other parts of the world: and it is, to the present day, a characteristic of the monuments alike of the pantheistic Hindus, and the idol-hating Muhammadans.

The remains at Sánchi and adjacent places, belong to one or other of the classes enumerated above, viz.:—

1st. A central Sthúpa, which was originally dedicated to the sun, fire, and elements, of which the Celestial or Adi Buddha was a type; and was, subsequently, converted into a purely Buddhist temple. (Sthúpa No. 1.)

2nd. Smaller Sthúpas, round or near the principal one; which were, probably, in the first instance, also emblematic; but some of which were, subsequently, converted into relic Sthúpas, or shrines over the remains of celebrated Buddhist saints. (Sthúpas 2 and 3.)

3rd. More or less numerous minor Sthúpas; which, whatever their original purport, were, in several instances, found to contain relics of minor Buddhist personages.

Most of the opinions heretofore maintained, as to the age, and purport, of the Sánchi Sthúpas, have been largely, if not entirely, based upon the foregone conclusion that the èra of Gautama, commonly called Sákya Buddha, was between 623 and 543 B.C.: and that the dissemination, throughout India, of his reformed religion, three hundred years after his nirvána or decease, was the work of Asoka, or Priyadarsi; the Devánampiya Piyadasi of the láth and pillar edicts; and the grandson of Chandra Gupta Maurya of Pátaliputra.

This opinion rests upon the following propositions:

1. That Chandra Gupta Maurya, the ruler of Pátaliputra, is the Sandrocoptus of Pálibothra, mentioned by contemporary Greek historians of the fourth century B.C.
2. That Asoka, the grandson of this Chandra Gupta, according to both Buddhist and Bráhman writers, is the Devánampiya Piyadasi of the rock and pillar edicts; who adopted and promulgated a new faith.
3. That the religion so adopted and inculcated was the Buddhism of Sákya.

The first of these propositions, seems quite indisputable: but the second and third have long been contested, by eminent scholars; and are, I venture to think, still so open to question, as to be untenable, in the present state of our knowledge.

The second is, in fact, based, not so much upon anything contained in the edicts themselves, as upon statements in the "Dipawanso" of Ceylon, and other Buddhist works, and in the Bráhmanical Puránas: the earliest authentic dates of which, are in the fifth century A.D.; or about a thousand years after the epoch which they are held to fix!

The Páli edicts contain no mention of or allusion to the name or title "Asoka"; and no name at all, for their promulgator, save "Devánampiya Piyadasi," or Priyadarsi, the beloved of the gods; an essentially *un*-Buddhist appellation: while neither in the Buddhist Mahâwanso—the chief source of Buddhist history—nor in the Bráhmanical Puránas, is there any indication that Asoka was called Piyadasi, or by any name analogous thereto.(1)

As to the third proposition, that the edicts of Devánampiya Piyadasi refer to the Buddhism of Sákya; it was pointed out, in 1837, by their first decipherer, James Prinsep, that they contain no reference, whatever, either to the deified mortal Sákya, under any of his titles, or to his relics, or their worship.

He adds, "In another place I have rendered a final expression, 'agnim namisati,' 'shall give praise to Agni'; a deity we are hardly at liberty to pronounce connected

(1) Sir A. Cunningham, however, ("The Bhilsa Topes," 109), quotes the Cingalese Buddhist work, the "Dipawanso," as identifying Piyadasi with Asoka; and according to other Buddhist works, "Devánampiya Piyadasi" was the appellation of the ruler of Ceylon, when Buddhism was introduced there by Mahindo, or Mahendra, the son of Asoka: which is tantamount to saying that Ceylon was part of the Indian monarch's dominions.

The *title* "beloved of the gods" was, doubtless, common, among the Bráhmans, long before the time of Sákya; and may have been derived from the ancient Persians; whose kings had an analogous title. The Indian title "Devánampiya" may, also, be compared with the Assyrian royal title "Devenbar," which had a similar meaning.

with the Buddhist worship; *though points of agreement and harmony may be adduced.* But in any case, Agni, if rendered, generally, as god, keeps him distinct from Buddha, the teacher; of whose deification no evidence is afforded by the inscriptions: for neither is there any allusion to images of him, nor to temples or shrines enclosing his relics." ("Jour. As. Soc. Beng." VI. 569, 570.)

Professor Wilson considered it "doubtful, whether the edicts of Priyadarsi have any connection with Buddhism: the meaning of the inscriptions, to say the least, being equivocal."

He added, "There is nothing in the injunctions promulgated, that is decidedly and exclusively characteristic of Buddhism;" and remarked upon "the total omission of any allusion to Buddha himself; by any of his appellations, Sugata, Tathágata, Gautama, Sákya, or Sákya Sinha"; and upon the non-mention of "Sthúpas, Viháras, or Chaityas, or of the Bodhi, or Bo tree, everywhere else so freely adverted to."

The Professor further pointed out that the identification of Piyadasi with Asoka, rests upon the "Dipawanso" of Ceylon, "a work of rather doubtful character," written in the fourth century of the Christian era: and he remarked upon the inexplicable omission of the appellation Asoka, or Dharmasoka: and concluded by instancing against the identification, "chronological difficulties, of which it is not easy to dispose." (See "Jour. Roy. As. Soc." Vol. XII., Part I., pp. 236 to 244.)

In "The Bhilsa Topes," pp. 101 to 113, Sir A. Cunningham summarized under five heads, the above objections of Professor Wilson; and replied to them, seriatim: his counter arguments being, in effect, as follows:—

Firstly; That "Dharma," which is the key-stone of all the edicts, means, emphatically, the religious law of *Buddha.*

Secondly; That the term "Bhagavána," which occurs in the Kapurdigiri edict, "is almost peculiar to the Buddhists"; whereas the common Bráhmanical term is "Bhagavat." And that the Bhabra edict mentions all three members of the orthodox Buddhist triad, Buddha, Dharma, and Sangha."

Thirdly; That the "Dipawanso," though re-written, in Páli, by Buddha Ghosa, between 410 and 432 A.D.; was based upon the Cingalese version of the original Páli, compiled by Mahendra, the son of Asoka, and introducer of Buddhism into Ceylon: and that Mahendra, in his version, made use of the recorded discourses of Buddha, and the dissertations thereon, of Sári-putra and others.

Fourthly; That, at the date of the Piyadasi edicts, it was "the common custom, for a prince at least, to have two names." And that their promulgator used his own self-assumed name only; while in the annals written by others, he was called by the name "which he had always borne; and by which he was best known to the people."

Fifthly; That the minor difficulties of chronology mentioned by Professor Wilson, arose from the "erroneous assumption that Priyadarsi must have been a contemporary of Antiochus the Great"; whereas the learned of Europe have, generally, agreed that the "Antiyako" of the edicts refers to Antiochus Theos, of Syria, who flourished B.C. 262 to 247.

I cannot presume to discuss, generally, the conflicting arguments of two such high authorities: but, with reference to previous portions of this book, I venture to urge the following objections to some parts of these replies.

The term "dharma," which is that used in all the Páli edicts of which I have seen copies, and in every Páli inscription to which I have had access, is distinct, both in spelling, and in meaning, from the unquestionably Buddhist term "dharmma" (see pages 100, 101): and, as regards the terms "Bhagaván" and "Bhagavata," Sir A. Cunningham's own researches at Bharhut, have shown that the word commonly used by the *Buddhists* was Bhagavato or Bhagavata; and that it was expressly applied to Sákya Muni himself (see pages 60, 99).

The Páli term, used in the Bhabra edict, is, I believe, as it is in all the Páli inscriptions at Sánchi, "Budha," not "Buddha" (see pages 100, 101): and the two are, as elsewhere shown, quite distinct both in spelling and meaning. Its occurrence, therefore, in one of the Piyadasi edicts, does not, any more than does the use of "Dharma," *prove* that the religion indicated is that of Sákya Buddha!

As regards the use, in the edicts, of the title and name "Devánampiya Piyadasi," and the absence of the names Asoka or Dharmasoka; it seems, to say the least, improbable, that a monarch, just converted from Bráhmanism to Buddhism, and seeking to disseminate and popularize his new faith, should, instead of using his old and familiar name, use a new and unfamiliar one; and the improbability is all the greater, when we consider that the new title and name were of a *Brahmanical* character, and so calculated to recall the discarded faith; while the old names were in no respect opposed to the new religion!

The explanation seems to me to be, that "Devánampiya Piyadasi" was the old and the real, designation of the promulgator of these celebrated edicts: that, at their date, the Buddhism of Sákya had no existence: and that the Buddhist name and title, Asoka, and Dharma Asoka, were subsequent inventions; dating probably from the time when both Buddhist and Bráhman religious history were, purposely, falsified.

I may add, in conclusion, as an additional proof of the comparatively modern date of the Buddhist Asoka, that though used in both Buddhist and Bráhman literature—which, as before stated, dates from the fourth century A.D., *at earliest*—no such name appears in *any* of the more ancient inscriptions of India; nor has it, so far as I am aware, ever been found on any ancient Indian coin.

CHAPTER XIV.

THE MITHRAIC NATURE OF PRIMITIVE BUDDHISM: AND THE COMPARATIVELY MODERN DATE OF THE BUDDHISM OF GAUTAMA OR SAKYA.

In the foregoing chapters, I have stated such views, as to the nature and origin of the form of religion represented at Sánchi, as were suggested by the sculptures, symbols, and inscriptions, successively described.

Stated connectedly, the several conclusions to which the Sánchi remains originally led me; and which have been strengthened by such study of the subject as I have, since, had opportunities for, are as follow:—

I. That, in the sixth century B.C., the existing religion of the countries north-west of India Proper was either replaced, or largely modified, by the sun, fire, and elemental worship imposed on the conquered race, by the Persians.

II. That further modifications and innovations resulted from Greek influence, between B.C. 327 and 57: and that the Sákas, or Scythians, who entered India, by the Indus route, about the latter date, and eventually ousted the Greeks from Bactria, adopted, with modifications of their own, the deities and symbols which had been engrafted on the old local mythology, by the Persians and Greeks.

III. That this composite system, of sun, fire, and elemental worship, mingled with some features of the primitive local religion, spread, gradually, southwards, through India: and was the "old," or former, religion—the "budha-dharma"—which is represented, by Buddhist writers, as the worship of "former Buddhas"; namely the Bhagavatas Krakuchanda, Kanaka, and Kásyapa; the predecessors of the Bhagavata Sákya Muni; that is, of Gautama, the "Buddha" of the books; the deified mortal, Prince Siddhártha; variously named Sugata, Tathágata; and, from his Scythian origin, Sákya Muni, and Sákya Sinha, the sage, and the lion of the Sáka tribe.

IV. That the so-called "Buddhism of Sákya" was a reform of the old sun, fire, and elemental worship; and of its priestly, and other abuses: but that it retained, for a time, many of the old observances and symbols.

V. That this reformed religion, which, eventually, borrowed largely from the Bible, and other foreign sources, and in which the enshrinement of relics became a prominent feature, arose, or at any rate was widely adopted, in the valley of the Ganges, about, or perhaps shortly before, the commencement of the Christian era: and *not*, as has been asserted, on the authority of comparatively recent Buddhist works, in the sixth century B.C.

Before I discuss these several propositions, I would remark that many allusions, in ancient authors, to the worship of fire, should, apparently, be regarded as referring, equally, to sun-worship: the two cults having, anciently, been identical. The word "pur"—the root of pyramid—though now read as "fire" only; was, in its true, and original sense "the sun"; both in Greek and Egyptian. (See O'Brien's "Round Towers of Ireland," 148; Notes on Sir H. Elliot's "Historians of Muhammadan India," in the *Calcutta Review*, No. XXIV. p. 383; and Thomas's "Sáh Kings of Saurāshtra," 26, 27, and Note 4.)

In the Bráhmanical Puránas, we find "Pur" as synonymous with "Bhava," the sun; and, also, with Íswara, and Mahat; both of which terms were adopted by the Buddhists, as titles of the supreme, or celestial, Ádi Buddha; the embodiment of spirit, light, intelligence, and mind.(1)

In the Váyu and Vishnu Puránas, the association, as objects of worship, of the sun and fire, and their mutual connection, is the subject of the following explanation:—

"The radiance of the solar orb, when the sun has set, is accumulated in fire; hence fire is visible at a greater distance by night than by day: and during the latter, a fourth of the rays of fire blend with those of the sun; and, from their union, the sun shines with greater intensity by day." (Wilson's "Vishnu Purána," 220, and Note 9; and "Rig Veda Sanhitá," 247, Note *b*.)

I. Professor Wilson ("Ariana Antiqua," 124) says, regarding the Indian conquests of the Persians, "Isfandiyár, son of Gushtasp (Darius Hystaspes), the contemporary of Zoroaster, invaded India; and compelled the Hindús to acknowledge his father's supremacy, and conform to his religious faith." And the old writers, whose statements he follows, have since been corroborated by the inscriptions of Darius, at Behistun; which mention India as one of the nations subject to Persia. (Sir H. Rawlinson, in the "Jour. Roy. As. Soc." X. 280, 282.)

Ferishta, the Persian historian, of Akbar's time, appears to allude to this suppression or modification of the local Indian faith, when stating that "some centuries prior to Vikramáditya, the Hindús abandoned the simple religion of their ancestors; made idols, and worshipped the host of heaven." (Tod's "Rájasthán," I. 219.)

II. The figures and symbols of the Persian Ahuramazda and Mithras (themselves derived from Assyria) merged into the Pur, Helios, and Mithras, seen on the Græco-Bactrian coinage: and these were, in turn, adopted, and further modified, by the Indo-Scythic successors of the Greeks: assuming, eventually, the composite forms found in the coinage and sculpture of the Bráhmans, Buddhists, and Jainas.

The gradations and transitions are clearly traceable, in the coinage and sculpture found in various parts of India (see Chapter X.); and nowhere more

(1) "Bhava," and "Mitra" are both titles of the Bráhmanical sun-god "Súrya": who is called, also, in the Puráuas, "fire, and the moon"; "the impersonation of the mystic Om;" "the eye of the universe;" all of which epithets are, also, applicable to Buddha; who combines the attributes of Súrya, Agni, Soma, Vishnu, and "Mahat," or embodied intelligence.

strikingly than in Afghánisthán and the Panjáb; more particularly in the region, between Swát and the Indus, anciently called Gandhára; where the oldest, best executed, and most Greek-looking Buddhist figures have been found.

III. The close connection between what has been called "primitive Buddhism," and sun, fire, and elemental worship, is proved,—

Firstly: by the indications of such worship, in the Sánchi sculptures, in juxtaposition with the worship of other objects which are, admittedly, associated with the Buddhism of Sákya.(1)

Secondly: by numerous allusions, in the Sánchi inscriptions, to sun and fire worship; and by the frequent use, therein, of sacred terms, which, however common in Buddhism, are equally, if not more common, in Bráhmanism; and indicative of a foreign, Mithraic origin. (See pp. 9, 11—13, 21, 29—40, 46—52, 59—62, 68, 71, 73, 82—93, 98—101, 117.)

Thirdly: by the universal use, in sculpture and on coinage, long recognized as Buddhist, of Mithraic figures, attributes, and symbols.

Fourthly: by the manifestly Mithraic character, and origin, of many of the names and titles given to Gautama, or Sákya, and to his predecessors as Buddha. (See pp. 27, 28, 46, 80, 83, 87, 99, 101, 124.)

Fifthly: by the evidence of Buddhist literature, itself. (See pp. 17, 31, 45, 49.)

In addition to the many illustrations, under this head, given in other chapters, I may mention the following:—

The discovery, many years ago, near Kábul, of a figure of Buddha, with flames rising behind him. ("Jour. As. Soc. Beng." III., Plate 26, Fig. 1.)

The common representation of Buddha as crowned by triple, or quintuple, jets of flame. (See Coleman, "Hind. Myth.," Plate 29, Figs. 4, 5.)

The description, in the Maháwanso, of a figure of Buddha, shown by the Nága King, to Asoka and his Court, as "surrounded by the halo of glory, and surmounted by the lambent flame of sanctity." The occurrence, on the pedestals of Buddhist figures, from Gandhára (now in the Lahore Museum), of various forms of "fire-altars," in conjunction with the Mithraic wheel, and "disc-and-crescent": and, the discovery, in some of the older Ceylon Sthúpas, in association with figures of Buddha and the Nága, of obeliscal stones, such as are known to have been symbolical of the solar ray, and its product, fire.

IV. That sun and fire worship was a characteristic of the form of religion *antecedent* to Sákya's Buddhism, needs, I think, no further illustration: and as regards the reformed system of Sákya, we learn from Buddhist writers themselves, that the founder of their sect encountered, and subdued the "great fire spirit" or "fiery dragon"; and converted, and admitted into his community, many fire-worshippers. We are also told, on like authority, that the worship of fire, and the

(1) Compare my Plates IV.; VIII.; XIII., Fig. 2; and XXVI.; with those of Sir A. Cunningham's "Stupa of Bharhut," Plates XIII., Fig. 3; XXXI., Fig. 2; and XXXIV., Fig. 4.

There are, also, as shown in my descriptive notes, other indications of fire-worship, which are not given in my illustrations.

sun, was not formally excluded from Buddhist ritual, until three centuries after Sákya's death.

In Sákya's time (the *date* of which is a separate question) there were, as pointed out in "The Bhilsa Topes" (pp. 16 to 20, and 36, 37), two great sects of religionists, in India; the Bráhmans, and their opponents, the Swástikas. The former followed the old Mithraic idolatry; and believed in the immortality of the soul, after purification by a long succession of earthly transmigrations; while the latter taught that the soul's existence is "finite; and limited to its connection with the body."

Sákya is said to have tested, and successively rejected, both these systems; and in their place to have preached a new faith, which, while adopting, in a modified form, some of the features of both, had for its leading dogmas, "morality, charity, abstinence, and the more speedy attainment of Buddhahood; with the abolition of caste, and of the hereditary priesthood." He also, it may be added, instituted "relic-worship"; and—to quote Sir A. Cunningham—"either invented, or adopted, the theistical triad of Buddha, Dharma, and Sangha; in which triad, Buddha, or 'supreme intelligence,' is the creator of all things."

Then, following Brian Hodgson, Sir A. Cunningham adds, "In the transcendental and philosophical sense, Buddha means mind; Dharma, matter; and Sangha, the concretion of the two former in the sensible or phenomenal world. In a practical or religious sense, Buddha means the mortal author of this religion (Sákya); Dharmma, his law; and Sangha, the congregation of the faithful."

In other words, Sákya engrafted a reformed system upon that previously in popular favour: retaining, and adapting, partly out of former reverence, and partly from motives of policy, old forms of sacred buildings, and the names, triad, symbolism, and some of the rites and ceremonies of the older cults: and inculcating the worship, as relic-shrines, of the Sthúpas, which, apparently, had previously been sacred as emblematic structures.

It is, apparently, this earlier, and semi-Mithraic Buddhism, which is represented at Sánchi. Its *later* phase, such as we find it in Buddhist literature; in the sculptures of Amarávati; and in other comparatively modern sculptures and coins; shows, besides other corruptions, a progressive recurrence to the pantheism which had preceded it: and this explains the striking analogies, in the latest, as well as in the earliest Buddhism, to the old Mithraic worship: and the many illustrations afforded by Buddhism, in common with Bráhmanism, of the often-repeated remark, long ago made by Sir Wm. Jones, that most mythological deities mean, merely, "the powers of nature, and principally the sun; expressed in a variety of ways, and by a multitude of fanciful names."

J. Prinsep remarked, as follows, on this point:—"It is not surprising, that, on the Indian side of the Persian monarch's dominions, we should find the fire altar and the image of the sun, replaced by Krishna among the Hindus, and Buddha among the Buddhists: both of them personating the sun, in their respective mythologies." ("Jour. As. Soc. Beng." VI. 455; and IX. 850).

All the infinitely varied forms of the "sun-god," had a common origin in the primeval myths of the Akkadians, Assyrians, and Babylonians; which embodied the earliest corruptions of Biblical traditions: and the primitive "Budha" of India, besides combining the characteristics of various more ancient divinities, was invested with many Biblical traits. Hence it is that Buddha has come to be identified, by different writers, with so many sacred, and mythical personages: with the Biblical Noah, Nimrod, and Moses; with the Assyrian Bar, Bel or Baal, Nebo, and Sver or Sur; with the Egyptian Sur, or Osiris, Noub or Noum, Thoth, and Sesostris or Sheshak; with the Persian Auramazda, Bhaga, and Mithras; the Greek Dionusos, Iacchos or Bacchus, Pur, Hermes, Helios, and Mithras; the Bráhmanical Pur, Súrya or Mitra, Bhaga, Bhava, Budha, Agni, Indra, Jagannáth, and Krishna; and the Scandinavian and Mexican Woden or Votan!

The identity of the earlier "Budha" of India with Mercury or Hermes the Roman and Greek representatives of the Egyptian Taut, or Thoth—is not only indicated by the resemblance of their symbols, if not of their names (see p. 87), but by their parentage. The Egyptian Hermes (Thoth) was the son of Osiris by Maya: Mercury was the son of Jupiter (the Vrihaspati of Brahmánical mythology) by the Pleiad Maia: and Buddha, the deified son of Suddhodhana Súryavansi, was also the son of Maya.(1)

Then, again, we have the significant fact that Mercury, Budha, Woden, and the Mexican Votan, were all worshipped on the same day of the week, the middle day, Wednesday! (2)

Sir A. Cunningham, in noticing some of these "numerous and striking" coincidences, further compares Buddha (who is called "Bhaga," the dispenser, or distributor; see p. 99), with the ancient Welsh deity "Buddwás," called "the dispenser of good." ("The Bhilsa Topes," Pref. vi.-viii.)

Among many other points of resemblance between Buddha, and the Bráhmanical sun-god, Súrya, Aditya, Bhaga, Bhava, or Mitra, one of the most striking is that figures of Buddha (as well as those of Jaina Tirthankaras) often have below their thrones, or cars, the single wheel which, in representations of Súrya, is his chariot-wheel. The shape of this is as shown in Fig. 17 of Plate XL.; and its Sanskrit name, "bhámandala," means a circle, crown, or diadem of light; or a garland of solar rays.

Professor Wilson, in his notes to the "Vishnu Purána" (p. 218, Note 5), says: "In images of the sun, two equal and semi-circular axles connect a central wheel with the sides of the car": and the Purána itself describes it as "a wheel with

(1) According to the Bráhmanical Púranas, the planetary "Budha," or Mercury, is the ninth avatára of Vishnu; and the illegitimate son of Soma, the moon, by Tára (a star), the wife of Vrihaspati, the Indian Jupiter. The object of the incarnation was to beguile the too-powerful Daityas from their pure Vedic worship; and thus to secure their defeat by the gods. ("Vish. Purán." 340, 341, Note 8, and 393.) The legend is a clumsy allusion to the rise of the Buddhist and Jaina sects.

(2) The learned Humboldt, in an unpublished letter, quoted in the "New York Weekly Tribune" of 22nd October, 1853, said, "certainly the coincidence of the naming of the third day of our week, after Votan, Woden, and Buddha, in three different parts of the world, is a very interesting one; and it seems to be about time to get some critical insight into the matter."

three naves, five spokes, and six peripheries; consisting of the ever-during year: the whole constituting the circle or wheel of time." (Ibid. p. 217, Note 3.)

I have, elsewhere, traced this single chariot-wheel from the simple disc, which, before the use of images, represented the luminary itself; rays or spokes being added, to convey the idea of rapid motion (pp. 39, 40): and I have, also, noticed the connection of the five-rayed wheel, with the five-rayed star of Egypt, formed by the intersection of two, triple-pointed, arrow-heads. (See Fig. 24, Plate XXXIX.)

On some of the Bactrian coins, noticed in chapter X., which are classed as Buddhist, the single-wheeled chariot of the sun-god appears; and the occupant of the car—perhaps the king, with the costume, and attributes of the deity—closely resembles some of the common representations of Súrya. Compare, for instance, the figures, attitude, and accessories on the coins (Figs. 6, 7 of Plate XXXIX.) with those of the Súrya shown in Fig. 8 of Plate XL.

The explanation of the very *un-Indian* appearance of such figures, is, doubtless, that both Bráhmans and Buddhists originally invested their deity with the dress of the people from whom they derived him: like the Greeks; who, as we learn from Hyde, always represented their god Mithras, in the costume of a Persian king; that is, with boots, or leggings, and other peculiarities. (See Prinsep, and quotations from Hyde, and Guignaut, in the "Jour. As. Soc. Beng." III. 450, 452.)

The Buddhists, who, eventually, discarded the direct worship of fire, which had once formed part of their ritual, also discontinued, at any rate for a time, many other Mithraic rites, figures, and symbols: but the Bráhmans have retained the old forms and symbols to the present day; and their booted figures of the sun-god, still recall its Persian origin. As in the case of "Jagannáth," elsewhere noticed, an absurd legend attempts to explain the peculiarity, in figures of "Súrya," which denotes his foreign derivation. (See my Plate XL., Figs. 7 and 8.)

The Vishnu Purána (p. 267, Note 3) says, "To diminish his intensity, Viswakarma placed the luminary on his lathe, to grind off some of his effulgence; and, in this manner, reduced it an eighth—for more than that was inseparable. . . . . The Matsya Purána says, he trimmed the sun everywhere, except in the feet; the extent of which he could not discover. Consequently, in pictures, or images, the feet of the sun must never be delineated, under pain of leprosy." From the portions of "the divine Vaishnava splendour, residing in the sun," thus filed off, were formed the "chakra," "trisula," and other weapons or symbols; which were sacred among both Bráhmans and Buddhists; and, like the figures of the deity themselves, derived from a foreign source.

I cannot attempt a detailed examination of the numerous points of analogy, between Budha, the Indian Súrya or Mitra, the Græco-Persian Mithras, and other solar impersonations; whose common prototype was the ring-encircled figures of the supreme deity of Assyria. I can only, again, urge; and I have, I think, shown, much ground for the argument, that the representations and attributes of the Indian Budha, correspond, strikingly, with those of very many other deities of an admittedly Mithraic character, and of the highest antiquity: and that, such being the case, it is at least more probable, that the primitive Buddhists of India adopted the ancient figures and symbols which had been handed down to them, than that such widely separated races as the Assyrians, Persians, Egyptians, and Greeks should, successively, have borrowed ideas and figures from India!

V. The new, composite, religion introduced by Sákya about the commencement of the Christian era, eventually required, for its prestige and success, a fictitious antiquity: and, in the Buddhist books which tell us all we know about the subject, we find plentiful indications of a concocted chronology. Indeed, many European scholars have characterized Buddhist sacred history, as even more untrustworthy than that of the Bráhmanical Purånas!

Even as regards the all-important epoch of the nirvâna of Sâkya, Buddhist writers, themselves, have dated it, variously, from 1336 B.C.—or even earlier—to 300 B.C.: while Muhammadan authors, who, of course, had no inducement to falsify Buddhist chronology, give it dates of B.C. 76 and B.C. 7.(¹)

As even the *earliest* of the Buddhist books, whence the above discrepant dates are derived, cannot be conclusively shown to be older than the fourth—or perhaps fifth—century, of the Christian era, it must, I think, be admitted, that they are scarcely a reliable authority for the date of an event, which, according to the ordinarily accepted chronology of Buddhism, occurred about a thousand years before any of them were written!

How far the compilers of Buddhist religious history were cognizant of the history and myths of other nations, can only be conjectured: but it is, at least, worthy of notice that the commonly received era of Gautama, or Sákya Buddha, is synchronous with the following events and epochs; all more or less connected with India, and depending upon other than Buddhist data.

1. The reformation of the Mithraic religion in Egypt; and the flight, thence to India, of a Magian priest; in the time of the Persian Cambyses. (Maurice, "Ind. Ant." II. 305; and "Anc. Hist. of Ind." II. 480; and Kæmpfer's "Japan," I. 38.)
2. The defeat, by Darius, of the Magian Gomates Bardius—or Gomata Badiya—who had usurped the Persian throne, during the expedition of Cambyses to Egypt: and the prohibition of certain rites instituted by Gomata. ("Jour. Roy. As. Soc." X. 200-206; and "West. and For. Quart. Rev." April, 1850, 42-44.) The names "Comata Badiya," are suggestive of a Páli imitation in "Gotama Budha"; but the connection is not very apparent.
3. The invasion of Upper India, by the Nâga, Takshaka, or serpent race: that is, the sun and fire worshippers, who preceded Sákya's reform; and, doubtless, gave rise to the common designation of his sect as "followers of the serpent." (Tod's "Rájasthán," I. 57.)

(¹) See, as to these discrepant dates, "Jour. Roy. As. Soc." VI. 23, 27, 318, 319; Laidlay's "Travels of Fa Hian," Chapters XXIV., Note 4; XXVI., Note 4; XXXII., Notes 1, 2; and XXXVIII., Note 19; Spence Hardy's "Eastern Monachism," 173; Rhys Davids' "Buddhism," 212; Sir A. Cunningham's "The Bhilsa Topes," 73 to 75; Sir E. Perry's "Bird's-eye View of India," 52-54; and the works of Rashíd-ud-din, and Al-Masudi, elsewhere quoted.

This refers, primarily, to the Persian invasion, in the time of Darius, already alluded to as the source of the earlier Buddhism: but, in Buddhist, as in Bráhmanical garbled history, it is a common thing to find several separate incidents or personages classed as one; and there is probably, an allusion, also, to the much more recent inroads, some 500 years later, of the Sákas, or Scythians, the race to which Sákya himself belonged.

4. The era, according to Pinkerton—ap. Torfœus—of the Scythian invader, and reformer, Woden or Odin. (Tod's "Rájasthán," I. 57, 64.)

The date of Odin's invasion of Scandinavia is, by some authorities, given as B.C 70; which tallies with the *modern* date which I have assumed for Sákya.

5. The epoch of the Chinese philosopher and reformer Confucius.
6. The generally accepted era of Zoroaster; the reformer, if not the founder of the Persian Magian religion; and the reputed author of the Zend Avesta; who is said to have resided at Babylon, during the Jewish captivity; and to have there acquired the Biblical knowledge which characterizes parts of the Zend Avesta.

Possibly, we may trace, to this source, some of the Old Testament resemblances observable in both Buddhism and Bráhmanism.

7. Lastly, the ancient date assigned to Buddha corresponds with that given, by Hindú astronomers, to the Mahábhárata, or "great war"; that is, between 575 and 540 B.C.

The date of the "Mahábhárata," however, is as much a "vexed question" in Bráhmanical history, as is that of the "Nirvána," in Buddhist history: and it has been variously stated at periods between the fourteenth century B.C., and the twelfth century A.D.

The poem mentions both the Greeks and the Scythians; and must, therefore, have been composed after the appearance, in India, of the latter; that is, after the commencement of the Christian era: and, on the other hand, it must have been in existence for a considerable time before A.D. 1030; as, according to Al-Masudi, who wrote in that year, it was then, already, a standard work in India.(1)

The true date of the work is of special importance, in regard to the history of Sákya's Buddhism: as there seems no reason to doubt that it describes, in mythological style, the prolonged contests between the Buddhist reformers, of Sákya's sect, represented by the Pándavas and Krishna; and the Bráhmanical Kurus, or Kauravas: an idea first, I believe, started by Dr. Bird. These contests, though dated, in the concocted histories, as far back as the sixth century B.C., really commenced soon after the rise of the new sect of Buddhists, and the establishment of the Indo-

(1) For various dates for the "Mahábhárata," and speculations as to its historical allusions, see Reinaud's "Fragmens Arabes et Persans, relatifs à l'Inde," 100; Sykes, in the "Jour. Roy. As. Soc." VI. 438; Bentley's "Hindu Astronomy," 90, 91; Wilson's "Aria. Antiq." 197; and Preface to "Vishnu Purána," iii., ix., and lviii.; Sir Stamford Raffles' "Hist. of Java"; Prichard's "Phys. Hist. of Man," IV. 101, *et seq.*; Coleman's "Myth. of the Hindus," 250; "Jour. As. Soc. Beng." IX. 856, 858; and No. 1 of 1850, 18; and "The Bhilsa Topes," 136, 137.

Scythic rule: that is, about the commencement of the Christian era: and they lasted for several centuries, with varying success; the final result being the expulsion of the Buddhists from India; and their migration to Tibet; where, we learn from independent testimony, Buddhism was introduced in the seventh century A.D.

I have already quoted the "Jami-ul-tawárikh" of Rashíd-ud-dín, as giving about 75 B.C. as the date of Sákya Buddha. Another Muhammadan writer—Al-Masudi—affords us further information as to a slightly later period, by the statement that schism in the Hindu religion occurred in the time of "Korish" (perhaps a corruption of Krishna), 320 years after the death of Porus; that is, about 7 B.C.

According to Professor Wilson, "the Buddhist heresy prevailed in the Punjáb, soon after, if not shortly before, the Christian era." And, as regards the contemporaneous Scythians, to whose race he elsewhere assigns Sákya Muni, he says, "By the first century A.D., the Scythians had wrested the country along the Indus, from the Greeks; and Scinde was called Scythia." ("Ariana Antiqua," 197, 211, 213.)

Krishna, though, like Buddha, placed back, in his purposely falsified history, to the sixth century B.C., was not really added to the Bráhmanical pantheon until after A.D. 600; which is his date, according to his horoscope: and we have further proof of his being an invention of a later period, in the significant fact that there is no allusion to him in the works of the observant Chinese travellers Fa Hian and Hwan Thsang.

The mention of Krishna, in the Mahábhárata, is a further indication that, whatever the events related, the poem itself is as recent as the seventh century A.D.: about which time, according to Bentley, and other authorities, "the avatárs of Vishnu, and especially Krishna, and parts of his history, were invented, as an offset to the incarnation and history of our Saviour" . . . Krishna being "placed back, in the new works, as a contemporary of Yudhishthira, to give him the prestige of antiquity, and to preclude investigation." ("Hindu Astronomy," 90, 91.)

It seems to me, on a consideration of the above various data, that they fortify the general conclusion, that the Buddhism of Sákya was introduced into India—*viá* Sindh and the Panjáb—about, or shortly before, the commencement of the Christian era: that it was, originally, a comparatively simple and pure form of religion, largely mixed up with Mithraic features: and that it gradually changed its character, until it assumed the complex form presented in the Buddhist works written four or five centuries after its first introduction.

Finally, I have to consider the evidence, as to the comparatively modern date of the Buddhism of Sákya, which is derivable from purely literary sources. This may be summarized as follows:

Firstly: There is no mention of, or allusion to, any of the usual names or titles of Buddha, or any Buddhist structures, sculptures, symbols, or rites, in *any* work, Greek, Persian, or Indian, older than the Christian era: while such allusions are frequent, and unmistakable, in both Christian and pagan writings of later dates.

Secondly: The only Buddhist books which contain particulars of the history and tenets of Sákya Buddha, though said to be, in some instances, based upon ancient oral traditions, are, themselves, of dates at least a thousand years posterior to the usually accepted era of Sákya.

Thirdly: Even these Buddhist works are utterly discordant as to the date they are supposed to establish.

Fourthly: The history and adventures of Sákya Buddha, as related in these books, besides containing many resemblances to various pagan legends—some ancient, and some post-Christian—show a large admixture of Biblical incidents, from both the Old and the New Testaments; and of early Christian legends: which proves that a knowledge of *Christianity* existed, in India, when the history of Sákya was written.

Fifthly: The local literature of China, Ceylon, Burmah, Tibet, and other countries where Buddhism, as taught by Sákya, still prevails, shows that it was introduced, from India, at various dates; all of which are *subsequent* to the Christian era.(1)

All this is consistent with the theory that Sákya's reformed Buddhism arose, in India, about, or, at earliest, shortly before, the commencement of the Christian era: and is *inconsistent* with the theory of its having so originated as far back as the sixth century B.C.

As an appropriate conclusion to this chapter, I quote the following remarks, by Mr. Brian Hodgson; one of the best-known Indian writers on the subject of Buddhism. In the sixth volume of the Bengal Asiatic Society's Journal, after describing the Buddhism of Sákya, as a reformation of an older religion, and an opposition to its priestcraft, and other abuses, he said:

"I can trace something very like Buddhism, into far ages and realms: but I am sure that that Buddhism which has come down to us in the Sanskrit, Páli, and Tibetan books of the sect, and which only, therefore, we do or can *know*, is neither old nor exotic.

"That Buddhism (the doctrines of the so-called seventh Buddha), arose in the middle of India, in comparatively recent times; and expressly out of those prior abominations which had long held the people of India in cruel vassalage to a bloated priesthood.

"The race of Sáka, or progenitors of Sákya Sinha, may have been Scythians,

(1) The following dates—some based upon very questionable authority, have been assigned to the spread of Buddhism, as now known to the several countries indicated: its primary source, in each case, being India:—

Java; 10, 24, and 57 A.D.—(Prinsep's "Useful Tables"; Raffles' "Java," II. 69; and "Foe-Koue-Ki," Chapter XL., Note 4.)

China; 60-62 A.D.—(Rhys Davids' "Buddhism," 241; and "Foe-Koue-Ki," Chapter VII., Note 5.)

Corea; 372 A.D.—(Rhys Davids' "Buddhism," 242.)

Ceylon; 420-430 A.D.—(Rhys Davids' "Buddhism," 13; and Spence Hardy's "Eastern Monachism," 1.)

Japan; 552 A.D.—(Rhys Davids' "Buddhism," 242.)

Nepál; sixth century A.D.—(Rhys Davids' "Buddhism," 247.)

Tibet; 632 A.D.—(Rhys Davids' "Buddhism," 247.)

or Northmen, in one sense: and so, probably, were the Bráhmans, in that same sense; namely, with reference to their original seat.

"If one's purpose and object were to search, backwards, to the original hive of nations, we might, as in consistency we should, draw Bráhmanism and Buddhism, Vyása and Sákya, from Tartary.

"All I say is, that *quoad* the known and recorded man, and thing, Sákya Sinha, and his tenets, they are, indisputably, Indian and recent."

In endeavouring, to the best of my ability, to maintain a theory, as to the nature and origin of the Buddhism of Gautama, or Sákya, which runs counter to generally accepted opinions, I have quoted, freely, those writers of established repute, whose opinions support my argument. Had space allowed, I could have easily added to my quotations; but I have, I trust, said enough to show that what I may call the popular view, as to Buddhism, however ably supported, is still open to dispute.

I am very sensible of many defects in this book: but I may, at least, hope that it will tend to a fuller and more conclusive treatment of the interesting subject of Indian Buddhism, by more competent scholars, and more practised pens.

FINIS.

INDEX.

A.

Ádi Buddha; the Celestial Buddha. 46; 83; 90; 101; 119.
Age and purport of Sánchi Sthúpas. 116-122.
Agni. 21, Note 1; 30, Note 1; 31; 98; 120; 121; 124, Note 1; 127.
Ahi, and its meanings. 62, Note 1; 98.
Amatory scenes. 22; 51, Note 1; 55; 58; 70.
Amshaspands, the thirty-two attendants of Ahuramazda, compared with the Trayastrinshas, or thirty-two attendants of Indra. 37, Note 2.
Animals, natural, representations of. 23, Note 1; 31-39; 42, Note 1; 47-49; 51-57; 62-66; 68-70.
Animals, supernatural, representations of. 31; 38; 47; 51; 52; 58; 60; 63; 65; 68, Notes 1, 2; 70; 71.
„ symbolical use of. 52, Note 1.
„ worshipping Sthúpas. 38, Note 1; 51; 64.
„ „ trees. 31; 38, Note 1; 51; 52; 63.
„ „ wheel. 54; 65.
Aom, or Om. 22, 23, Note 5; 89, Notes 1, 2, 3; 90; 124, Note 1.
Apes, connected with Scythia (*q.v.*). 42; 62; 63; 64.
Appropriation, by Buddhists, of old buildings, names, and symbols. 71; 114; 119; 126.
Ark symbol. 32, Note 1; 59, Note 1.
Arms, and Armed men. 20; 23; 48; 50; 51; 53; 56; 62-66; 69, Note 1.
Arrow-head, a sacred symbol. 19, Note 3; 128.
Asádrisa Játaka. 64, Notes 1, 2.
Ascetic class. 35; 36; 42-47, and Notes; 62.
Asoka, his date, and identification. 7; 75; 83; 96; 102, Note 1; 103; 109-111; 117, Note 1; 120, Note 1; 121; 122.
Aswattha. (See Pipala.)
Attributes, deification of. 91, Note 1.
Ávasatha, meaning of. 105, Note 1.
Avatáras of Buddha. (See Játaka.)
„ of Vishnu. 26, Note 1; 27, Note 1; 28; 59, Note 1; 68; 81, Note 2; 87; 127, Note 1; 131.

B.

Ball and Cross symbol, origin of. 86, Note 2.
Bámana. (See Bráhmana.)
Banian Tree. 27; 32; 38; 52; 64.
Bhaga; and its derivation and meanings. 99; 127.
Bhagava, or Bhagaván, a name of Vishnu. 99.
Bhagavata. 28; 40; 60, Note 1; 99; 121; 122.
Bhalli, arrow so called. 19; 64; 69, Note 1; 79.
Bhámandala, the chariot-wheel of Súrya. 127; 128.
Bhava, a name of Súrya. 124, Note 1.
Bhikhu (Bhikshu); a Buddhist mendicant priest. 43; 99.
Bhikshuka; a Bráhman mendicant. 99.
Bhikshuní, a female mendicant. 99.
Bhilsa, former names of. 104.
Biblical resemblances in the Buddhism of Sákya. 112, Note 1; 132.
Bident symbol, Assyrian, Egyptian, and Indian. 85, Note 1; 88, Notes 1, 2, 3; 90.
Birds, representations of, in sculptures. 37; 42; 47; 49; 51; 52.
Bird-symbol. 68, Note 1; 73.
Blade-shaped symbol. 19, Note 3; 55; 69, Note 1.
Boat and oar, a type of Buddha. 43; 59.
„ ordinary, representation of. 42; 43.
„ sacred „ 12; 31; 58; 59, Note 1.
Bodhi, meanings of. 29, Note 1; 33, Note 2; 40.
„ of Kanaka Bhagavata. 27; 28; 31; 33; 37; 99.
„ of Kásapa Bhagavata. 27; 28; 37; 38; 64; 99.
„ of Krakuchanda Bhagavata. 27; 28; 31; 37; 60; 99.
„ of Sáka Muni Bhagavata. 22, Note 5; 26-29; 37; 46; 55; 99.
„ of Sikhin. 27; 37.
„ of Vipaswi Bhagavata. 25-28; 31; 37; 42; 46-48; 58; 62; 63; 65; 99.
„ of Viswabhu Bhagavata. 27; 28; 37; 47; 48; 60; 65; 99.
Bodhisatwas as attendants on Buddha. 25, Note 2; 111.
„ how symbolized. 52, Note 1.
Bráhmanas. 43; 44, Note 1; 45; 98; 126; 133.
Bráhmanical resemblances in Buddhism. 82.
„ sculptures at Sánchi. 76.
Bucranium. (See Bull's-head symbol.)
Budha, a distinct term from Buddha. 100; 101; 121; 122.
„ images of. (See Images.)
„ mention of, in the Piyadasi edicts. 122.
„ mention of, in Sánchi inscriptions. 100.
„ ninth or last Avatára of Vishnu. 13; 26, Note 1; 27, Note 1; 59; 127, Note 1.
„ primitive, Mithraic and Biblical resemblances in. 127-128.
„ the planetary Hermes, or Mercury. 83; 86, Note 2; 87; 127, Notes 1, 2.
„ Various names of, and their Mithraic allusions. 124, Note 1.
Buddha, a distinct term from Budha. 100; 101; 122.
„ Butta of Clemens Alexandrinus. 45.
„ names of. 46; 121; 123; 126.

Buddha, not mentioned in any pre-Christian work. 131.
- „ not mentioned in the Piyadasi edicts. 121.
- „ not mentioned in Sánchi inscriptions. 100.
- „ not represented in any of the older Sánchi sculptures. 13; 16.
- „ representations of, with flames and other Mithraic symbols. 125.
- „ various resemblances of, to other deities. 21, Note 1; 82; 83, Note 1; 87; 124; 127, Notes 1, 2.
- „ with his two Bodhisatwas, Sáriputra and Mahámogalana, compared to Christ between Moses and Elias. 111; 112, Note 1.

Buddhism, foreign origin of. 29, Note 2; 30; 82; 92; 123; 125.
- „ of Sákya, modern date of. 92; 117; 118; 120; 123; 126; 130-133.
- „ „ „ not that of the Piyadasi inscriptions. 120-122.
- „ preceded by Fire and Sun worship. 123-126.
- „ relapse of, into Pantheism. 41.
- „ two periods of. 112, Note 1; 123; 126.
- „ when introduced into Burmah, Ceylon, China, Japan, and Tibet, respectively. 132, Note 1.

Buddhist books, discordance of, as to dates. 129; 131; 132.
- „ buildings not mentioned in any pre-Christian work. 131.
- „ formula, "Ye dharmma," etc. 74; 76; 100, Note 2; 106.
- „ railing, Burmese variety of. 12, Note 2.
- „ „ construction of. 11; 13; 21, Note 3; 24, Note 1.
- „ „ how used in the sculptures. 11-13; 24; 33; 47; 58.
- „ rites, sculptures and symbols, not mentioned in any pre-Christian work. 131.
- „ triad, compared with that of Jagannáth (*q.v.*). 55; 89, Note 1.

Buildings represented in the sculptures, remarks on. 23; 24.

Bull, or ox, metaphorical use of. 52, Note 1.

Bull's head symbol, its meaning and origin. 17; 83; 87; 88, Notes 1, 2, 3.

C.

CADUCEUS. 83, Note 1; 86, Note 2.

Cars, yoked, Buddhist metaphor of. 52, Note 1.

Caves, and cave-temples. 30; 74.

Centaurs. 68, Note 2.

Chaitiya, Chaitya or Chetiya, a relic-Sthúpa. 3; 45; 119; 121.
- „ caves, structural imitation of. 74.
- „ earliest mention of, is by Clemens Alexandrinus. 45.
- „ symbol of Mithraic origin. 30; 39; 79, Note 2; 80.

Chaitya-hall (R). 7; 74.

Chaka or Chakra. 18, Note 2; 39; 40; 80, Note 1; 88; 100, Note 1; 128.

Chakravartti, meaning of. 41.

Chandragupta Maurya. 96; 120.
- „ of the Sánchi inscriptions. 102, Note 1; 103, Note 1; 105; 106.

Character of Páli inscriptions, not a conclusive test of age. 95; 114; 116.

Chariots. 32; 33, Note 1; 35, Note 2; 57; 65.

Chariot-wheel of Súrya. 40; 127; 128.

Chaturanga, whence Shatranj (chess). 50, Note 1.

Chaumukhti, or four-faced Mahádeva. 73, Note 1.

Chequers, meaning of. 21, Note 2.

Chetiyagiri. 3; 4; 7; 75.

Chinese evidence as to Buddhist use of images. 17.

Chronology, fictitious, of Bráhmans and Buddhists. 81, Note 2; 96, Note 2.
- „ only slightly illustrated by the Sánchi inscriptions. 94; 98; 107.

Chuḍamaha, or Chuṛamaní. (See Hair-Relic.)

Circumambulation ceremony. (See Padakhinán and Parikrama.) 9, Note 1; 31; 63; 76, Note 1; 117.

Classical authors quoted. 28; 33; 44, Note 1; 45; 56, Note 1; 61, Note 1; 62.

Cloud and Serpent, connection between. 62, Note 1; 98.

Coins bearing the disc-and-crescent symbol. 80-83; 88, Note 2.

Conception of Maya. 49, Note 1.

Contests between Bráhmanism and Buddhism. (See Mahábhárata.)

Costume, foreign. 23, Note 2; 32; 48; 49; 56.
- „ Indian. 23-25; 32-35; 46; 48-51; 54-60; 63-65; 69; 70.
- „ of Ascetic, or priestly class. 25; 43, Note 1; 44, Note 1; 47, Note 2; 62.

Crescent symbol. 20; 32; 66; 69, Note 1; 79; 91.

Crook symbol. 20; 21.

Cross, an elemental symbol. 86.
- „ in combination with disc. 11, Note 2; 12, Note 1; 18, Note 2; 50, Note 2; 86, Note 2.

D.

DÁNAM, or votive Páli inscriptions. 98, Note 1, to 105.

Dancers, and dancing. 35; 37; 38; 42; 50; 51, Note 1; 54; 55; 60; 64.

Date of enclosures of Sthúpas. 67; 96; 116, Note 1; 117; 118.
- „ of gateways of Sthúpas. 13; 34, Note 1; 56, Note 2; 57; 95; 96; 115; 117; 118.
- „ of inscriptions. 94-96; 102; 105; 106; 107; 114; 115; 117.
- „ of relic deposits. 113, Note 1; 114; 115.
- „ of Sákya. 56, Note 1; 120, Note 1; 122; 123; 129-133.
- „ of Sthúpas. 16, Note 2; 67; 116, Notes 1, 2; 117; 118.

Deer, natural. 42, Note 1; 47; 52; 54; 62; 63; 65; 68.
- „ symbolical use of. 52, Note 1.
- „ winged. 38.

Devánampiya, "beloved of the Gods," an Assyrian and Persian as well as Indian title. 120, Note 1.
- „ Piyadasi, edicts of. 45; 120, Note 1; 121; 122.

Dhama. (See Dharma.)

Dhama Chaka, or Dharma Chakra. (See Chaka.)

Dharma, a distinct term from Dharmma. 100, Note 2; 101; 106; 122.
- „ meanings of. 83; 100; 121; 126.
- „ mentioned in, and principal subject in, the Piyadasi Páli edicts. 121; 122.
- „ mention of, in the Sánchi Páli inscriptions. 100; 122.

Dharma, second member of the mystical or celestial Buddhist triad. 25; 26, Note 1; 29, Note 1.
Dhammma, a distinct term from Dharma. 100, Note 2; 101; 106; 122.
„ mention of, in the Kutila inscriptions at Sánchi. 74; 76; 100, Note 1; 106.
„ second member of the personal, or modern triad of Buddhism. 29, Note 1.
Dhyáni, or five celestial Buddhas. 37, Note 1; 90.
Dipawanso, conflicting views as to authority of. 120, Note 1; 121.
Disc symbol. 20, Note 1; 32; 39; 56; 66; 68; 79; 80; 88, Note 3; 89, Note 2; 90; 91.
„ „ and triangle analogous: and both represent the sacred number three. 88, Note 3.
Disc-and-crescent symbol, an elemental symbol. 83; 84; 85.
„ „ „ „ compared with Bull's head symbol. 17; 83; 84; 87; 88, Notes 1, 2, 3.
„ „ „ „ detail of its uses at Sánchi. 78.
„ „ „ „ double. 79.
„ „ „ „ general remarks on. 78-92.
„ „ „ „ no trace of, in India, prior to the Greek era. 81, Note 1.
„ „ „ „ on coins. 79-83; 88, Note 2.
„ „ „ „ Páli letters, composing it. 85-87.
„ „ „ „ preceded images as a representation of Buddha. 17; 36; 43.
„ „ „ „ quadruple. 68; 78; 79; 90.
„ „ „ „ representations of, in inscriptions. 79.
„ „ „ „ representations of, in sculptures. 18; 19; 32; 38; 40; 50-52; 54; 55; 64; 66; 68; 78; 79, Note 1.
„ „ „ „ represents the Buddhist Chaitya. 79, Note 2; 80.
„ „ „ „ represents the elements. 84; 85, Notes 1, 2.
„ „ „ „ represents the Mithraic as well as the Buddhist triad. 79, Note 2; 80; 89, Note 1.
„ „ „ „ resemblance of, to Jagannáth figures. 55; 89, Notes 1, 3.
„ „ „ „ resemblance of, to other mythological figures, and symbols. 83, Note 1; 84; 85, Note 3; 86; 90; 91.
„ „ „ „ triple, 55; 79, Note 2; 80; 88, Note 2.
Disc within bident or crescent. 90; 91.
Domestic scenes. 48; 59; 60.
Dream of Máya. (See Máya.)
Dwarf Capitals. 58; 70.
Dwarfs, representations of. 48, Notes 1; 53; 58; 70.

E.

EASTERN Gateway of No. 1 Sthúpa. 42-52.
Elemental worship, indications of. 13; 83-85; 117; 123; 125.
Elements, symbols of. 83; 84, Notes 2, 3; 85; 86.
Elephant Capitals. 34; 42; 50; 69.
„ dedication of. 51, Note 2; 52.
„ Játaka. 38.
„ representations of. 22, Note 3; 35-39; 42, Note 1; 47-49; 50-53; 57; 63; 65; 68; 69.
„ symbolic use of. 14; 21; 52, Note 1; 61.
Enclosure. (See Buddhist Railing.)
Enclosures of Sthúpas. 10; 11, Note 2; 12-14, Note 1; 46; 67; 68; 70; 98, Note 1; 116, Note 1; 117.
„ of Sthúpas, the origin of the passages round shrines of structural temples. 76, Note 1.
Entrances, Swastika plan of. 11; 12; 67; 97.
Eras synchronous with the Buddhist era. 129-131.
Ether, symbol of. 84; 85, Note 1.
Eye symbol. 46.

F.

FALSIFICATION of history, by Bráhmans and Buddhists. 122; 129.
Fauns, figures resembling. 37.
Female figure, anointed by elephants (see Máya). 36, Note 2; 38; 49, Note 1; 51; 52; 82.
„ musicians, and other attendants. 37; 51, Note 1; 53-55; 57; 58; 60.
„ power in nature, symbols of. 26, Note 1; 83.
„ priesthood, Buddhist. 35; 44, Note 1; 62.
„ „ of other races. 44, Note 1.
Females, association of, in worship. 23; 26; 31; 33-36; 50; 51, Note 1; 53-57; 60; 62; 63; 65; 69; 70.
Fir-cone symbol. 85, Note 1.
Fire altars. 38; 47; 79; 85, Note 2.
„ and Sun, both represented by the word "pur." 124.
„ caves dedicated to. 30; 47.
„ temples „ „ 12; 47; 105, Note 1.
„ worship, indications of. 13; 30; 39; 44; 47; 52; 55; 61; 63; 71; 105, Note 1; 117; 125, Note 1; 128.
„ worship introduced into India from Persia. 123; 124.
„ „ not among the heresies mentioned in Buddhist works. 85, Note 2.
Fish Avatára of Buddha and Vishnu compared. 21; 59, Note 1; 87.
„ pair of, an Egyptian, Jaina, and Zodiacal symbol. 20; 21.
„ symbol, Biblical origin of. 59, Note 1.
Fisherman Játaka. 48.
Five-disc symbol. 86, Note 1.
„ -rayed star and wheel. 127; 128.
„ sacredness of number. 37, Note 1.
Floral work, and flowers. 18; 19; 34; 35; 38; 42; 43; 51; 55; 58; 68.
Foot-print, sacred. 18, Note 2; 51.
Foreigners, representations of. 23, Note 2; 32; 48; 49; 54, Note 2; 56; 65, Note 2.
Former Buddhas, their names, symbols, and worship. 27; 28; 123; 125.
„ Buddhism, the "Budha-Dharma," or old faith. 123.
„ names of Sánchi. 3; 4.
„ notices of Sánchi. 2; 5; 6; 13, Note 1.
Four Buddhas, the. 14; 106; 114; 115; 117.
„ predictive signs. 23; 30; 50.

G.

GANDHÁRA, Greek character of the Buddhist sculptures from. 125.
Gateways of sacred buildings, etc., represented in the sculptures. 30; 31; 63.
„ of Sthúpas Nos. 1 and 3. 10; 11; 13; 18-66; 71; 117.
„ of various secular buildings, etc., represented in sculptures. 22; 23; 30; 32; 42; 47; 48; 51; 53; 56; 65; 68.
General description of the Sánchi ruins. 5-8.
Gift, mode of confirming a. 35.
Gigantic figures, representations of. 37; 38; 53; 65.
„ head, representation of. 63.
Giri (hill), names ending in. 39, Note 1; 104; 105.
Goat symbol. 21, Note 1.
Good and evil, conflict between—how allegorized. 29, Note 2; 62, Note 1.
Greek influence, traces of. 22, Note 3; 32, Note 2; 45; 53, Note 1; 68, Note 2; 73; 82; 123; 124.
Greeks mentioned in the Mahábhárata. 130.
Gryphon. 58; 60; 63; 68.
Gumnosophai, or Gumnosophistai. 44, Note 1.
Gupta inscriptions. 94; 102; 105; 106.
„ meaning of term. 103.
„ mention of term (as Guta) in the old Páli inscriptions. 101-103.
Guptas and Pándavas compared. 101; 102; 103, and Note.
„ and their dates. 61; 101-103; 105; 106.

H.

HAIR, modes of wearing. 24, Note 4; 30; 32; 35, Note 1; 42; 43, Note 1; 46; 48; 49.
„ relic of Buddha. 49, Note 2; 54.
Hand symbol. 90.
Hansa. 42; 43; 73.
Hanumán, connection of, with Scythia (*q.v.*). 23, Note 1.
Hare, symbolical use of. 52, Note 1.
Hariswámini inscription. 106.
Headgear, varieties of. 24, Note 4; 43, Note 4; 44; 49, Note 2; 54; 58; 62; 74.
Hermes and his symbols. 36, Note 2; 66, Note 1; 83, Note 1; 86, Note 2; 87; 127.
History, falsification of, by Bráhmans and Buddhists. 96, Note 2; 112.
Hog. 63.
Homa, the sacred tree of Persia. 28.
„ sacrifice of India. 76.
Honeysuckle symbol. 18; 19; 34; 37; 53, Note 1; 62; 73.
Horn and Ray analogous. 49, Note 2; 88, Note 2.
Horned divinities of Assyria, Greece and India. 88, Notes 1, 2, 3.
„ head-dresses. 49, Note 2; 54; 58.
Horses, dedication of. 32; 33, Note 1; 51, Note 2; 57; 65; 66.
„ representations of. 22; 30; 32; 35; 38; 42; 48; 51; 53; 56; 57; 63-66.
„ sacredness of. 98; 99.
„ sacrifice of. 33, Note 1; 51, Note 2; 52; 66.
„ symbolical use of. 52, Note 1.
Human-faced animals. 30; 68.
„ figure, derivation of, from symbol. 89.

I.

IMAGES of Buddha, at gateways of No. 1 Sthúpa. 14.
„ „ „ in other places. 16; 74-76.
„ „ „ date of. 16; 17; 43.
„ „ „ no trace of, in the sculptures of enclosures and gateways. 16.
„ preceded by symbols. 17; 36, Note 2; 40; 43.
„ use of, in India, traceable to Greek influence. 17.
„ worship of, a comparatively recent feature of Buddhism. 14; 16, Note 3; 17; 43; 76; 83; 88; 106; 117; 123.
Indo-Scythians. 23, Note 1; 52; 61, Note 1; 82; 118; 123; 124; 130.
„ mentioned in the Mahábhárata. 130.
Indra. 34; 37, Note 2; 62, Note 1; 127.
Inscriptions, Gupta. 14; 73; 94; 102; 105; 106; 115; 117.
„ Kutila. 15; 16; 74; 76; 94; 100, Note 2; 106.
„ Mithraic allusions in. 98, Note 2; 105, Note 1; 125.
„ Nágari. 75; 94; 106; 107.
„ Páli. 11; 39; 46; 54; 57; 60; 63; 67; 69; 70; 73; 94-105; 117.
„ Páli, character of, not a sure test of age. 94; 95.
„ Relic. 70; 71; 108-115.
„ Small chronological importance of. 94; 95; 98; 107.
„ unconnected with relic deposits. 94 to 107.
Introductory remarks. 1-4.
Ironwork, traces of. 74, Note 1.
Isolated pillars. (See Sthambhas.)
Íswara, a Brahman as well as Buddhist term. 83; 101; 124.

J.

JAGANNÁTH and Buddha compared. 26, Note 1; 55; 89, Note 1; 127.
Jaina, sect and works. 16, Note 2; 74; 98, Note 2; 124.
Janitor figures. 7; 24; 25, Note 2; 31; 46; 48; 53; 58; 63; 74; 75.
Játakas, or former incarnations of Buddha. 21; 27, Note 1; 35; 36; 49; 51; 59, Note 1; 62-64, Note 2; 68; Note 1; 87; 115.

K.

KA, meanings of. 87.
Kachchapa, or Tortoise (*q.v.*).
Kalpadarma, or Kalpavriksha. 22; 26; 33; 58.
Kanaka, the fifth of the seven Mánushya, or mortal Buddhas. 27; 37; 114; 123.
Karna (a horn or ray), and its equivalents. 49, Note 2; 88, Note 1.
Kásapa (Kásyapa), the sixth of the seven Mánushya, or mortal Buddhas. 27; 37; 63, Note 1; 66, Note 1; 68; 114; 123.
Kauravas, or Kurus, the Bráhmanical opponents of the Buddhists. 130.
Khormousda—a Mongol name for Indra—compared with Ahuramazda. 37, Note 2.
Kinnara, and their resemblances. 24; 29-32, Note 2; 36-38; 46; 50-52; 54; 56; 57; 60; 63; 65; 66; 70; 71.
Krakuchanda, the fourth of the seven Mánushya, or mortal Buddhas. 27; 37; 60; 114; 123.
Krishna, his date and resemblances. 81, Note 2; 127; 130; 131.

L.

LADDER symbol. 33; 34.
Láths (see Sthambha), called Bhima Gaja. 103.
Linga, and Linga worship. 8; 11, Note 2; 14; 15; 16, Note 1; 30; 50, Note 3; 51, Note 1; 84; 86.
„ and Yoni, analogous to the ring-encircled figures and symbols of Assyria and Egypt. 11, Note 2; 86.
„ a pole or staff. 50, Note 3.
Lion, a solar symbol. 30, Note 1.
„ capitals. 38; 51; 53; 69; 70; 73; 95.
„ pillars. 51; 73.
Lions, fish-tailed. 31; 63; 68.
„ horned. 52.
„ human-faced. 68.
„ natural, representations of. 36; 38; 42, Note 1; 52; 53; 63; 64; 68; 69; 70; 73.
„ winged. 37; 38; 51; 60; 65; 66; 73.
Lotus. 18; 20, Note 1; 31; 42.

M.

MA, meanings of. 87; 89, Note 3; 90. (See also Aom, and Disc-and-Crescent.)
Mahábhárata and its date. 130, Note 1; 131.
Mahámáya. (See Máya.)
Mahámogalána. 26, Note 1; 71; 111-113.
„ compared with Moses. 112, Note 1.
Mahásrámana, a title of Buddha. 45.
Mahat. 101; 124, Note 1.
Mahendra (Mahindo), a son of Asoka. 7; 75; 102; 103 and Note 1; 121.
„ a son of Chandra Gupta Vikramáditya. 102 and 103, Note 1.
Makara. 21, Note 1; 42; 43; 59, Note 1; 68; 87.
Mánushya, or mortal Buddhas. 27; 37, Note 1; 63, Note 1; 66, Note 1; 68; 114; 123.
Mathura, Sthúpas of Mahámogalána and Sáriputra at 111; 112.
Máya, conception, and dream of. 49, Note 1.
„ mother of Buddha. 26; 36, Note 2; 49, Note 1; 83; 127.
„ mother of Mercury. 83; 127.
„ resemblances to, in Assyrian, Brahmanical, Egyptian, and Greek mythology. 36, Note 2; 49, Note 1.
Menander and Sákya, similar legend as to. 56, Note 1.
Mendicants of both sexes. 99; 100.
Mercury. (See Hermes.)
Meru. 25; 37, Note 2; 61.
Metaphors, Buddhist, recent date of. 39; 40; 52, Note 1.
Miscellaneous remains at Sánchi. 7; 8; 16; 72-77.
Missions and Missionaries, Buddhist. 109; 110; 113.
Mita, Páli form of Mitra (*q.v.*).
Mithra, or Mithras, of Greece and Persia. 11, Note 2; 82; 101; 128.
Mithraic allusions, and resemblances, in Buddhism. 11, Note 2; 12; 13; 21, Notes 1, 2; 33, Note 1; 37, Notes 1, 2; 39; 40; 46; 47; 52; 61; 63; 68-71; 73; 74; 79-93; 99-101; 104; 105; 107; 123; 124, Note 1; 125-133.
Mitra, name of the Indian Súrya. 11, Note 2; 82; 124, Note 1.
„ various meanings of. 98, Note 2; 101.
Moon, junction of with the sun, in mythology. 29; 83.
„ symbols, and worship. 29; 56; 83; 87; 90.
Musical instruments and musicians. 24; 30; 32, Note 2; 37; 48; 50; 51; 54; 57; 60; 64; 65.

N.

NAGA (root of Nága), meanings of. 61; 101.
Nága—descended tribes. 52; 61, Note 1; 62.
„ emblem of Buddhism. 62; 129.
„ „ „ Páraswanátha. 74.
„ „ „ the sun. 47, Note 1.
„ „ „ water. 19, Note 1; 59, Note 1; 60; 61; 71.
„ meanings of. 30; 61; 62, Note 1.
„ mention of, in inscriptions; 101.
„ overshadows and supports Vishnu. 59, Note 1.
„ worship not represented at Sánchi. 47, Note 1.
Nágas, historical. 52; 61; 62; 129; 130.
„ invasion of India by. 61; 129; 130.
„ mythological. 25; 30; 52; 60-62; 68; 71; 74; 75.
„ representations of. 47; 52; 57; 60; 68; 70; 71; 74; 75.
Nágnis, or female Nágas. 60; 68; 75.
Names, former, of Sánchi. 3; 4; 7; 75; 97.
„ of persons, in miscellaneous inscriptions. 96, Note 1; 97; 98; 101-103; 106; 107.
„ „ „ in relic inscriptions. 108-113.
„ of places, in miscellaneous inscriptions. 103-107.
„ „ „ in relic inscriptions. 109; 110.
„ of Sthúpas. 68.
Nebo and Noub compared with Agni and Buddha. 21, Note 1; 30, Note 1; 127.
Necklaces of sacred symbols. 18-21; 85, Note 1.
Nirvána, discrepant dates of. 129, Note 1.
Nude figures, rarity of. 22, Note 1.
Numbers three, five, and seven, sacredness of. 37, Note 1; 88, Note 3.

O.

OM. (See Aom.)
Omega, an Egyptian and Phœnician symbol. 91.
Orientation of temples, etc. 67, Note 2.
Ornaments. 18; 19, Note 2; 20; 24, Note 4; 35, Note 1; 49, Note 2; 50; 54.

P.

PADAKHINÁN, the Buddhist ceremony of circumambulation. 9, Note 1; 31; 63; 76, Note 1; 117.
Pagan legends in Buddhism. 132.
Páli character (old), still in use in the first century A.D. 95.
Pándava, a term used in the Pali inscriptions. 101; 102;
Pándavas (Pándus) and Guptas, compared. 102; 103.
Párijáta tree of Indra's paradise. 22; 26; 33; 37; 58.
Parikrama, or parkarma, the Bráhman ceremony of circumambulation. 9, Note 1; 76, Note 1.
Peacock, a sacred bird. 22, Note 4; 23.
„ representations of. 22; 23; 37; 47; 68.
Persians, introducers of fire and sun worship in India. 123; 124; 130.
„ myths of, traceable in India. 34; 61, Note 1; 124; 130.
„ references to, and resemblances in sculptures. 33; 34; 43, Note 1; 61, Note 1; 82; 123; 124; 130.
Phallic worship, in India. 51, Note 1.
Phallos, a pole, or staff. 50, Note 3.
Pillars. (See Sthambha.)
Pipala tree. (See Bodhi and Tree.) 22, Note 5; 26; 27; 29; 46; 55.

Piyadasi. (See Devánampiya Piyadasi).
„ edicts, and their connection with Buddhism. 45; 120, Note 1; 121; 122.
„ „ evidence of, as to the terms Bámana and Sámana (*q.v.*). 45.
Plants, sacred. 47; 49; 55; 58; 62; 63; 65.
Pratyeka class, how symbolized. 52, Note 1.
Prayer, attitudes in. 26, Note 3.
Processions, representations of. 22; 23; 30; 32; 42; 48; 50; 51; 55-57; 65.
Pur, a solar term, common to Egypt, Greece, and India. 124; 127.

R.

Ra, meanings of. 87.
Ram, a symbol of fire and the sun. 30, Note 1; 31; 91.
„ -headed divinities. 30, Note 1; 31.
„ human-faced. 30.
„ representations of. 30; 51; 52; 63.
„ zodiacal sign of, a trident reversed. 91.
Rath-játra of Jagannáth, derived from Buddhists. 89.
Relics, caskets for. 56; 57; 65; 70; 71; 108-112.
„ contests for. 56, Note 1; 66.
„ date of deposit of. 113, Note 1; 114; 115.
„ deposit of, in buildings already old. 71; 114; 115.
„ in Chaitya Hall (R). 74; 108; 112.
„ in No. 2 Sthúpa. 70; 108-110; 114, 119.
„ in No. 3 Sthúpa. 71; 110; 111; 114; 119.
„ not found in No. 1 Sthúpa. 108; 114-116.
„ not mentioned in the Piyadasi edicts. 120.
„ „ „ „ Sánchi enclosure and gateway inscriptions. 114.
„ processions with. 65; 66.
„ removal of, from place to place. 114.
„ where discovered. 108.
„ worship of, indications of, in the sculptures. 12; 54; 56; 65; 66.
„ „ „ introduced by Sákya. 123; 126.
Ring encircled figures of Assyria, the prototype of figures of Buddha, Mitra or Mithras, Súrya, and the Linga. 11, Note 2; 85; 86; 89, Note 2; 90; 128.
Runic K, a double crescent. 79.

S.

Sacred terms used in the inscriptions. 43; 45; 97-101; 105-110; 113.
Sacrifices of animals. 51, Note 2; 52; 56.
Sákas. (See Scythians.)
Sakti, or female form of divinity. 26.
Sákya, a tribal appellation only, from Sáka, a Scythian. 23, Note 1; 51, Note 1; 52; 61; 99; 102, Note 1; 103; 118; 123; 131-133.
„ Buddha, both a Bráhmana and a Srámana. 45.
„ date of. 44, Note 1; 56, Note 1; 113, Note 1; 114; 120; 123; 129-133.
„ history of, borrowed from many sources. 56, Note 1; 129-133.
„ not mentioned in any inscription at Sánchi. 117; 118.
„ „ „ in the Piyadasi edicts. 120.
„ not represented in the enclosure or gateway sculptures at Sánchi. 117; 118.
„ reformed religion of. 56, Note 1; 61; 118; 123 to 133.
Sákya, the seventh or last of the seven Mánushya, or mortal Buddhas. 27.
„ tree of. (See Bodhi of Sáka.)
„ worship of tree by. 36, Note 3; 37.
Sama Játaka. 62; 63.
Sámana. (See Srámana.)
Samudra Gupta and Vindusára compared. 102; 103, Note 1.
Sánchi not mentioned by any Buddhist writer. 114; 115; 118, Note 1.
Sangha, and its meanings. 25; 29, Note 1; 83; 111; 112, Note 1; 126.
Sáriputa (Sáriputra). 26, Note 1; 71; 111-113.
Sátakarni Rája, and his date. 57; 96; 97.
Scroll-shaped symbol. 18; 19; 31, Note 2; 66.
Sculptures of Gandhára, superiority of. 53, Note 1.
„ three epochs of, at Sánchi. 16; 126.
Scythia, an old name of Sindh. 23, Note 1.
„ called "the land of apes." 23, Note 1; 52; 64.
Scythians. 23, Note 1; 32; 33; 51; 52, Note 1; 61, Note 1; 64; 82; 83; 99; 102, Note 1; 103; 118; 123; 124; 130.
Serpent. (See Nága.)
„ myths. 61, Note 1; 62, Note 1.
„ symbolical of fire and the sun. 30, Note 1; 47; Note 1.
„ „ of Buddhism. 62.
„ worship, not represented at Sánchi. 47, Note 1.
„ worshipping fire. 47.
„ „ tree. 52.
Seven, sacredness of number. 37, Note 1; 71; 111.
Seven-fold groups of objects of worship. 7; 34; 37; 55; 71; 111.
Seven-stepped ladders of the Buddhists, and Persians. 34.
Sheep, representations of. 47; 48; 52, Note 1.
„ symbolical use of. 52, Note 1.
Shields, various. 50; 65; 66.
Shrines, hut-shaped. 12; 24, Note 2; 63.
„ of the four Buddhas. 14; 106; 117.
„ round sacred trees. 50; 55; 65, Note 1.
Siege, representation of. 56.
Sikhara, or temple tower, derived from the Sthúpa. 15; 16; 75, Note 2; 76.
Sikhin, the second of the seven Mánushya, or mortal Buddhas. 27; 37.
Siva; his names and symbols. 8; 11, Note 2; 14-16, Note 1; 30; 50, Note 3; 51, Note 1; 84; 86; 91; 99; 101.
Sola Sapne, or sixteen dream portents. 20; 21; 49, Note 1.
Soma, the Indian moon-god; and also a name of the sun-god. 124. Note 1.
„ tree or plant of India, the Homa of Persian mythology. 28.
South, and south-east, both sacred quarters. 67, Note 2; 70; 111, Note 1.
Srámana, and Bráhmaná, as to the analogy between. 45; 101.
„ a title of Buddha. 45.
Srámanas, general remarks on. 43, Note 1; 44, Note 1 45; 101; 105, Note 1.
„ mention of, in the Piyadasi edicts. 45.
„ not mentioned in any of the older Pali inscriptions at Sánchi. 105, Note 1.
„ the Semnoi of Clemens Alexandrinus. 45.
Sráwaka class, how symbolized. 52, Note 1.
Standards and standard-bearers. 32; 37; 38; 48; 50; 53; 56; 57; 65; 66; 69.

Star symbol, five and eight-rayed. 20, Note 1; 89, Note 2.
Sthambhas, or isolated pillars; and their representations in the sculptures. 7; 18; 36; 51; 69; 70; 103.
Sthúpa, a type of Buddha. 55.
„ „ „ of fire and the sun. 11, Note 2; 55.
„ „ „ of Meru. 25; 61.
„ building, representation of. 46.
„ meanings of term. 3; 84.
„ No. 1. 6; 7; 9-17; 97; 114; 116, Notes 1, 2; 117, Note 1; 119; 120.
„ No. 2. 7; 67-70; 108-110; 116, Note 1.
„ No. 3. 7; 70; 71; 116, Note, 1; 119.
Sthúpas and trees, worshipped alike, and in conjunction. 30; 38; 57; 66.
„ classification of. 119; 120.
„ Indo-Scythic origin of. 118.
„ mentioned by Clemens Alexandrinus. 45.
„ miniature models of. 7; 14; 15; 76; 84.
„ Nos. 4 to 8. 7; 71.
„ not mentioned by any pre-Christian Greek writer. 118.
„ old, adopted, as relic shrines, by Sákya. 118; 126.
„ relative height of, a test of age. 6.
„ relative position of, and its significance. 7; 71.
„ relic deposits in. (See Relics.)
„ representations of, in the sculptures. 31; 34; 36; 38; 46; 50; 56; 57; 64; 66; 69; 70.
„ worship of. 31; 34; 36; 37, Note 1; 38, Note 1; 44; 47; 50; 52; 55-57; 64; 66; 69; 70.
Stone bowl (L). 7; 76; 77.
Subjects of the sculptures, detail of. 9; 13; 68; 70; 71.
Sun and Fire both represented by the Egyptian and Greek word "pur." 124.
„ and moon worship, the basis of all mythology. 39; 126.
„ god of India (see Súrya). 11, Note 2; 13; 33; 39; 46; 61, Note 1; 62, Note 1; 117; 125-128.
„ god of other countries. 11, Note 2; 13; 33, Note 1; 39; 61, Note 1; 123; 126-128.
„ and moon represented on shields and standards. 56.
„ and on Sati pillars. 90.
„ the symbol of the male or supreme power in Nature. 83.
„ symbols. 15; 30, Note 1; 31; 39; 40; 87; 88; 91.
„ worship. (See Sun-god.)
„ „ and tree worship, connection between. 29, Note 1.
„ „ not among the heresies mentioned in Buddhist works. 85, Note 2.
Súrya or Mitra, the sun-god of India, and his resemblances to other deities. 11, Note 2; 21; 39; 82; 124, Note 1; 127; 128.
Swastika, a cross, with arms bent to the right. 93.
„ an ecclesiastical, and heraldic symbol. 92, Note 1.
„ a Trojan symbol. 93.
„ form of entrances to Sthúpas. 11; 12.
„ form of relic-chambers. 121, Note 1.
„ general remarks on and meaning of. 19, Note 1; 92, Note 1; 93.
„ not an exclusively Buddhist symbol. 93.
„ places where met with. 92.
Swástika sect—the Tao-tsse of China. 92, Note 1; 93; 126.
Sword-blade symbol; and its connection with the letter N. 19, Note 3.
Symbol of life. 20; 86, Note 2; 89.
Symbols, Buddhist, ancient origin of. 19-21; 29, Notes 1, 2; 34; 37, Notes 1, 2; 39; 40; 47, Note 1; 59, Note 1; 61; 68, Notes 1, 2; 73; 78 to 93; 123-126; 131.
„ deification of. 91, Note 1.
„ Elemental, viz., of—
Air. 84, Note 3; 85.
Earth. 84, Note 3; 85.
Ether. 19; 20; 84, Note 3; 85.
Fire. 19; 21, Note 1; 30, Note 1; 39; 40; 84, Note 3; 85; 91; 93; 124; 125; 128.
Water. 19, Note 1; 22, Note 2; 59, Note 1; 84, Note 3; 85-87.
„ of lightning. 91; 93.
„ of the moon. 29; 83; 85-88.
„ of the sun. 11, Note 2; 12; 13; 19; 29; 30, Note 1; 39; 47, Note 1; 83; 85; 88-90; 93; 124-128.
„ preceded images. 43; 83; 88, Note 2.
„ various references to. 14; 15; 18, Note 2; 19-23; 25; 29; 32-34; 36, Note 2; 38; 43; 46; 47, Note 1; 50, Note 2; 51-59; 61; 62, Note 1; 63, Note 1; 64; 65; 66, Note 1; 68; 69, Note 1; 70; 73; 74; 78-93; 124; 125; 127; 128; 129.
„ zodiacal. 20; 87; 91.
Synchronism of the Indo-Scythic epoch and the introduction of relic-Sthúpas. 118.
„ between Buddhist events and personages, and those of Egypt, India, and Persia. 129; 130.

T.

TAKSHAKAS, same as Nágas (q.v.).
Tao-tsse of China, the Swástikas of India. 92, Note 1.
Thor, hammer or sacred axe of. 93.
Thoth and his resemblances. 86, Note 2; 87; 127.
Three, sacredness of number. 37, Note 1; 88, Note 3.
Ti, chatta, or umbrella of Sthúpas, Nos. 1 and 3. 13; 70.
„ triple. 31; 36.
„ worship of. 36, Note 3; 48.
Tortoise, or Kachhapa, representations of. 62; 63; 66; 68.
„ symbol of Kásyapa. 63, Note 1; 66, Note 1; 68.
„ „ „ Hermes or Mercury. 66, Note 1.
„ „ „ Vishnu. 68.
Towers of deliverance. 15; 84, Note 2; 85.
Trayastrinshas. (See Amshashpands.)
Tree, connection of, with sun-worship. 29, Note 1.
„ „ „ with the Nága, or serpent. 30; 61.
„ „ „ with the worship of Venus. 28; 29.
Trees and Sthúpas worshipped alike, and together. 30; 57; 66.
Trees, sacred, of India. 22; 24-29; 32; 33; 36, Note 3; 37; 38; 48; 50-52; 55; 57; 58; 60; 63-66.
„ „ of other countries. 26-29; 31, Note 1; 33.
Trees, seven-branched. 55.
„ triform and triple. 12; 24; 46.
„ worship of, general remarks on. 26-30; 51, Note 1; 61.

Trees, worship of, not exclusively Buddhist. 27; 28; 29, Note 1; 30.
,, ,, representations of. 12; 24; 26; 30-34; 36, Note 3; 37, Note 1; 38, Note 1; 42; 44; 46-48; 50-52; 55; 57; 58; 60; 62-66; 70.
Triads, and triple groups:
,, Bráhmanical. 25; 26, Note 1; 37, Note 1; 55; 79, Note 2; 80; 89, Note 3; 90; 126.
,, Buddhist. 25; 26, Note 1; 37, Note 1; 55; 78; 79, Note 2; 80; 89, Note 3; 90; 111; 112, Note 1; 121; 126.
,, of other creeds. 25, Note 2; 26, Note 1; 37, Note 1; 79, Note 2; 80; 85; 88, Note 3; 89, Note 2.
Triangle and disc, both represent the sacred number three. 88, Note 3.
Trident. 83; 86, Note 2; 90; 91; 128.
Triple buildings. 30; 46; 55.
,, disc-and-crescent symbol. 30; 37, Note 1; 39; 55; 78; 89.
,, gem symbol, or "tri-ratna." 78; 79, Note 2; 80; 89-91.
,, ladder. 34.
,, O, represented by the disc-and-crescent symbol. 91.
,, Sthúpas. 30; 31; 37, Note 1.
,, symbols. 30; 34; 39; 55.
,, Ti. 30; 31; 36.
,, trees. 30; 37, Note 1; 46.
Trisula (see Trident) a solar symbol. 128.

U.

UMBRELLA, a mark of royalty and sanctity. 23.
Union-Jack, resemblances to. 50, Note 2; 66.

V.

VAJRA or thunderbolt symbol, and its resemblances. 23; 50; 79.
Venus, and her symbols and worship. 28; 29; 86, Note 2.
Vihára, large (U). 7; 75.
,, mention of, in inscription. 105, Note
,, small (W). 7; 76
Vihára-temple (V). 7; 75; 76.
Vikramáditya; his date and identification. 81, Note 2; 102, Note 1; 103.
Vipaswi, the first of the seven Mánushya or mortal Buddhas. 27; 37; 46.
Vishnu, avatáras of. 59, Note 1; 68, Note 1; 127, Note 1.
,, names of. 28, Note 1; 68, Note 2; 99; 101; 124, Note 1.
Viswabhavana, one of Vishnu's names. 28, Note 1.
Viswabhu, the third of the seven Mánushya, or mortal Buddhas. 27; 28, Note 1; 37; 60.
Votan, of Mexico, compared with Buddha and Woden. 127, Note 2.
Vritra, and its meanings. 62, Note 1.

W.

WATER, a type of the deity. 62.
,, how represented. 19, Note 1; 22, Note 1; 84.
,, the abode of the mythological Nágas. 59, Note 1; 60; 61.
Water-vase symbol. 21, Note 1.
Weapons, deification of. 91; Note 1.
Wessanagara, and its identification. 104.
Wessentara Játaka. 35; 36; 51; 62.
Wheel, metaphorical use of. 39-41.
Wheel-symbol, derivation and meanings of. 39-41.
,, ,, general remarks on. 18, Note 2; 39-41; 81.
,, ,, various representations of. 12; 18, Note 2; 36; 38-40; 42, Note 1; 47; 51; 55; 57; 64-66; 69; 70; 80, Note 1; 88; 125.
,, ,, worship of. 51; 54; 65; 69; 70.
Winged globe, an Assyrian, Egyptian, Persian, and Mexican symbol. 85, Note 3.
Woden of Scandinavia. 87; 127, Note 2; 130.
Wooden origin of Sánchi enclosures and gateways. 21, Note 3; 23; 24, Note 1; 54, Note 1.

Y.

YAKSHAS and Yakshinis. 25.
Yoni (see also Linga). 8; 11, Note 2.
Yu-gai. (See Chandragupta.)

Z.

ZEND AVESTA, Biblical allusions in. 130.
Zodiacal signs. 20; 21; 87; 91.
Zoroaster, era of, compared with that of Buddha. 130.

PLATE I.

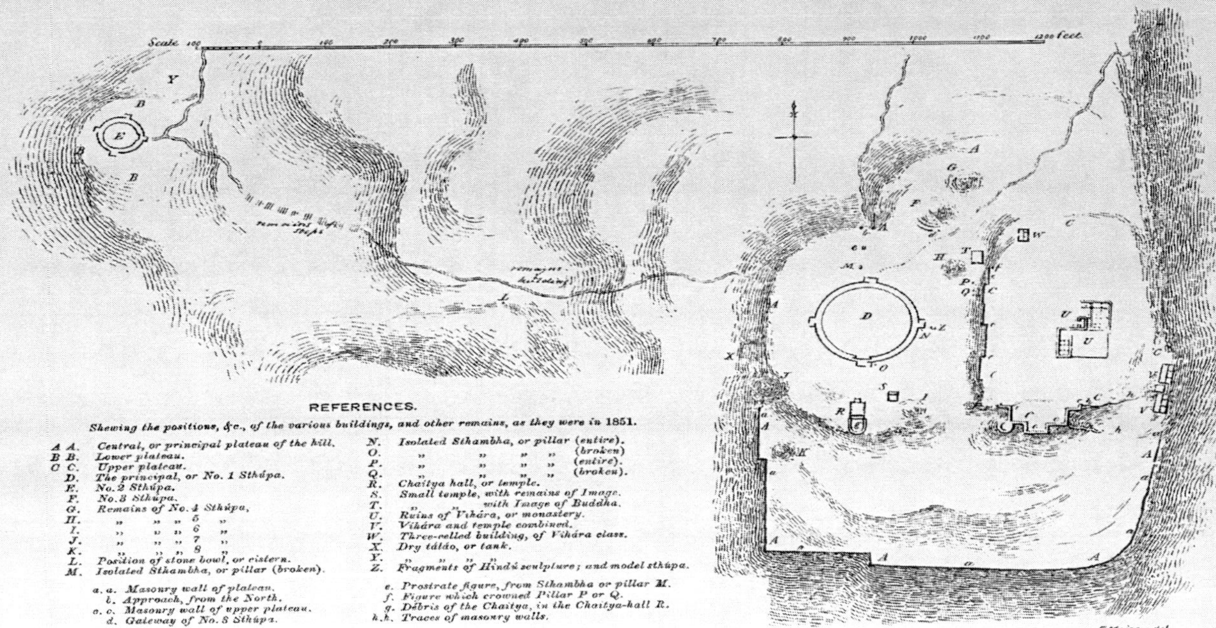

REFERENCES.

Shewing the positions, &c., of the various buildings, and other remains, as they were in 1851.

- A A. Central, or principal plateau of the hill.
- B B. Lower plateau.
- C C. Upper plateau.
- D. The principal, or No. 1 Sthúpa.
- E. No. 2 Sthúpa.
- F. No. 3 Sthúpa.
- G. Remains of No. 4 Sthúpa,
- H. " " " 5 "
- I. " " " 6 "
- J. " " " 7 "
- K. " " " 8 "
- L. Position of stone bowl, or cistern.
- M. Isolated Sthambha, or pillar (broken).
- N. Isolated Sthambha, or pillar (entire).
- O. " " " " (broken)
- P. " " " " (entire).
- Q. " " " " (broken).
- R. Chaitya hall, or temple.
- S. Small temple, with remains of Image.
- T. " " with Image of Buddha.
- U. Ruins of Vihára, or monastery.
- V. Vihára and temple combined.
- W. Three-celled building, of Vihára class.
- X. Dry táláo, or tank.
- Y. " " "
- Z. Fragments of Hindú sculpture; and model sthúpa.

- a. a. Masonry wall of plateau.
- b. Approach, from the North.
- c. c. Masonry wall of upper plateau.
- d. Gateway of No. 3 Sthúpa.
- e. Prostrate figure, from Sthambha or pillar M.
- f. Figure which crowned Pillar P or Q.
- g. Débris of the Chaitya, in the Chaitya-hall R.
- h. h. Traces of masonry walls.

W. Griggs & Sons, Photo-litho.

F. Moisey del.

PLATE II.

Fig. 1. *Restored plan of large Sthûpa (No. 1).*
„ 2. *Restored elevation of ditto (south).*
„ 3. *Actual condition of ditto in 1851.*
„ 4. *Section on m, o, p, s, m of Fig. 3.*
N.B.—In the plans (figs. 1, 3) the enclosing palisade a. a. a. is represented as an unbroken wall; though, as seen in fig. 2, it is not actually so.

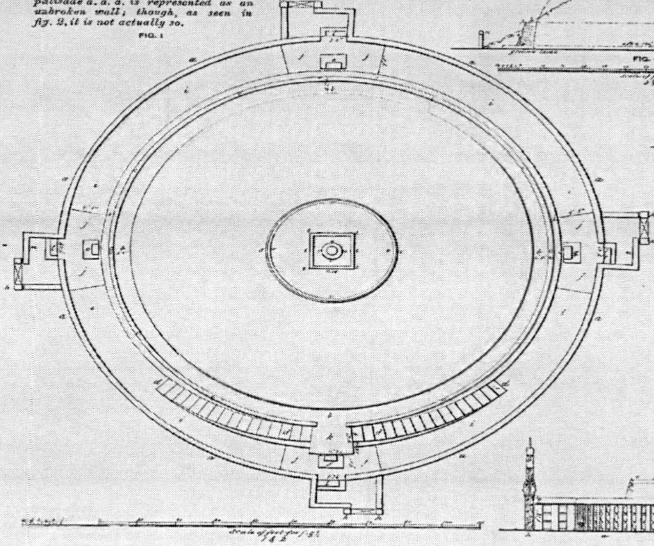

FIG. 1

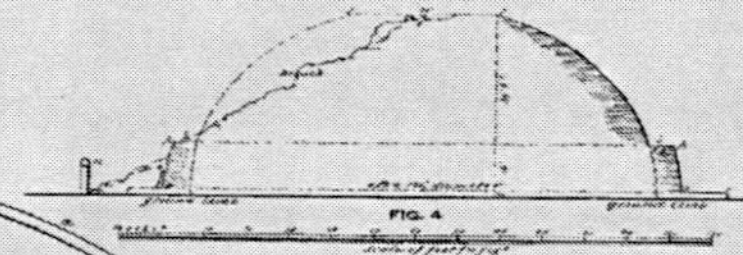

FIG. 4

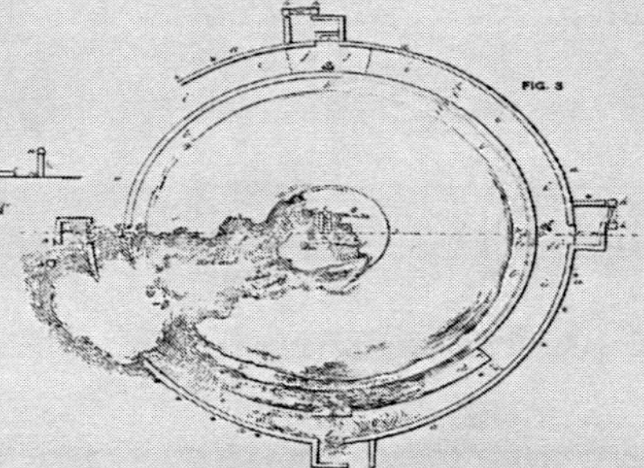

FIG. 3

EXPLANATION.

a.a. Enclosing wall or palisade.
b.b. Basement, berm, or drum.
c.c. Parapet of the berm, pieces of which are still remaining: restored from an existing specimen at Andher.
d.d. Steps leading on to berm.
e.e.g. Seated Image. f. Standing do.
h.h. Uprights of sculptured gates.
i.i. Enclosed passage round Sthûpa.
j.j. Stone pavement supporting images.
k. Landing of the staircase.
l.l. Steps into enclosure.
m.n. Enclosing palisade.
o.p. Slope of basement.
s.s. Top of Sthûpa.
t.t. Enclosure round tî, or chatta.
u.u. Tî, or kalas, or chatta. (portions of t and u are seen in fig. 3).
*v.v. Top enclosure or balustrade. The portions of the enclosing wall marked * lean either outwards or inwards.*
(The various portions of all the figs. are lettered to correspond).

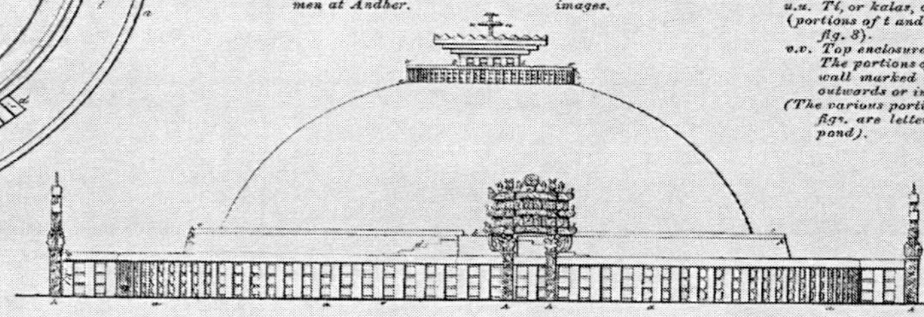

FIG. 2

F. Maisey del.

PLATE III.

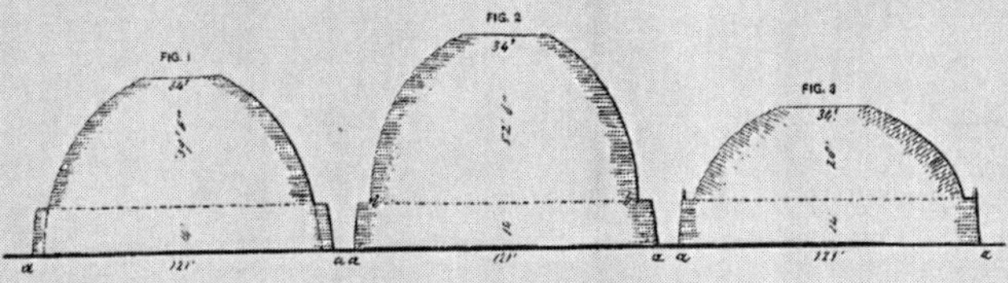

Figs. 1, 2, 3. Comparative sections of the large, or No. 1 Sthúpa; as represented by different writers on Sánchi.

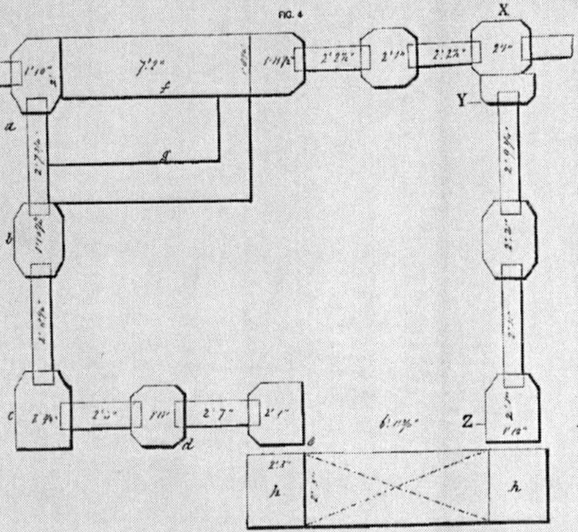

Fig. 4. Ground plan of the Northern entrance to the large, or No. 1 Sthúpa (h h are the sculptured Gate-pillars).

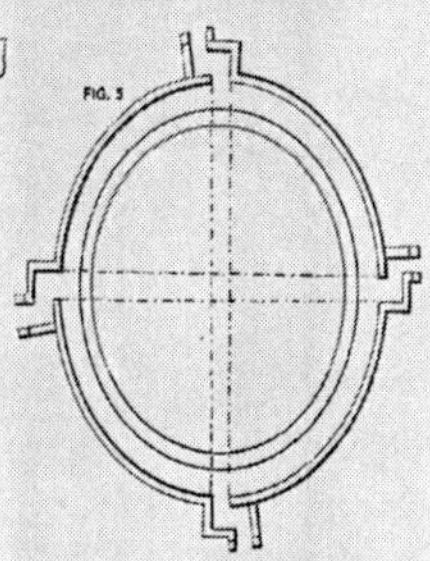

Fig. 5. Sthúpa, with its enclosure and entrances; showing the analogy to the Swástika cross.

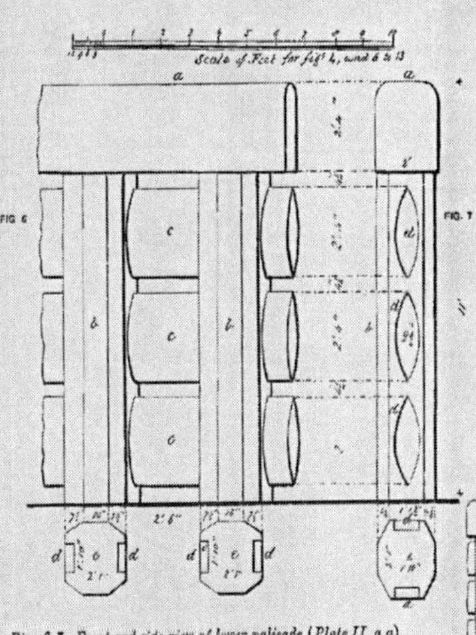

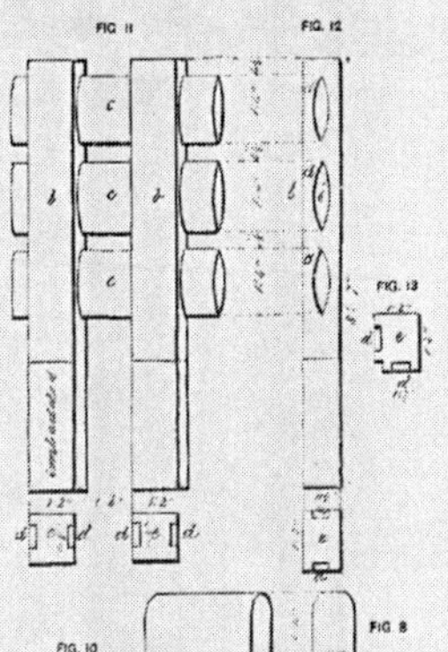

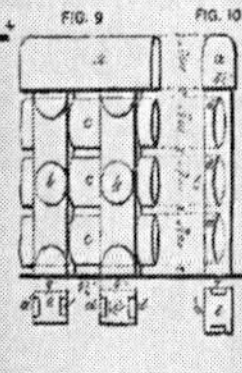

Figs. 6, 7. Front and side view of lower palisade (Plate II. a.a).
„ 8. Rail or balustrade, which probably encircled Berm (Pl. II. c.)
„ 9, 10. Front and side view of upper palisade (Pl. II. v.v.)
„ 11, 12. „ „ „ „ enclosure round Tee.
„ 13. Angle of do. (Plate II. t.t.)

EXPLANATION.

a.a. Coping or entablature.
b.b. Uprights (those of figs. 6, 9 are only shown above ground).
c.c. Cross bars of double convex section.
d.d. Sockets for ditto.
e.e. Plan, or horizontal section of the uprights.

PLATE IV.

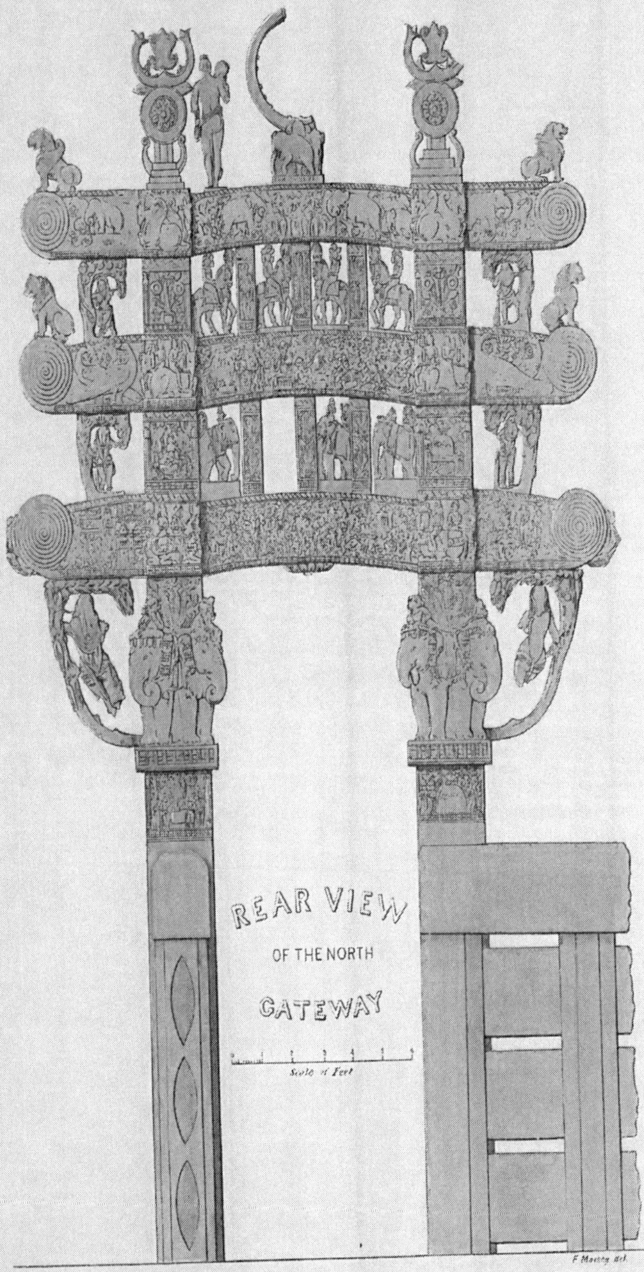

PLATE V.

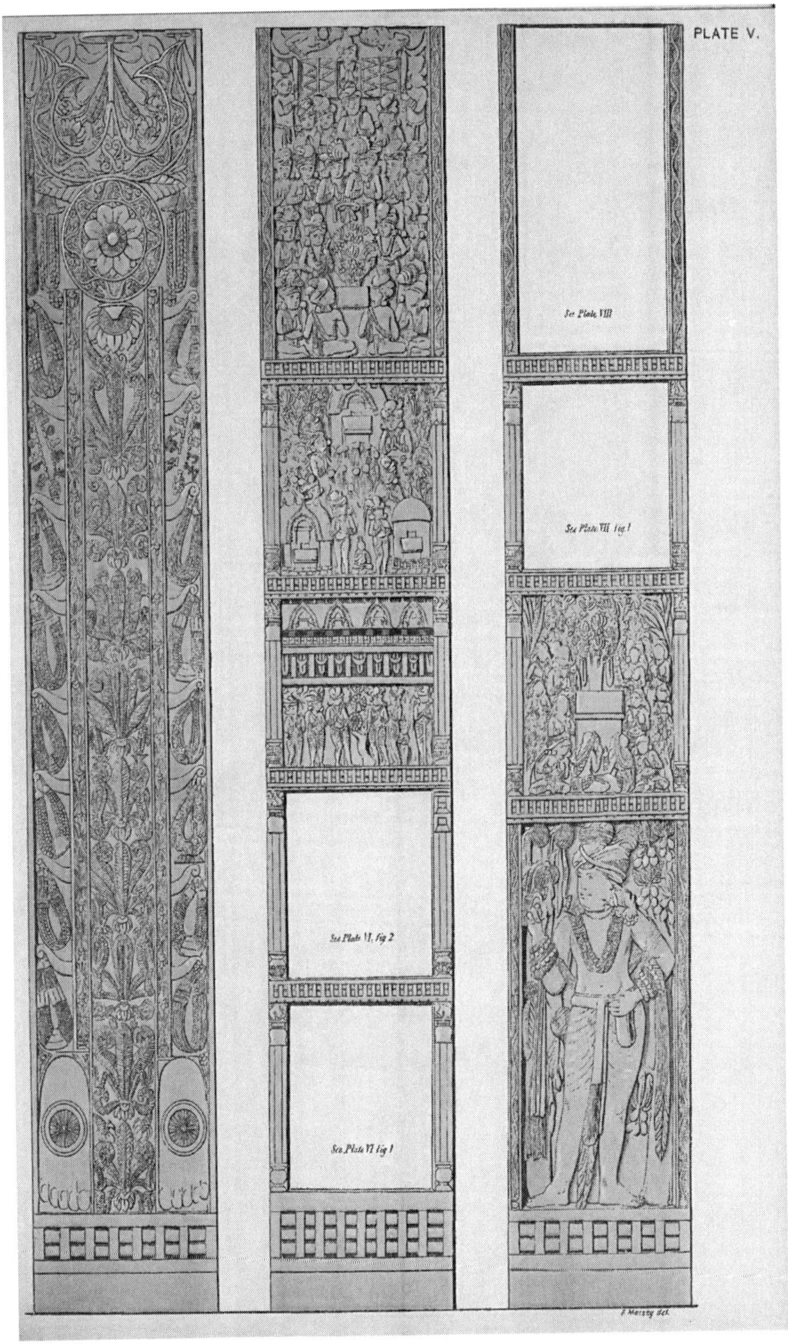

See Plate VIII
See Plate VII fig 1
See Plate VI fig 2
See Plate VI fig 1

PLATE VI.

FIG. 1

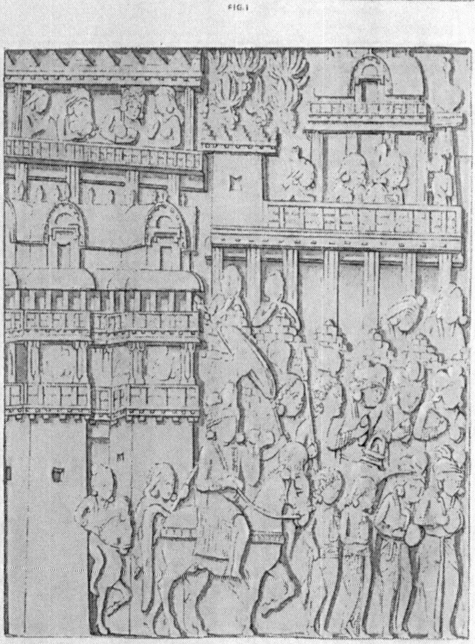

FIG. 2. F. Maisey del.

PLATE VII.

FIG. 1.

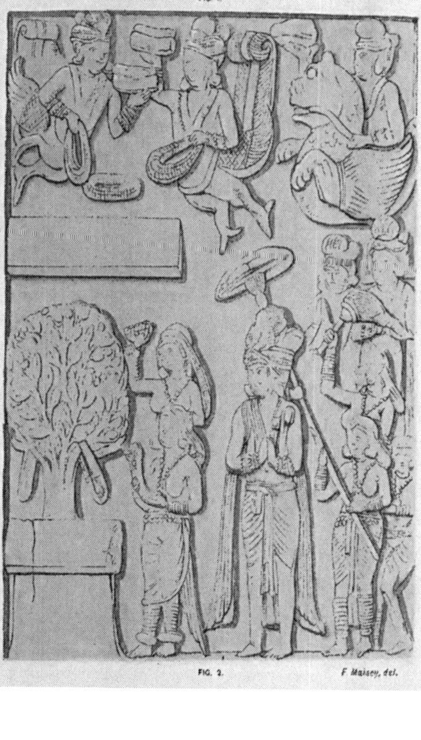

FIG. 2.

F. Maisey, del.

PLATE VIII.

F. Massey del.

PLATE IX.

FIG. 1

FIG. 2 F. Maisey, del.

PLATE X.

F. Massey del.

PLATE XI.

F. Nash del.

PLATE XII.

FIG 1

FIG 2

F Maisey, del.

PLATE XIII.

FIG. 1

FIG. 2

F. Maisey del.

PLATE XIV.

FIG. 3

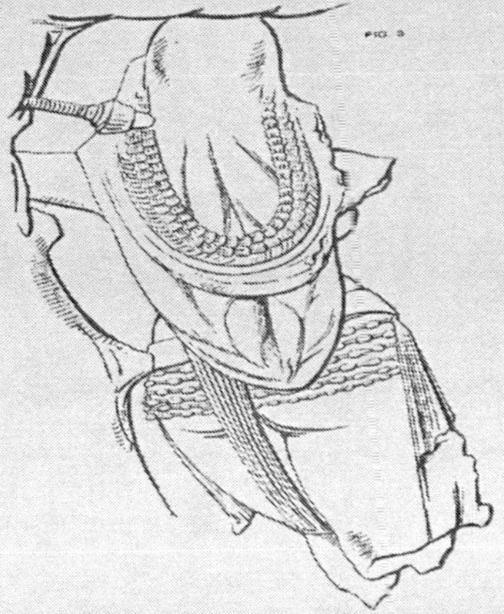

FIG. 5

FIG. 2

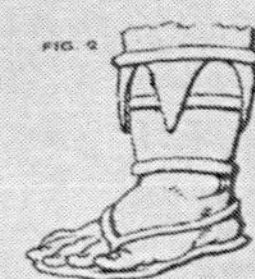

FIG. 6

FIG. 4

FIG. 1

FIG. 7

F. Massey del.

REFERENCES.

Fig. 1. *Image of Buddha, at S. Entrance of No. 1 Sthûpa.*
Fig. 2. *Enlarged sandal, from Plate X.*
Fig. 3. *Dancing figure, at N. Entrance.*
Fig. 4. " " " *W.* "
Figs. 5, 6. *Head-dress of dancing figure at E. Entrance.*
Fig. 7. *Head-dress of another dancer at W. Entrance. N.B.—The tuft is added from a different figure.*

PLATE XV.

FIGS. 1 2 3 4 5 6

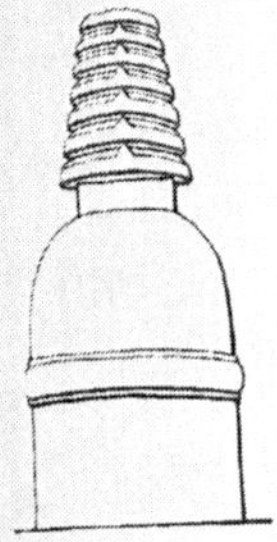

FIG. 7

FIG. 10

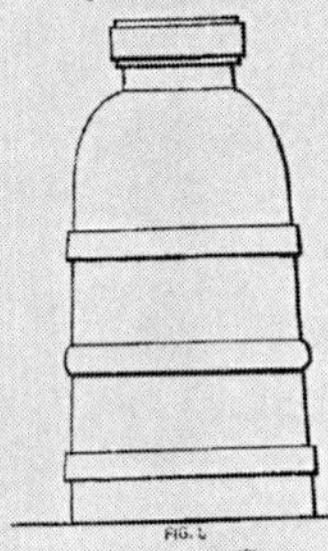

FIG. 8

FIG. 9

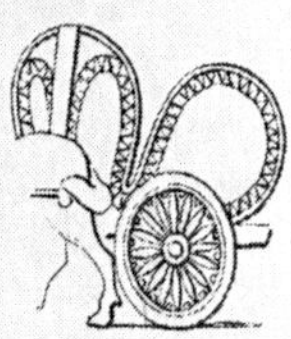

FIG. 11

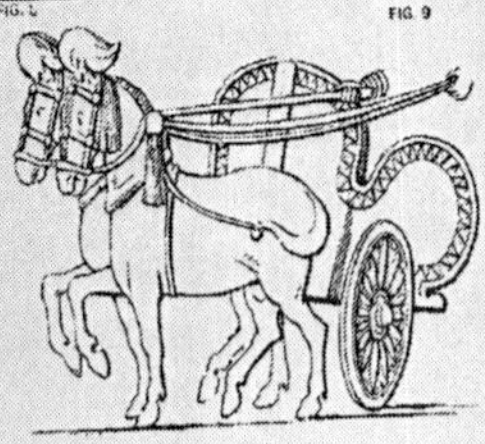

FIG. 12

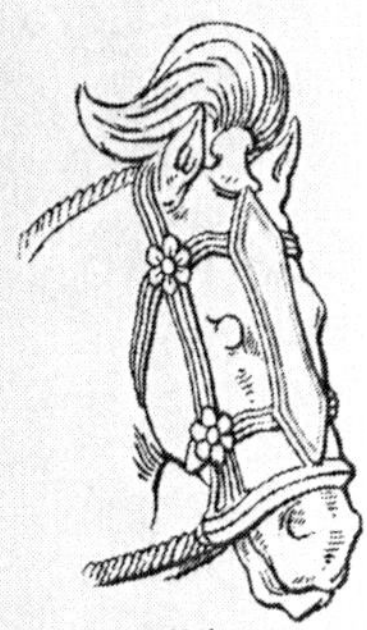

FIG. 14

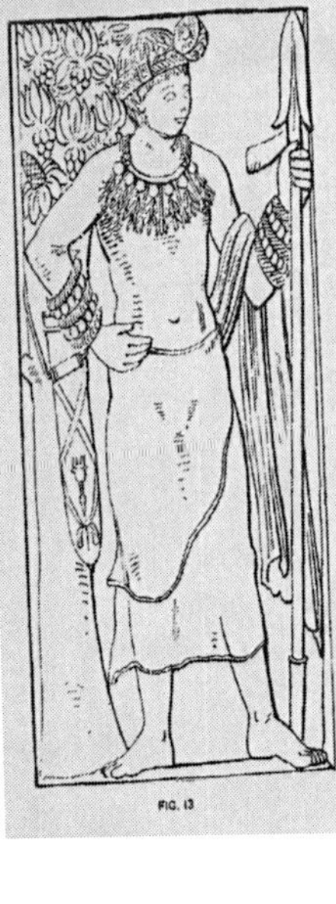

FIG. 13

REFERENCES.

Figs. 1 *to* 5. *Specimens of miniature Sthûpas.*
,, 6. *Shape of the ordinary Linga and Yoni.*
,, 7, 8, 9. *Specimens of miniature Sthûpas.* (*There is an inscription, in the Kutila character, at a.b. of figure 9; and another, or a continuation, on one of the other sides*).
,, 10. *Head of image of Buddha at N. Gate.*
,, 11. *Chariot, from entablature of N. Gate.*
,, 12. *Chariot, from S. Gate.*
,, 13. *Door-keeper, from W. Gate.*
,, 14, 15 *Head-stalls of Horses from entablature of W. Gate.*

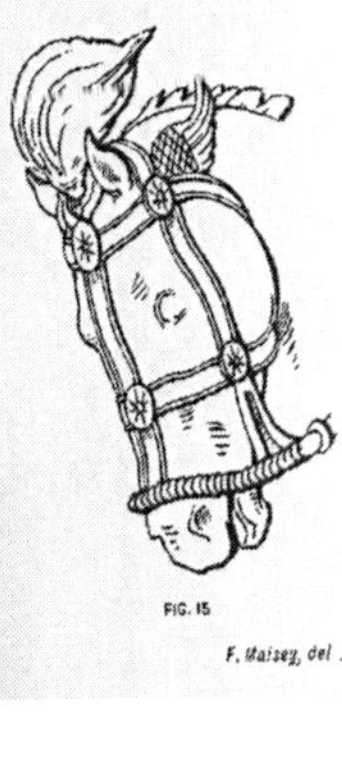

FIG. 15

F. Maisey, del.

PLATE XVI.

F. Maisey, del.

PLATE XVII.

F. Maisey del.

PLATE XVIII.

PLATE XIX.

FIG. 1

FIG. 2

F. Maisey del

Fig. 1. Lion Capital of the pillars of Southern Gateway of No. 1 Sthûpa.
Fig. 2. " " of Sthambha near " " " "

PLATE XX.

F. Maisey del.

PLATE XXI.

PLATE XXII.

FIG. 1

FIG. 2

F. Maneg del.

PLATE XXIII.

FIG. 1

FIG. 2

F. Maisey, del.

PLATE XXIV.

F Moisey del

PLATE XXV.

F. Maisey del.

N.B.—The top moulding of this Capital is, by oversight, imperfectly represented in this Plate: there being lotus flowers between the battlements. The full ornamentation is shown in Plate XXXVI fig. 17.

F. Mnisey del.

PLATE XXVII.

F. Maisey del.

PLATE XXVIII.

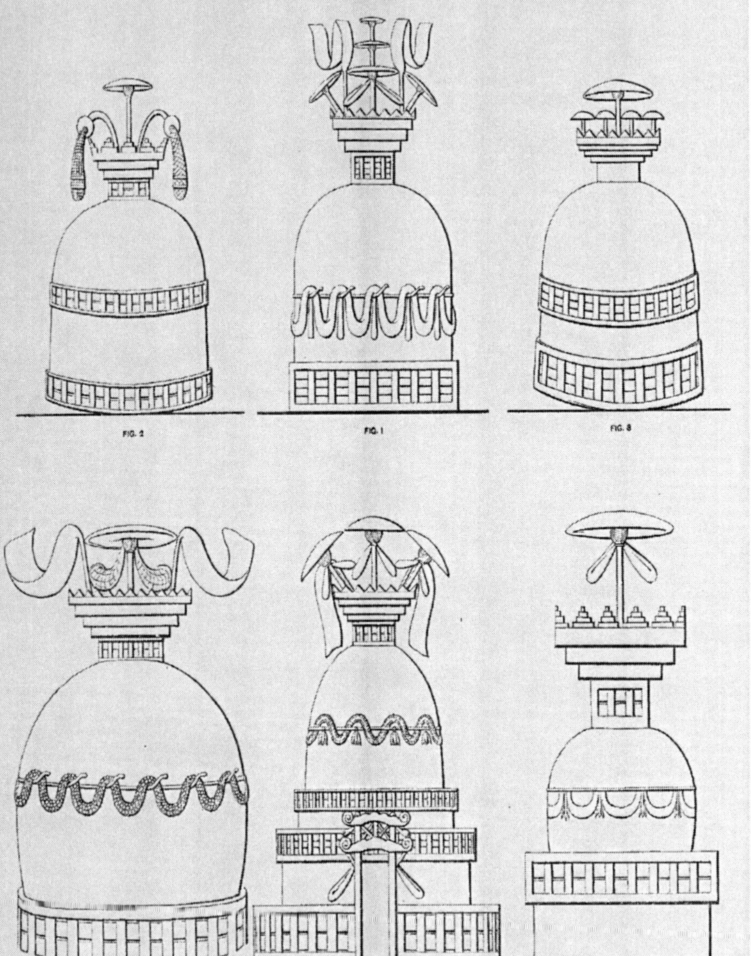

REFERENCES.

Fig. 1. *Sthúpa from the sculptures of the top lintel, Eastern Gateway.*

Figs. 2, 3. *Sthúpas from one of the lintels of the Southern Gateway; on which Sthúpas and trees alternate, as objects of worship. On fig. 3 is the Inscription of Sri Sátakarni.*

Fig. 4. *Sthúpa from one of the lintels of the Western Gateway.*

Fig. 5. " *from the left pillar of Gateway of small Sthúpa, No. 3.*

Fig. 6. *Restored elevation of the Sthúpa shown in Plate X.*

PLATE XXIX.

Fig. 1. Restored plan of the small, or No. 2 Sthúpa (E. Plate I.) with the parapet of Berm restored as in large Sthúpa.

Fig. 3. Present section on a.b.

Fig. 2. Restored section on a. b. c. d. e. f. g. h. i. j. k. of Fig. 1, with the staircase E. and the enclosing palisade shown in elevation

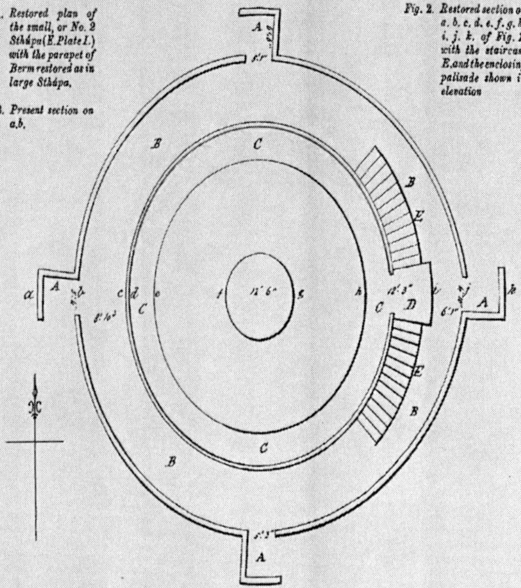

FIG. 1

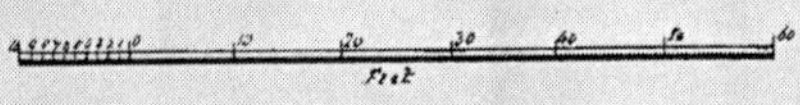

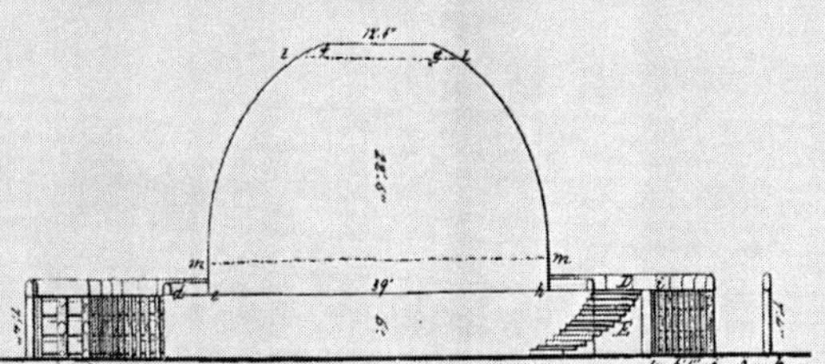

FIG. 2

N.B.—The dotted line l.l. shows the top diameter, of 19', as measured by Capt. Fell, in 1819. m.m., 3' 6'' above the basement, is the line whence the curve springs.

FIG. 3

n. is the position of the relic cell.

F. Maisey del.

A. A. recessed entrances to the passage, B. B.
B. B. enclosed passage round the Sthúpa.
C. C. basement, drum or berm.
D. landing of the staircase E. E.

PLATE XXX.

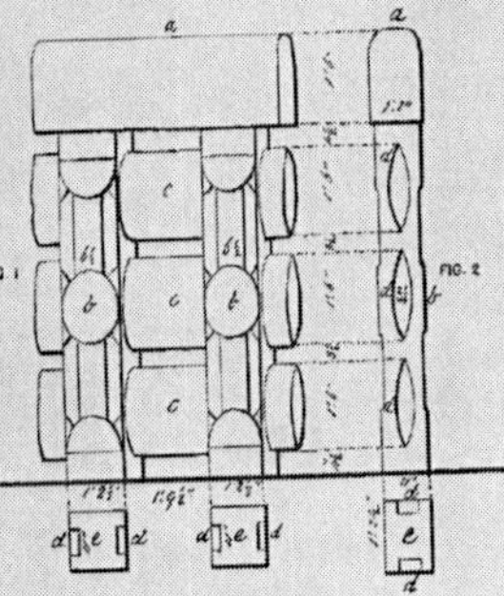

FIG. 1 FIG. 2

FIG. 4

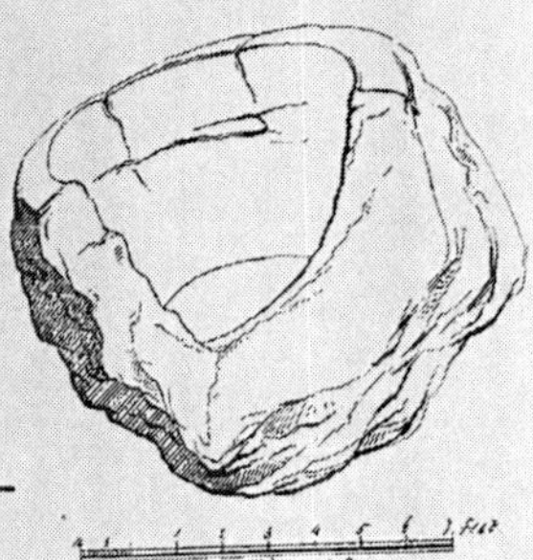

FIG. 3

Fig. 1, 2. *Front and side views of palisade of small Sthúpa* (*No.* 2).
a.a. coping: b.b. uprights: c.c. cross pieces: d.d. sockets for do.: e.e. section of uprights.

Fig. 3. *Upright on a large scale, showing the style of decoration of the basses.*

Fig. 4. *Stone cauldron or cistern, between the large and small Sthúpas; interior dimensions,* 4′ 6″ *diam.* 2′ 6″ *deep.*

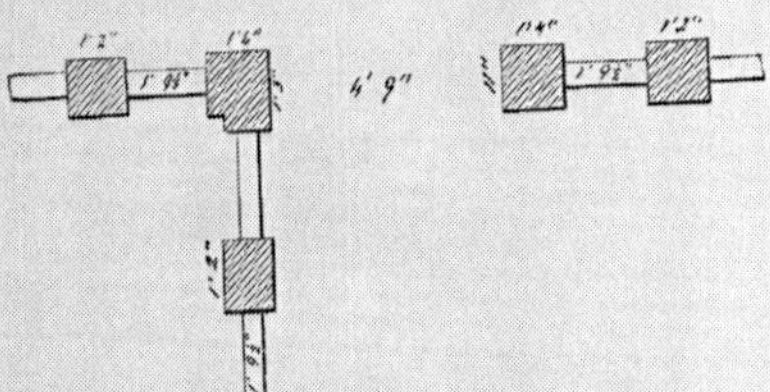

FIG. 5

Fig. 5. *Plan of the entrances to the railed enclosure of No.* 2 *Sthúpa.*

Fig. 6. *Female figure, riding on a "Nara," or Centaur: from one of the basses, or centre medallions of the enclosure pillars of No.* 2 *Sthúpa.*

FIG. 6

F Mussey del.

PLATE XXXI.

FIG 2 FIG. 3 FIG 1 FIG 4 FIG. 6 FIG. 5

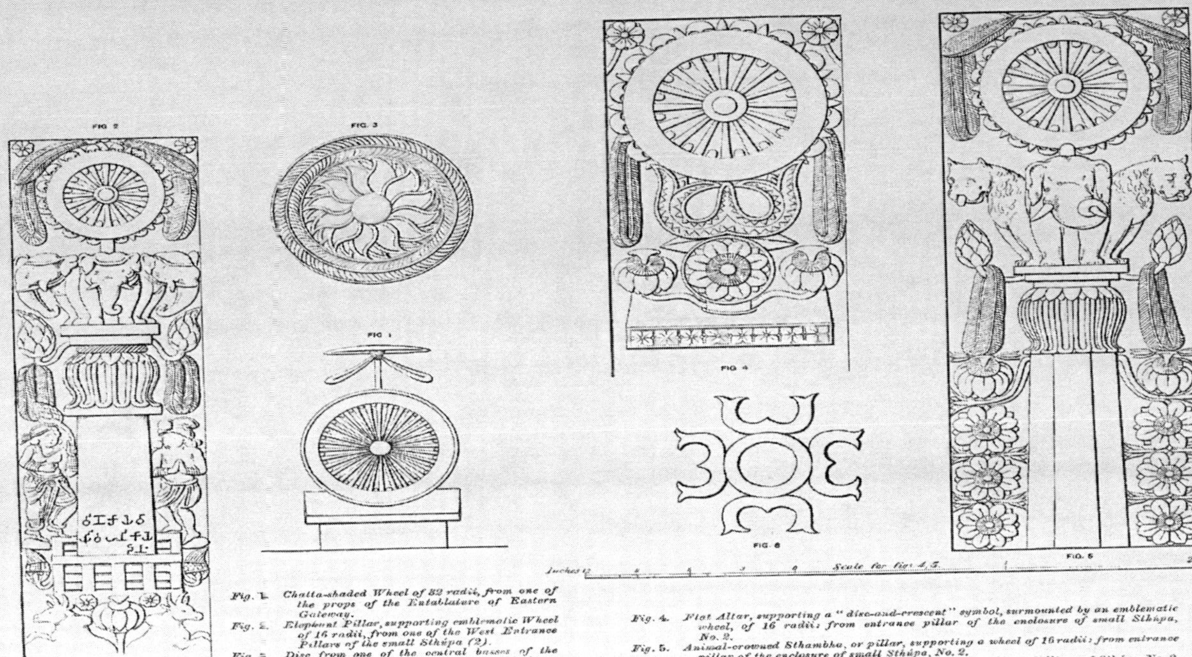

Inches Scale for Figs. 4, 5. 2 Feet

Fig. 1. *Chatta-shaded Wheel of 32 radii, from one of the props of the Entablature of Eastern Gateway.*

Fig. 2. *Elephant Pillar, supporting emblematic Wheel of 16 radii, from one of the West Entrance Pillars of the small Sthûpa (2).*

Fig. 3. *Disc from one of the central bosses of the enclosure pillars of small Sthûpa, No. 2.*

Inches Scale for Figs. 1, 2, 3. 2 feet

Fig. 4. *Flat Altar, supporting a "disc-and-crescent" symbol, surmounted by an emblematic wheel, of 16 radii: from entrance pillar of the enclosure of small Sthûpa, No. 2.*

Fig. 5. *Animal-crowned Sthambha, or pillar, supporting a wheel of 16 radii: from entrance pillar of the enclosure of small Sthûpa, No. 2.*

Fig. 6. *Quadruple disc-and-crescent symbol; from one of the medallions of Sthûpa No. 2. (a similar, but more elaborate symbol is on one of the pillars at Andher).*

F Maisey del

PLATE XXXII.

Figs. 1, 2. *Capital, and part of the crowning figure of a broken Láth near the North Entrance of Large Sthúpa.*

Figs. 3, 4. *Pillars of a small Temple (T) to N.E. of the Large Sthúpa.*

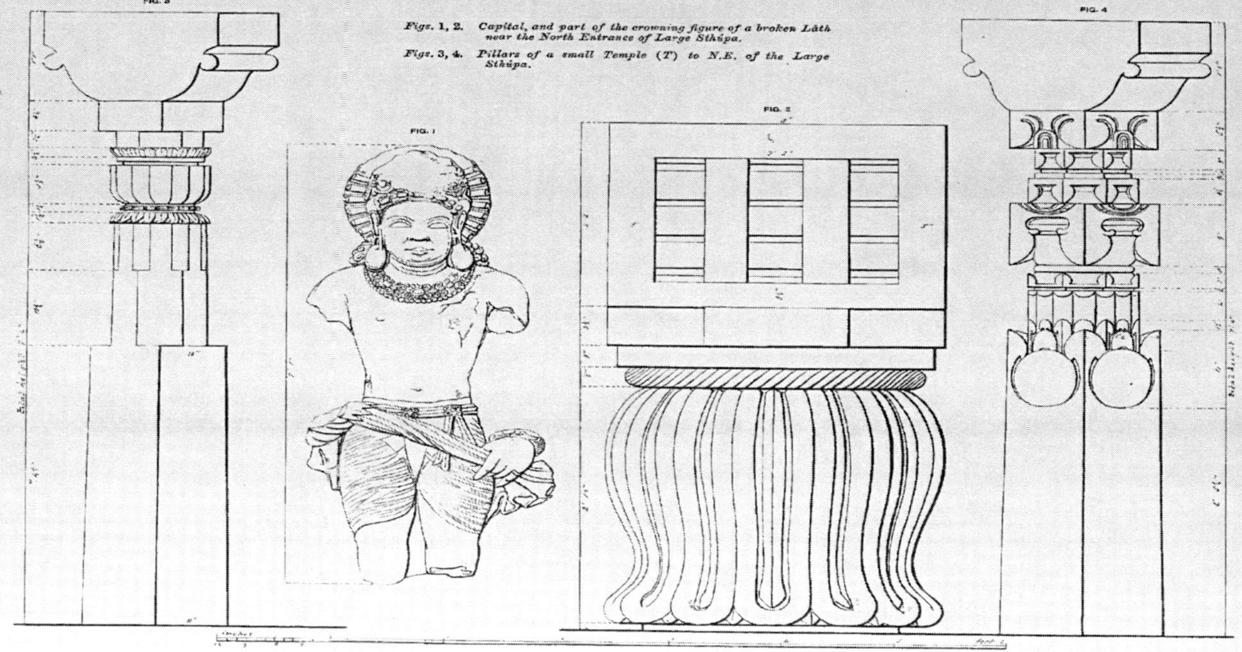

F. Waesey del.

PLATE XXXIII.

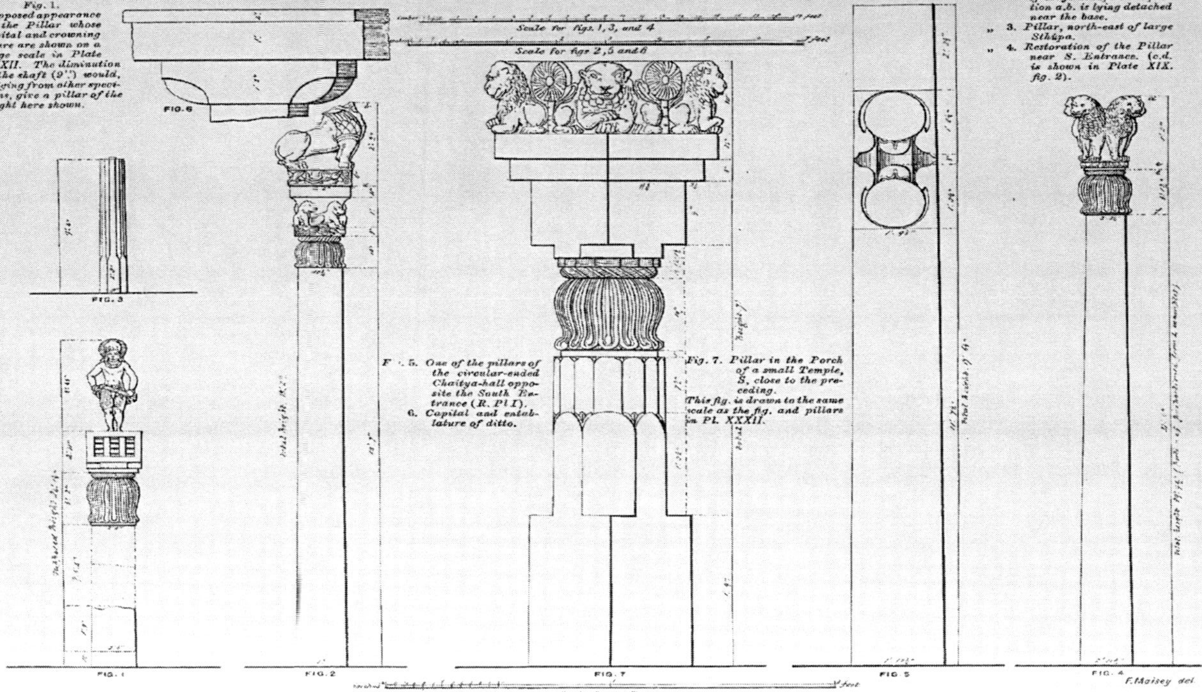

Fig. 1. Supposed appearance of the Pillar whose capital and crowning figure are shown on a large scale in Plate XXXII. The diminution of the shaft (9″) would, judging from other specimens, give a pillar of the height here shown.

Fig. 2. Pillar near East Entrance of large Sthûpa: the portion a.b. is lying detached near the base.
" 3. Pillar, north-east of large Sthûpa.
" 4. Restoration of the Pillar near S. Entrance. (c.d. is shown in Plate XIX. fig. 2).

Fig. 5. One of the pillars of the circular-ended Chaitya-hall opposite the South Entrance (R. Pl I).
6. Capital and entablature of ditto.

Fig. 7. Pillar in the Porch of a small Temple, S, close to the preceding.
This fig. is drawn to the same scale as the fig. and pillars in Pl. XXXII.

PLATE XXXIV.

F Maisey del.

Total height 8 feet 2 inches.

PLATE XXXV.

REFERENCES.

Figs. 1, 2, 3. *Female drummers from a procession (from Entablature of Eastern Gateway).*
,, 4, 9. *Male drummers, in a procession (Plate XXVII).*
,, 5, 6, 7, 8, 10. *Varieties of drums and tabors, from various sculptures, not shown in my Plates.*
,, 11 to 14. *Other drums, from Plates X. and XXIII. fig. 1.*
,, 15. *Female shell-blower, from East Gateway.*
,, 16, 17. *Male shell-blowers, or players on some shell-shaped instrument (see Plate XXVIII).*
,, 18. *Female flute-player (from East Gateway).*
,, 19. *Male* ,, ,, ,, ,,

Fig. 20. *Man playing double pipe (Plate X).*
,, 21. *Trumpeter, from Eastern Gateway.*
,, 22. ,, *from Plate X.*
,, 23. *Hand lyre, played by a man (Plate VI. fig. 1).*
,, 24. *Lyres, played with plectrum, by women (Plate XXIII, fig. 1).*
,, 25, 26. *Swords, carried and slung (E. Gateway).*
,, 27, 28. *Swords, slung (Plates XXI. and XXVII).*
,, 29. *Javelin-bearers (Plate VI. fig. 2).*
,, 30 to 34. *Shields of various kinds, some with spears (Plates XX. and XXVII).*

Fig. 35. *Two-handed Club; Fig. 36. Trident; and Fig. 37. Axe; held by Giants, on a fragment of the W. Gate entablature.*
,, 38. *Archer, from Eastern Gateway.*
,, 39. *Archer, with semi-circular bladed arrow (Plate XXII. fig. 2).*
,, 40, 41. *Double-curved bows, and arrow notches (Plate XXIII. fig. 2).*
,, 42 and 45. *Poles, with emblems and streamers (Eastern Gateway).*
,, 43, 44, 46, 47, 48. *Standards (Plates X; XXI. fig. 1; and XXVII).*

F. Maisey del.

PLATE XXXVI.

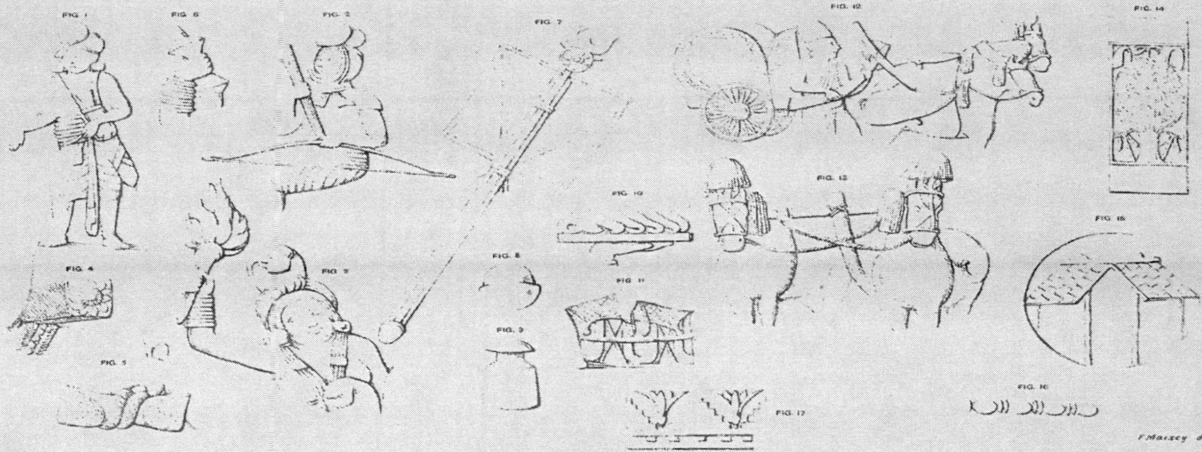

REFERENCES.

Figs. 1, 2. *Sword-bearer, and archer (on an elephant), from end of lintel shown in Plate XX.*

,, 3. *Female Chaori-bearer, attending on a Nâga-hooded male figure (South Gate).*

,, 4, 5. *Ear ornaments, such as are worn by most of the male figures.*

,, 6. *Vajra, or thunder-bolt mace, or sceptre held by the King, or principal figure, in a compartment of right pillar, E. Gate.*

Figs. 7. *Standard and Staff (South Gate lintel).*

,, 8, 9. *Covered vessels carried by men. (2nd and 3rd compartments, front face, left pillar, South Gate).*

,, 10. *Offering carried by a bullock-rider (South Gate lintel).*

,, 11. *Throne or Stool of the mace bearer, whose mace or sceptre is shown in fig. 6.*

,, 12. *Unharnessed Chariot, from North Gate lintel; showing the pole, yoke, and supporting bar. It has four horses, of which the two wheelers only are shown.*

Fig. 13. *Horses harnessed in Chariot (E. Gate).*

,, 14. *One of the small props of N. Gate lintels.*

,, 15. *Tiled-roof gateway, from one of the pillars of No. 2 Sthûpa: (a mounted elephant is emerging from it).*

,, 16. *Bead and reel ornament, from the enclosure pillars of No. 2 Sthûpa.*

,, 17. *Top Moulding of Capital in Plate XXV.*

PLATE XXXVII.

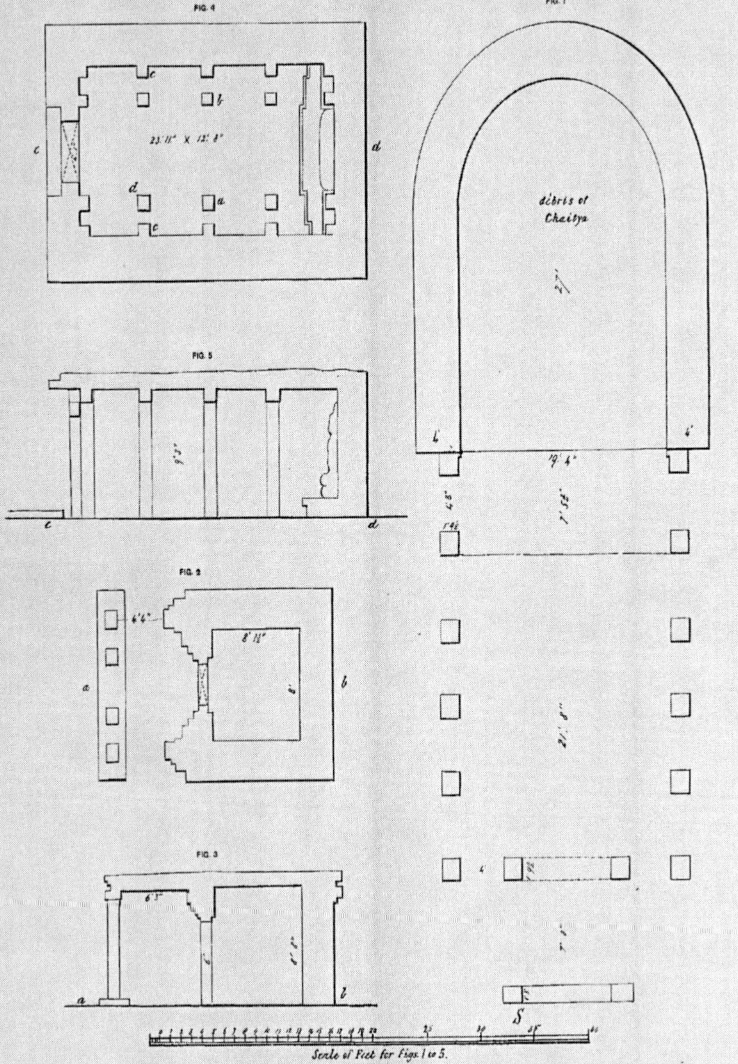

F. Massey del.

REFERENCES.

Fig. 1. *Plan of Chaitya-hall, or temple (R. in Plate I).*
Fig. 2. *Plan of small temple, marked S. in Plate I.*
Fig. 3. *Section on a.b. of Figure 2.*
Fig. 4. *Plan of temple, marked T. in Plate I.*
Fig. 5. *Section on c.d. of Figure 4.*

N.B. No cement used in the above buildings.

PLATE XXXVIII.

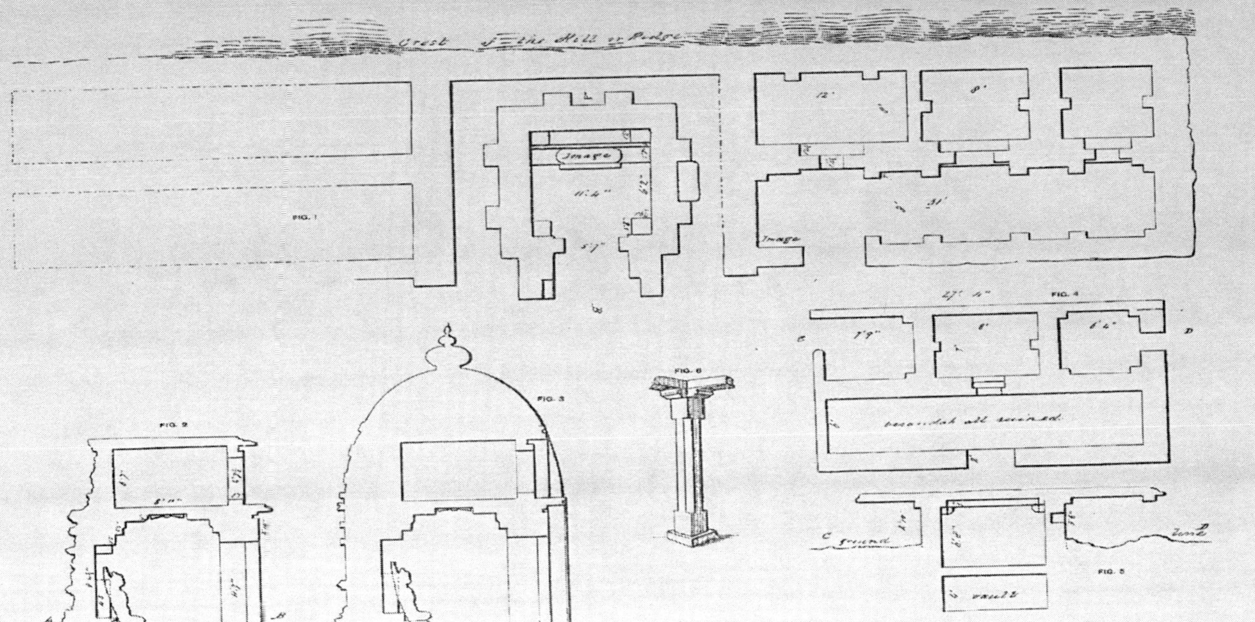

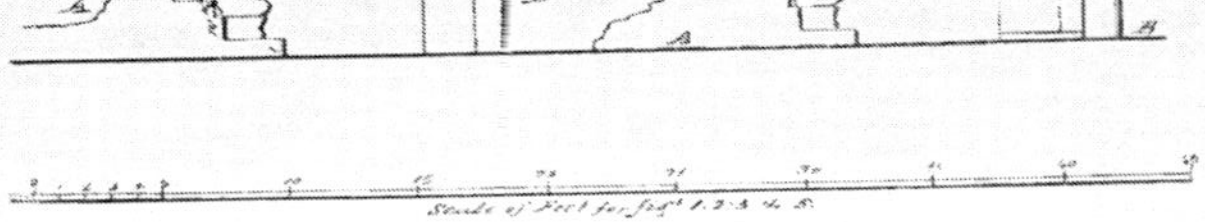

REFERENCES.

Fig. 1. *Plan of a Vihára-temple, to the East of the large Sthúpa (V. Plate I).*
" 2. *Existing Section, on A.B., of figure 1.*
" 3. *Restored Section, " "*
" 4. *Plan of small building to North-east of the large Sthúpa (W. Plate I).*
" 5. *Section on C.D. of fig. 4.*
(N.B. No cement used in any of the above buildings).
" 6. *Specimen of the pillars in the ruined Vihára (marked U. in Plate I).*

F. Maisey, del.

PLATE XXXIX.

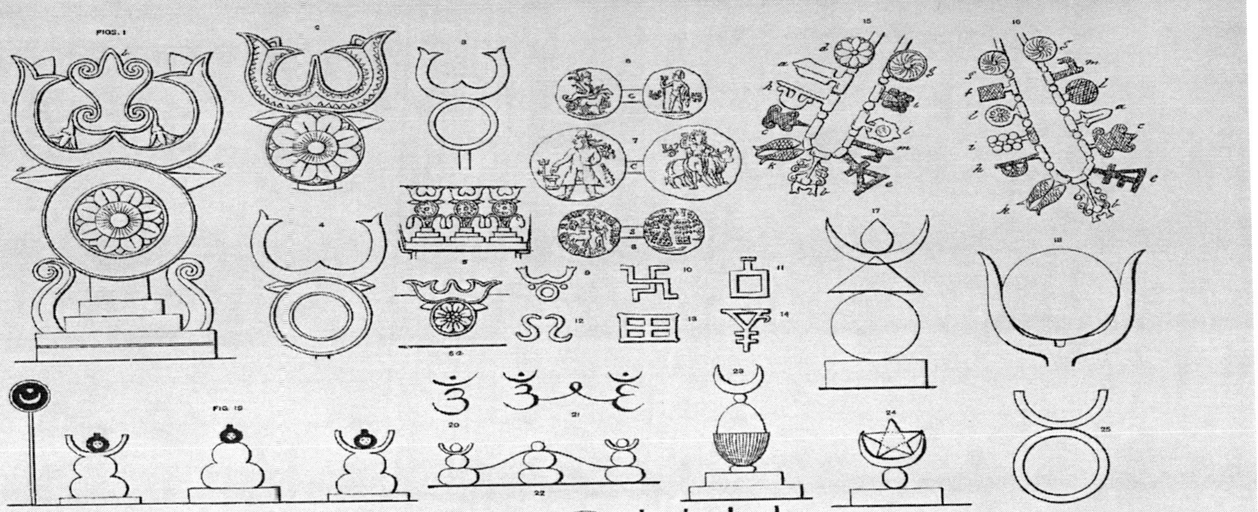

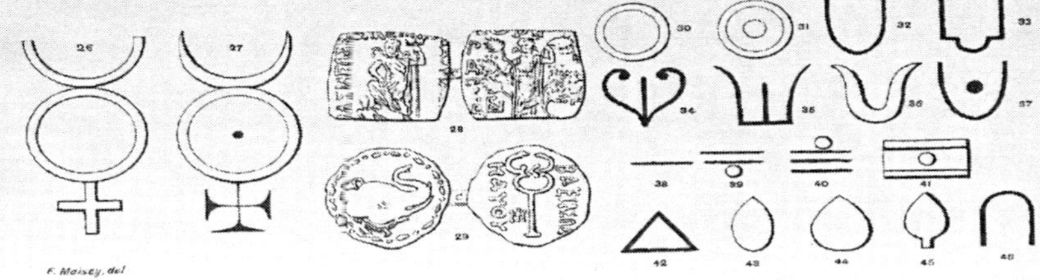

F. Maisey, del

REFERENCES.

Fig. 1. *Disc-and-crescent Symbol, from N. Gateway (Plate IV.)*
" 2. " " " " *on Altar (Plate XXXI.)*
" 3, 4. " " " " *on Standards.*
" 5. " " " " *triform; on Altar (Plate XVIII.)*
" 5a. " " " " *on Altar (Plate XII.)*
" 6, 7. *Coins of Kadphises (figs. 9, 17, Pl. X. "Ariana Antiqua.")*
" 8. *Coin of Amogha Bhata (fig. 23. Pl. XV. "Ariana Antiqua.")*
" 9 *to* 14. *Wilson's Coin Monograms, Nos.* 156, 158, 164*a*, 164*b*, 165, 166.
" 15, 16. *Necklaces of Symbols, on a votive Pillar (Plate V.)*
" 17. *Symbol called by Fa Hian a "tower of deliverance."*
" 18. *Symbol on the head of Apis and Isis.*
" 19 *to* 22. *The Jagannáth triad, and its connection with the "Prânava," or sacred syllable "Aom" or "Om," from Faber's "Anc. Myth." II. figs.* 11, 16, 17, 18.
" 23. *The God Lunus of Heliopolis* } *from Faber's "Anc. Myth."*
" 24. *The lunar God of the Carrhenians.* } *II. figs.* 19, 22.
" 25. *The zodiacal sign Taurus, or the Bull.*
" 26. *Astronomical sign of Mercury. Fig.* 27. *Caduceus.* [*Pl. VIII. fig.* 11.
" 28, 29. *Coins of Mauas, or Mayes ("Aria. Ant." Pl. VII. fig.* 5; *and*
" 30 *to* 46. *Vaishnava and Saiva Sectarial Marks; typical of water and fire, respectively.*

PLATE XL.

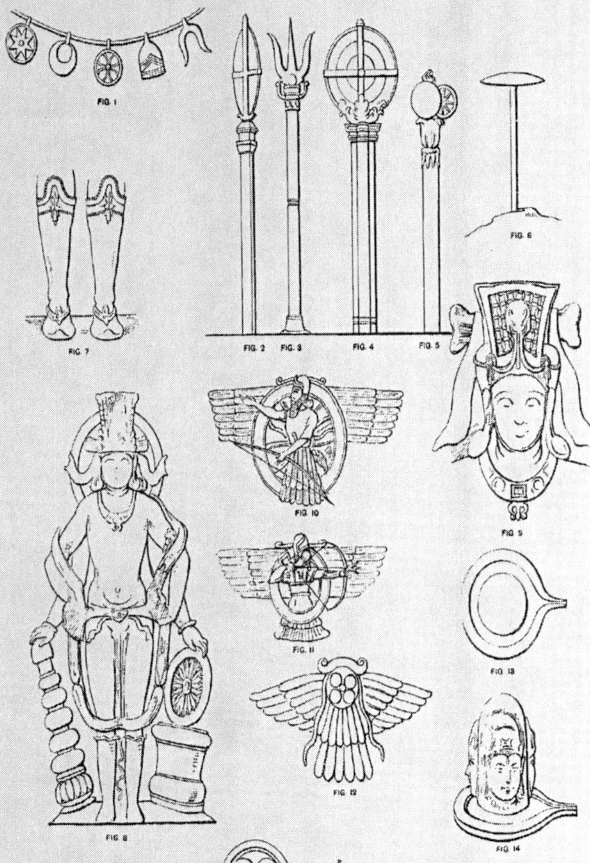

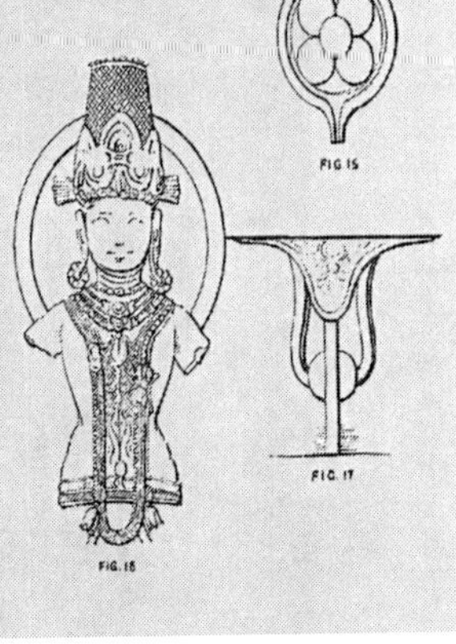

REFERENCE.

Fig. 1. *Necklace of sacred symbols: from Assyria.*

Figs. 2 *to* 6. *Symbols on pillars, at Bangalor.*

Fig. 7. *Boots of Súrya; from a temple at Kajuráha.*

Fig. 8. *Figure of Súrya; from Udáya-giri.*

Fig. 9. *Head of Súrya;* „ „

Figs. 10, 11, 12. *Winged figures and disc; from Assyria; representing the deity (the Sun): see Layard, "Nineveh and its Remains," II.* 447, 448.

Figs. 13, 14. *Siva, as Mahádeva, in the Linga form, with Párbati, as the encircling Yoni.*

Fig. 15. *Siva as the Panch-ánan, or Panch-Mukhti Linga (compare with Fig.* 12*).*

Fig. 16. *Súrya; from a temple at Gyaraspur.*

Fig. 17. *The single wheel beneath the thrones or cars of Buddhist and Jaina images; called "Bha-mandala," or the solar disc.*

F. Maisey, del.